'An extraordinary book on an extraordinary man.
The definitive story of Brother Walfrid, the father of Celtic,
and the legacy he bequeathed to Scottish culture. A story of
poverty, politics and faith that has a powerful significance
and an enduring resonance today.'

Hugh McDonald, journalist

'I would like to congratulate Dr Michael Connolly for this
excellent and definitive biography based on his academic
study. Brother Walfrid is a hugely important figure in the
history of Celtic Football Club and his massive contribution
to Celtic and Scottish society deserves such a tribute. He
gave people hope in times of desperation, in adversity he
brought people together by creating a Club open to all, and
his dedication to helping others has left a phenomenal
legacy. It is Brother Walfrid's vision of charitable purpose and
community through football which Celtic will always hold
dear and will strive to honour in all it does. Indeed, we are
proud that Brother Walfrid's spirit remains so strong at Celtic
as we continue to make a positive difference to the lives
in people in need. It is important for all Celtic supporters to
know and understand the history and true core values of
Celtic that Michael's writing defines so well.'

Peter Lawwell, Celtic Football Club

'We are indebted to Michael Connolly for producing such a
well-researched and fascinating account of Brother Walfrid's
life. I am his great grand niece but our family does not have a
lot of information on many aspects of his life. This book
helps to fill in the gaps and it also gives valuable and
welcome insights into Brother Walfrid's character and
personality.'

Alison Healy, journalist and author

'The powerful force of good that Celtic fans can deliver to the wider community is something that I have been aware of since a very early age. A charitable conscience and a caring work ethic are attributes that helped Brother Walfrid create one of the most powerful charitable sports organisations in the world. As we all know Celtic is more than a football club. Brother Walfrid set our football club up with the mission to bring hope and joy on and off the pitch and I believe that has been achieved in good measure over the years. That mission will continue into the future as the embodiment of Brother Walfrid's ethos and spirit lives on in the hearts of the Celtic supporters. Michael Connolly's account of his life will help deliver that mission globally.'

Paul McStay,
former Celtic and Scotland captain

'When I was growing up in Parkhead and being taken by my father to football matches at Celtic Park, little did I realise that the Marist Brothers would come to play such an important part in my life. When I joined the Marist Brothers in 1975, I learned about Brother Walfrid and the foundation of Celtic Football club in 1888 to provide funds for the Poor Children's Dinner Tables. It is highly likely that some of my own forebears benefited from his foresight and organisational skills. Michael Connolly's research provides fascinating and important information on the life and work of a man who had a significant impact on the development of the city of Glasgow. He shows that Walfrid's work in Glasgow was consistent with work he undertook in London and Grove Ferry in Kent, where the combination of his Irish heritage, Marist formation, passion for sport, and religious faith brought improvement to the lives of the poor children.'

Brother Brendan Geary, F.M.S., PhD.,
Provincial of the Marist Brothers, 2010 – 2019

'*Walfrid* is the poignant, authoritative account of an Irish migrant who transformed society by his dedication and commitment to the poor. Dr Michael Connolly has provided a narrative that goes well beyond the Celtic story, with timeless thoughts for this age as well as of years past. This is a story of founding a football club, but also of overcoming human suffering. It highlights education as the ladder out of poverty. My great grandfather who accompanied Walfrid out of Ireland would be proud.'

Professor Bart McGettrick,
Emeritus Professor and Dean Emeritus,
Faculty of Education, University of Glasgow

'Managed to read this lovely book on long haul flights this week! Who knew that when my children were cheering on Glasgow's legendary Celtic football team that the club's foundational story was of an altogether different kind of heroism and one that richly deserves this scholarly telling. History has for too long overlooked the seminal role in Celtic's narrative of Brother Walfrid, a humble Irish monk whose life was one of utterly unselfish but visionary service far from home. Michael Connolly, in this beautifully told biography, makes Brother Walfrid visible again as he deserves to be. Congratulations and best wishes for its success. I loved the book!'

Mary McAleese,
President of Ireland, 1997 – 2011

[continued, see inside back page]

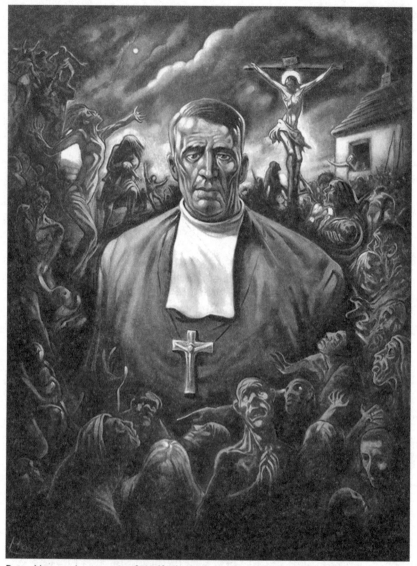

Peter Howson's portrait of Walfrid which hangs in St. Mary's parish church in Glasgow close to where Celtic FC was instituted on November 6th 1887. The work commemorates Walfrid's impact in life as a male religious. The painting also serves as a reminder of his cultural significance to Catholicism in Scotland, evoking his roots in Ireland and the horrors of *An Gorta Mor* which precipitated his emigration. A permanent memorial to that same dark episode in Ireland's history was unveiled at St. Mary's in Glasgow on July 25th 2021, shown on page 30.

Walfrid

A Life of Faith, Community
and Football

Michael Connolly

Best Wishes

Dr Michael Connolly

ARGYLL ✠ PUBLISHING

© Michael Connolly 2022

Second printing 2022
Third printing 2024
First paperback edition 2024

First published by
Argyll Publishing
an imprint of Thirsty Books
www.thirstybooks.com

The author has asserted his moral rights.

British Library Cataloguing-in-Publication Data.
A catalogue record for this book in available from the British
Library.

ISBN 978 1 7399922 3 1 hardback
ISBN 978 1 7393181 3 0 paperback

Typeset & design: derek.rodger21@outlook.com

Cover art: paulfwilkie@gmail.com

Printing: Bell & Bain Ltd, Glasgow

In tribute to Walfrid's religious service to others, the prayer recited daily by Marist Brothers worldwide is printed below. The influence of devotion to the Blessed Virgin Mary on his life is similarly reflected in the selection of Marian sky blue coloured endpapers on this book.

SALVE REGINA

Salve, Regina, mater misericordiae;
vita, dulcedo et spes nostra, salve.
Ad te clamamus exsules filii Hevae.

Ad te suspiramus gementes et flentes
in hac lacrimarum valle.
Eia ergo, advocata nostra,
illos tuos misericordes oculos ad nos
converte.
Et Iesum, benedictum fructum ventris tui,
nobis post hoc exsilium ostende.
O clemens, o pia, o dulcis Virgo Maria.

HAIL, HOLY QUEEN

Hail, holy Queen, Mother of Mercy.
Our life, our sweetness, and our hope.
To you do we cry, poor banished children of Eve.
To you do we send up our sighs,
Mourning and weeping in this vale of tears.
Turn then, most gracious advocate,
Your eyes of mercy towards us,
And after this our exile,
Show unto us the blessed fruit of your womb, Jesus.
O clement, O loving, O sweet Virgin Mary.

This book is dedicated to my Mum, Marie Connolly,
for instilling in me a passion for reading from my earliest years,
and my Dad, Phil Connolly, for imparting a love for football –
especially Celtic Football Club.

Contents

Introduction

Looking for all the world like a visitor from another dimension, an inauspicious figure dressed in the humble black soutane of a foreign religious order enters the plush reception of London's Caledonian Hotel. He asks in a clear gentle voice if he may call on one or two of their guests. It is still early in the day but the concierge, making an immediate judgement that the man before him is the genuine article relents.

It is a Mr Maley, a Mr Campbell, a Mr Kelly and a Mr McMahon he is enquiring after – they would have arrived off the overnight train from Glasgow. It is Friday 31st March 1893 and these named gentlemen are footballers in town for one of the early international matches between Scotland and England, this one to be held at Richmond Park the next day, Saturday 1st April. He gives his name and is shown upstairs to the shared rooms.

Willie Maley, James Kelly, Sandy McMahon and Johnny Campbell were Celtic FC players and also Scotland internationals. Johnny Campbell later recollected the meeting in the *Glasgow Star*:

> We left Glasgow at 9 o'clock on the Thursday night and arrived in London at 5 in the morning. We had a few hours sleep and I think the man to awaken us first was our old friend Brother Walfrid, who was at the inception of the Celtic Club, and one of the bright particular stars in the management of it until he was called away to London. We had a hearty handshake with him and a talk about old times.

The *Scottish Sport* also wrote in April 1893:

> Brother Walfrid, the father of Celtic, who is now resident in England, called at the Caledonian Hotel and shook hands with all old friends.

After a warm conversation and a good luck and God Bless, the men took their leave. The next day, overnight train journeys notwithstanding, Scotland, then a leading light in world football, were defeated 5:2 by England in front of 'not more than 20,000 spectators' at Richmond Park, Surrey. The four Celtic men are listed in the Scotland team.

Who was this figure? And why were the Scotland players not only not put out at being wakened but were glad to set eyes on so far from home? He gave his name only as Brother Walfrid.

Brother Walfrid (Andrew Kerins) was one of the most significant of the very many thousands of Irish immigrants to nineteenth century Britain. Despite knowledge around him as a prime founder of Celtic FC, Walfrid's story remains largely untold. Yet his nineteenth century legacy among the multi-generational Irish Catholic community in Scotland is arguably unparalelled. And is still evident today.

As with so many immigrants to a strange land, Andrew Kerins' origins were humble. His Co. Sligo birth in 1840 as the second son of a tenant farming family dictated his future. A poor childhood and a premature departure aged 15 as an economic migrant for Glasgow in 1855 were all too predictable. Surviving historical and archived documents show the effects of *An Gorta Mor* (the Great Hunger in Irish) and the stream of historical forces that preceded it,were unquantifiable on Kerins and his family. New information drawn from publications of the time and interviews provide the source material on this epochal figure of the Irish Catholic diaspora.

The socio-economic circumstances that were the backdrop to the emergence of Celtic FC – a unique representation of Irish migration in world sport – can be explained through Brother Walfrid's lived experience. Critically, the story also helps to understand Walfrid's role, motivations and achievements as a Marist Brother: especially with respect to his importance to Catholic religious, educational and charitable work and cultural identities in Scotland.

In this book Walfrid's integral role in the creation of Celtic FC is critically reappraised along with his faith and charity work amongst the poor and marginalised in Glasgow. By producing a full account of the life of Brother Walfrid, what emerges is a more substantive insight into a figure of totemic historical significance not just for the Irish Catholic immigrants that he helped, but for an often neglected aspect of Scottish history. Through the combination of faith, charity and football, Walfrid's life illustrates an historic contribution to Irish Catholicism in nineteenth century Britain.

Brother Walfrid died on 17th April 1915, aged 74 years. Over a century has transpired since the passing of the Irish Marist Brother and yet no biographical account, academic or popular, has ever been attempted on the life of a man indelibly associated with one of the most recognisable institutions in world sport. Research for the project that was to lead to a PhD thesis and which forms the basis of this book began in September of 2017 and was funded by the Nine Muses, an arts group based in Glasgow, who previously commissioned a portrait of Brother Walfrid by Scottish artist Peter Howson in 2008.[1]

Emma O'Neil of Nine Muses explained the rationale in funding a doctoral study of the life of Walfrid: to address 'questions left unanswered' concerning Walfrid's 'contribution to religious, social, economic and cultural life' in the places most closely associated with his life. The late Archbishop of Glasgow, Most Reverend Philip Tartaglia, offered endorsement on behalf of the Catholic Church, welcoming the opportunity for fresh research to 'shine an academic light on the person, faith and motivations of Brother Walfrid; on the underlying facts of his life and activity; and on the local and broader historical context'. Lastly, Peter Lawwell, then chief executive of Celtic FC, also lent support stating 'Brother Walfrid is a hugely important figure and someone whose contribution to Celtic Football Club and to wider Scottish society is most deserving of this kind of study'.[2]

It is in this context that this book and the thesis on which it is based present the first historical account of Walfrid's life from birth in rural County Sligo, just prior to the cataclysmic *An Gorta Mor*, through his survival and emigration to Scotland and to his subsequent life spent teaching in the community as a member of the French Catholic religious order, the Marist Brothers. The Marist motto, inscribed in Latin on the statue which pays tribute to Brother Walfrid, paid for by the donations of Celtic supporters and unveiled in 2005 at Celtic Park, reads:

Ignoti et quasi occulti in hoc mundo

['unknown and partially hidden in this world'].

Walfrid's devotion to his vocation as a Marist Brother and his willingness to live out his commitment to the order's original sacred vows of poverty, chastity and obedience perhaps to some extent explain why much of his story has remained *unknown* and *partially hidden* for so long.

The religious charism [the distinctive beliefs derived from devotion to the Blessed Virgin Mary] of the Marist Brothers promotes an ethos of humility, modesty and simplicity, which in many ways characterised the life of Walfrid. Brother Walfrid's association, however, with Christian charity and football, distinguish him as a figure of historical significance to religious, ethnic, social and cultural life in Scotland and beyond.[3] Finn has previously called for an 'overdue' academic reappraisal of Brother Walfrid's impacts in life.[4] To that end, I deemed it necessary to uncover and extrapolate new primary source information about his life towards the overarching goal of producing a critical historical biography. This approach aims at separating the man from the myth and fact from fiction. It remains an inspiring story.

Notes

1 The portrait was unveiled in November 2014 and features opposite the title page. The original is displayed beside the altar in St. Mary's, the Calton area of Glasgow, the birthplace of Celtic FC.

2 Available online at https://www.stir.ac.uk/news/2017/10/new-study-into-celtic-fc-founderbrother-walfrid accessed September 2021.

3 Bradley, J.M., 'Sport and the contestation of cultural and ethnic identities in Scottish society', *Immigrants & Minorities*, Vol. 17, No. 1 (1998), pp. 127-150.

4 Finn, G., 'Racism, Religion and Social Prejudice: Irish Catholic Clubs, Soccer and Scottish Society – II Social Identities and Conspiracy Theories', *The International Journal of the History of Sport*, Vol.8, No. 3 (1991), p. 388.

The ruin of Andrew Kerins' 1840 birthplace

CHAPTER 1

Sligo: 1840 – 1855

The man who became Brother Walfrid was born Andrew Kerins in Ballymote, County Sligo on the west coast of Ireland in 1840. The name Kerins is less well known, as are the historical context and ancestral origins of a somewhat mythical figure. Most popular historical, as well as the few academic references, have primarily focussed on the Marist Brother and his part in the foundation of Celtic Football Club. More substantive historical detail on the early years of his life is rare and often incomplete.

But our lives have meaning when set in their context. Analysis of family roots, socio-economic and cultural conditions into which Kerins was born is vital to aid understanding of where he was coming from and who he was.

Kerins' exact date of birth is recorded as 18th May 1840 on his headstone where he lays at rest in the cemetery of the Marist Brothers in Dumfries, Scotland. He was born to parents John and Elisabeth Kerins (née Flynn) in the parish of Emlafad, close to Ballymote in rural Sligo. The county of Sligo – together with Mayo, Roscommon, Leitrim and Galway – comprises one of the four provinces of Ireland, Connacht. Situated in the west of the island on the Atlantic coast, the inhabitants of the overwhelmingly agrarian area were 'least prepared' for what was to befall them and the majority of the population of Ireland in the years after Andrew's birth.[1]

Archival records held by the Marist Brothers in Rome show Andrew's father John was a '*cultivateur*' – a tiller farmer – while his mother Elisabeth is described as a '*ménagère*': this being French for homemaker.[2] Walfrid's parents were married on 25th June 1837 in the parish of Emlafad, in the Diocese of Achonry. The service took place in the Catholic Chapel of Ballymote, close to the Kerins' familial home and was witnessed by Martin and Andrew Kerins, brothers of Walfrid's father, John.[3]

Andrew Kerins was the second-born son to Elisabeth and John Kerins. The most recent complete census data shows that his older brother Peter was born in 1834. Peter was Andrew's only sibling.[4] Those later census returns show that both Irish and English were read and written within the Kerins household at Cartron Phibbs.[5]

The family name Kerins is an anglicisation of the Irish Ò'Céirín'. The name originates from the 'Ciarraige' people of Connacht, principally in County Mayo, but which by the nineteenth century had become prevalent in neighbouring Sligo.[6] The Kerins' family heritage – like most of those born of farming stock in the Connacht region – was distinctly Irish and Catholic in character, in stark contrast to the overwhelming majority of those who owned the land.

Cartron Phibbs – the farmstead where Kerins was born – lies two miles to the west of the town of Ballymote within the county of Sligo. The historic borders of the farm show the townland comprising an area of some nineteen acres, which places the land held by the Kerins family in the smallest 6% of landholdings in the county. Samuel Lewis' contemporary survey of Ireland first published in 1837 was backed by subscriptions and testament from the Church of Ireland, landed gentry and local Catholic clergy across Ireland. Lewis has previously been commissioned to complete similar topographical studies of England and Wales.

The text of the survey is significant in that it provides some of the most detailed descriptions, both qualitatively and quantitively, of the area where Andrew Kerins was born and spent his childhood. Lewis found that 'the best land in the entire county is around Ballymote'.[7] Lewis describes how 'around Sligo and Ballymote are some excellent dairy farms, and butter is made by all the small farmers, but much the greater part of which is shipped at Sligo for the British market'.[8]

This reflects Ireland's position within the Union at the time, as a subsidiary trading partner to Britain.

At the time of Andrew Kerins' birth, the extended family in Ballymote were of tenant farming stock. Family members would all have been required to work the land in order to pay rent as tenants of the Cartron-Phibbs farmland. In etymological terms, Cartron-Phibbs was originally known as 'Cartún Uí Choinéil', or O'Connell in English. The 'Parish Namebook' makes reference to the change of title as part of the 1836 Ordnance Survey. The official, John O'Donovan poses the question to his British superiors, 'Whether shall we call it after Phibbs or O'Connell?'[9] Many such placenames were anglicised at this time across Ireland during British colonial rule. Local historian Tom McGettrick contests:

> Baile An Mota (the original Irish for 'Ballymote') Townland names are an important part of our heritage, they are based on our native language. They are in most cases as old as our history and they will stay into the future regardless of what success the revival of our language may have. Many of them are captions for lost or forgotten local history, topography or genealogy which is now untraceable. Sixty-eight of these are in the Parish of Emlaghfad and Kilmorgan (Ballymote).[10]

The new 'Phibbs' part of the title, chosen as part of the Ordnance Survey, referred to the Phibbs family of landed Protestant aristocracy who owned substantial landholdings in County Sligo at the time.[11] Property information is extant for the Cartron Phibbs townland leased by the Kerins family from the Phibbs. The 'Tithe Applotments' were gathered to record which properties met the criteria which required the household to pay towards the Church of Ireland. These records for 1833 show a Martin Kerins as the occupier of Cartron Phibbs (then Cartron O'Connell). Martin Kerins was most likely the oldest brother of Walfrid's father John. The National Archives of Ireland describes the tithes as a tax equal to 'one tenth of the produce of agricultural land levied for the support of the official, state-established Church of Ireland and its clergymen'. By 1823, the Tithe Composition (Ireland) Act instructed how 'this was converted into a monetary tax and the

Tithe Applotment Books were compiled at various dates between 1823 and 1837'.[12]

Tithes were viewed as an unjust taxation and were especially unpopular amongst the Catholic majority of tenant labouring classes in Ireland. Harthwick explains that Catholic landholders were exasperated by 'having to pay what they considered an exorbitant rate of tithe – in itself a tax to support a [Protestant] church to which they did not belong and from which they received no benefit'. Coordinated resistance, varying from organised non-payments to mass protests, continued against the tax throughout the 1830s across Ireland, known as the 'Tithe War'.[13]

Nevertheless, to the benefit of the historian, the collection books survive as valuable genealogical sources, especially in light of the scarcity of complete nineteenth century census data for Ireland. The tithe taxation only applied to 'occupiers of agricultural holdings above one acre'.[14] The Kerins family is found to be leasing over nineteen acres in 1833 at Cartron Phibbs, three of which are classed as bog, and, as such, inarable. Only the head of the household was listed by the applotment registrars, which explains the eldest son's position as per the Irish custom of primogeniture.'[15]

By way of comparison, 61% of small farming families owned between one and five acres of arable farmland in Sligo county. This placed the Kerins family within the 4% of landholding families who held between fifteen and thirty acres as per the 1841 parliamentary report.[16] The three acres of bogland, listed separately, offered access to the Owenmore River which flows from nearby Templehouse Lake.[17] The Kerins family were in a comparatively privileged position in the locality given the size of their landholding. Nearby Templehouse, however – a 'handsome' country home built in 1825 and seat of the Perceval family estate – offers a visual reminder of the inequality prevalent in Ireland at the time.[18]

A recent article by Cummins and O'Grada on the structure of wealth in pre-famine Ireland's cautions that '[this] was a very unequal society, even by contemporary western European standards'. They describe how:

> . . . the chasm between the relatively small number of landowners who owned virtually all the land and the three million or so rural dwellers who relied almost solely on the potato for subsistence resonates more of serfdom and the *ancien régime* than of industrialising Britain.[19]

In November 1840, six months after the birth of Andrew Kerins, further property evidence sheds light on the position of the wider family. The Griffiths Valuation is the first example of British colonial efforts to map and evaluate all of the land and property on the island of Ireland. The Ballymote field book of 1840 shows John Kerins – head of the family – renting a house and offices from Sir Robert Gore Booth, the foremost landlord in the Sligo locality. Kerins also has a sub-tenant – Peter Langan – renting an adjacent property on Main Street, Ballymote. Catherine Kerins, an in-law, is also renting a property with an attached shop 'in good order' from Gore Booth on Main Street.[20] Member of Parliament for County Sligo for nearly a quarter century, Sir Robert Gore Booth took proprietorship of the town of Ballymote from the Fitzmaurice family in 1833. Rogers explains how 'for the most part he was an absentee landlord, which left the estate in the hands of an agent called Dodwell, whose name was synonymous with eviction throughout Co. Sligo'.[21]

Indeed, a John Kerins was incarcerated for debts on 15th April 1848, at the height of the famine.[22] It is entirely possible that this was Andrew's father given the widespread economic and humanitarian problems inflicted upon small farmers across the locality. John Kerins, however, is still shown as renting from Gore Booth in the 1858 Griffiths Valuation records of Ballymote Main Street.[23] The inability to make rent payments during the Great Hunger was a common occurrence for many families in rural Ballymote, as the Sligo prison registers attest.

Given the comparative size of the Kerins landholding at Cartron Phibbs, it is here where a young Andrew Kerins would have been required to labour as a child, particularly during harvest season in Spring and Autumn.[24] In 1857, the Griffiths Valuation lists Anne Kerins – sister of Walfrid's father – as occupier, renting land recorded at just over thirty one acres from Harlow Phibbs. Despite the turmoil of the famine years the Kerins family were able to keep their tenancy on the Cartron-Phibbs plot of farmland.

In 1852, while the Great Hunger continued to drive excess mortality and emigration across Sligo, *The Dublin Evening Post* reports the attendance of the Phibbs family at a 'Ball at Lissadell House', the seat of the Gore Booths. The report reads:

> Sir Robert and Lady Gore Booth gave a ball on the 14th, which was attended by the *elite* of the county of Sligo and the adjoining counties. Nothing could surpass the excellence of the arrangements in every department.[25]

Local newspaper reports of the funeral of the Kerins' landlord in 1871 shows that Phibbs was resident at Dublin and, like Gore Booth, far removed from the landholding in Ballymote rented to Walfrid's family.[26] Absentee landlords were common for rural tenants such as the Kerins family. The Irish National Folklore Collection is a key source for accessing cultural memory dating back to the nineteenth century, particularly in the west of Ireland.[27] One such entry in the Schools Collection records one family's experience of tenantry under the Phibbs family in Sligo. The entry describes how Phibbs was 'was considered to be a good landlord in comparison with the others of his class'. Instead, blame for evictions and deaths of tenants is ascribed to a local land agent – 'a cruel exterminator' – employed by the Phibbs family to collect rent.[28]

The cottier cabin, where Andrew Kerins is understood to have been born, remains standing from this time. The buildings are set within a grove clearing amidst the sizeable fields rented and worked by the extended Kerins family. This knowledge gives us understanding of the familial and socioeconomic situation Brother Walfrid was born into. As a rural farm boy on the eve of the catastrophe of *An Gorta*

Mor, his story of eventual departure for a better life away from his homeland reflects that of countless others caught up in similar circumstances across Ireland.

Further accounting of lived experience of small farmers was recorded by Gustave de Beaumont, a contemporary French sociologist who published field work findings based on his travels in Ireland in 1839. De Beaumont extensively considers what he perceived to be the 'feudal' nature of the landlord-tenant economic relationship in Ireland. He writes:

> ... lands are cultivated by the Catholic population,
> theoretically free to detach itself from the soil, but
> bound to it as the only means of existence, and in
> reality in a condition worse than that of the serfs during
> the middle ages.[29]

Reference to the Catholic religion of rural farming families in de Beaumont's survey is key in light of Emmet Larkin's description of a 'Devotional Revolution' in mid-nineteenth century Ireland. For Larkin, the shoots of this phenomenon could be traced to 'the enthusiasm and hope generated by the moral and political reform movements of Father Mathew and Daniel O'Connell'.[30] O'Connell's political movement aimed for the repeal of Ireland's union with Britain – bolstered by the achievement of the Catholic Emancipation Act in 1829 – and its famed 'monster meetings' reflected the widespread support of the Irish people.[31] Deignan describes how 'Co. Sligo was relatively quick off the mark in joining the Repeal campaign and on 1st August 1840 at least 20,000 people assembled at Ballymote to call for the Repeal of the Union' as reported by the *Sligo Champion*.[32]

Similarly, the Tipperary priest Father Theobald Mathew's speaking tours gained widespread press coverage, with his temperance pledge taken up by millions of Catholics in Ireland and Britain.[33] Larkin explains, in the decade of Brother Walfrid's birth, the mass appeal of 'both revival movements, which created not only an enormous enthusiasm but, because of the underlying anxieties created by population pressure and land hunger also contributed greatly to an already heavily charged emotional atmosphere'.[34]

The *Sligo Champion* records O'Connell addressing huge crowds in rural Sligo in May 1843 and again in October 1845, on the brink of the period of *An Gorta Mor*. Following the 1845 meeting, the Bishops of Sligo attended a dinner in honour of the 'Liberator' O'Connell.[35] Although the famine years dampened the fervour for repeal, Larkin argues that conditions for a 'Devotional Revolution' were already in place by mid-century Ireland, especially in the rural west.[36] Both the repeal and temperance movements of the early 1840s led by O'Connell and Father Mathew were able to garner mass appeal by availing of existing Catholic parochial organisation at a local level.

In the case of Ballymote and the Kerins family, it is crucial to understand how that 'Devotional Revolution' and the 'cultural importance of Irish Catholicism' began to manifest itself into the period between the onset of An *Gorta Mor* and Walfrid's departure from Ireland in 1855.[37] Lewis finds in 1837 that the Roman Catholic chapel for the surrounding area is a substantial building situated in Ballymote town itself.[38] Father Bernard O'Kane is listed as a subscriber to Lewis' topographical survey and is parish priest for Ballymote at the time.[39] O'Kane died at the height of the Famine and was replaced in the late 1849 by a Ballymote local, Father Denis Tighe, ordained after training in France.[40]

Both local priests, O'Kane and Tighe, would have been early spiritual influences on Andrew Kerins as a child growing up in Ballymote, particularly in terms of Catholic teaching and his later decision to devote his life to Catholic education as a Marist Brother soon after arriving in Glasgow. Education in mid-nineteenth century Ireland underwent a period of change with the implementation of the National Schools in 1831 and the later upheaval brought about by the famine conditions from 1845.

Fernandez-Suarez explores the enduring influence of the 'the native system of education' – the rural hedge school – during penal times, as well as on the new state system introduced in 1831.[41] She finds that only one in three Irish children attended the national schools in 1841, one year after Kerins' birth, meaning the majority of those engaged in education would have been taught at the traditional hedge school. The hedge schools tended to be funded by donations and run by the local parish clergy, with Fathers O'Kane and Tighe listed as schoolmasters in the Ballymote locality. However, Fernandez-Suarez explains:

> . . . the Famine marked their decline as the number of students decreased considerably and the families that survived were in such a state of dispossession that they would not be able to pay for the education of their children.[42]

O'Connell also attests to the enduring influence of hedge schools as a 'stronghold of Irish resistance to cultural domination by an outside power'.[43] Given that Irish was spoken and written within the Kerins family, it is likely that Andrew Kerins had some degree of education in the hedge school tradition in the Ballymote locality. Archbishop John MacHale of Tuam – 'the lion of the West' – was foremost in the Connacht region in decrying the lask of provision for the Irish language within the new imposed system. This explains why many families favoured paying for their children to be educated in the hedge schools. The leading Catholic Archbishop in the province referred to the National System as 'anti-national' and lobbied the Catholic hierarchy in Rome in 1839 to ensure some of the traditional character of the old Irish language schools was retained in the new system.

The likely source of Brother Walfrid's early education and spiritual teaching is found at Emlaghnaughtan. A survey of schools in County Sligo details how in 1832 Father Bernard O'Kane, then Ballymote parish priest, established 'a school known as Little Bridge'. Father O'Kane had the school reinstated as a National School in a new building by 1838. Although no roll books survive from the earliest years of its existence, by 1870 Emlaghnaughtan had 'an enrolment of 167 and an average attendance of 53'.[44] The folklore entries for *Imleach*

Neachtain (Emlaghnaughtan) school show schoolmasters 'used to teach Latin and Greek as well as Irish and a little English'.[45] Bordering the Kerins' Cartron Phibbs farmland directly to the east towards Ballymote town, the Emlaghnaughtan school is where Walfrid, most likely, first received formal education.[46] Hannan finds that the school was managed by the Ballymore parish priests, Father O'Kane followed by his successor Father Tighe, and is described as having the character of a hedge school. This indicates resistance against what Archbishop MacHale depicted as an 'anti-national' colonial system of education. As a product of this resistance, Andrew Kerins' personal conviction and strength of character – Catholic, Irish – endured throughout his life.[47]

The contemporary writings of William Carleton offer an insight into the workings of a traditional hedge school in Ireland:

> When a poor man, about twenty or thirty years ago, understood from the schoolmaster who educated his sons, that any of them was particularly 'cute at his larnin', the ambition of the parent usually directed itself to one of three objects – he would either make him a priest, a clerk, or a schoolmaster.[48]

Notes

1 Smyth, W.J., 'The province of Connacht and the Great Famine' in Crowley, J., Smyth, W. J. and Murphy, M., (eds), *Atlas of the Great Irish Famine* (Cork: University Press, 2012) pp. 281-290.

2 Microfiche of Brother Walfrid, No. 2998 held at the General Archive for The Institute of Marist Brothers, Rome. Translation is my own.

3 Marriages, Apr. 1837 to June 1837, Emlefad and Kilmorgan; County of Sligo; Diocese of Achonry. Microfilm 04228/07, p. 44. Accessed online at Catholic Parish Registers at the National Library of Ireland.

4 Census of Ireland 1901 and 1911, accessed online at http://www.census.nationalarchives.ie/.

5 *Ibid.*

6 O'Laughlin, M. C., *The Book of Irish Families: Great and Small; 1* (Irish Genealogical Foundation, 2002), p. 164.

7 Lewis, S., *County Sligo in 1837: A Topographical Dictionary* (The County Sligo Heritage and Genealogical Society: Sligo, 2003), p. 6.

8 *Ibid*, p. 8.

9 Information accessed online at https://www.logainm.ie/en/45705?s=Cartron+(Phibbs).

10 McGettrick, T., 'Townlands & Place Names', *Corran Herald*, Vol. 22 (1992), p. 6.

11 McTernan, J. C., *Worthies of Sligo: Profiles of Eminent Sligonians of Other Days* (Sligo: Avena Publications, 1994), p. 306.

12 Accessed online at https://www.nationalarchives.ie/article/tithe-applotment-records.

13 Harthwick, S. C., 'The Clergy Relief Fund, 1831: Tithe Defaulters', *Irish Genealogy*, Vol. 8, No. 1 (1990), p. 82.

14 Accessed online at https://www.nationalarchives.ie/article/tithe-applotment-records.

15 Tithe Applotment Books 1833, Parish of Emlafad. Accessed online at http://titheapplotmentbooks.nationalarchives.ie/reels/tab//004587439/004587439_00381.pdf.

16 Deignan, P., *Land and People in Nineteenth Century Sligo* (Sligo, 2015), p. 56.

17 Tithe Applotment Books 1833, Parish of Emlafad. Accessed online at http://titheapplotmentbooks.nationalarchives.ie/reels/tab//004587439/004587439_00381.pdf.

18 Lewis, S., *County Sligo in 1837: A Topographical Dictionary*, p. 22.

19 Cummins, N., and O'Grada, C., 'On the Structure of Wealth-Holding in Pre-Famine Ireland', *Irish Economic and Social History* (Feb, 2021), pp. 1-2. It is worth noting that Ireland was subsumed into the 'United Kingdom of Great Britain and Ireland' by parliamentary decree on January 1st 1801 unti the creation of the Irish Free State in 1922. Roman Catholics were barrred from participation in the political system until 1829.

20 Field book 27 Nov 1840 Accessed online at http://census.nationalarchives.ie/reels/vob/IRE_CENSUS_1821-51_007250687_00971.pdf.

21 Rogers, N., *Ballymote Aspects Through Time*, second edition (Sligo: Orbicon Print, 2010), p. 22. Countess Markiewicz, a name later synonymous with Ireland's revolutionary period at the beginning of the twentieth century, was a notable direct descendant of the Gore Booth family of Sligo.

22 Sligo Prison General Register 1843-1878, Book No. 1/34/3.

23 Griffiths Valuation 1858 Accessed online http://census.nationalarchives.ie/reels/vob/IRE_CENSUS_1821-51_007250687_00971.pdf.

24 County Sligo INTO Millennium Committee, *The National Schools of County Sligo* (Sligo: Carrick Print, 2000), p. 11.

25 *The Dublin Evening Post*, January 20th 1852.

26 *Roscommon and Leitrim Gazette*, June 10th 1871.

27 Glassie, H., 'The Irish Folklore Commission: International Scholarship, National Purpose, Local Virtue', *Béaloideas*, Vol. 78 (2010), p. 7.

28 The Schools' Collection, Vol. 0170, p. 0128. Accessed online at https://www.duchas.ie/en/cbes/4701702/4694113.

29 De Beaumont, G., *Ireland: Social, Political, and Religious. Vol. 1* (1839), p. 260.

30 Larkin, E., 'The Devotional Revolution in Ireland, 1850-75', *The American Historical Review*, Vol. 77, No. 3 (Oxford: Oxford University Press, Jun. 1972), p. 637.

31 *Ibid.*

32 Deignan, *Land and People in Nineteenth Century Sligo*, p. 86.

33 Larkin, 'The Devotional Revolution in Ireland, 1850-75', p. 636.

34 *Ibid.*

35 Deignan, *Land and People in Nineteenth Century Sligo*, p. 86.

36 Larkin, 'The Devotional Revolution in Ireland, 1850-75', p. 639.

37 Larkin, 'The Devotional Revolution in Ireland, 1850-75', p. 649-651.

38 Lewis, S., *County Sligo in 1837: A Topographical Dictionary*, p. 55.

39 Lewis, S., *County Sligo in 1837: A Topographical Dictionary*, p. x.

40 McTernan, J., 'The Tighes of Tighe's Town', *Corran Herald 1999/2000*, Vol. 32 (2000), p. 4.

41 Fernandez-Suarez, Y., 'An Essential Picture in a Sketch-Book of Ireland: The Last Hedge Schools', *Estudios Irlandeses*, No. 1 (2006), p. 45.

42 Fernandez-Suarez, 'An Essential Picture in a Sketch-Book of Ireland: The Last Hedge Schools', p. 48.

43 O'Connell, A., 'The Irish Hedge Schools: Rejection, resistance and Creativity (1695- 1831)', *Revue Civilisations*, (2011), p. 83.

44 County Sligo INTO Millennium Committee, *The National Schools of County Sligo*, p. 112.

45 The Schools' Collection, Vol. 0184, p. 333. Accessed online at https://www.duchas.ie/en/cbes/4725004/4699129.

46 Emlaghnaughtan townland information accessed online at https://www.townlands.ie/sligo/corran/emlaghfad/owenmore/emlaghnaghtan/.

47 Hannan'The Children Don't Sing Here Anymore', *Corran Herald* 199/1000. Vol 32 p. 20

48 Carleton, W., *Illustrated Stories and Tales of the Irish*, Vol. 3 (Project Gutenberg Edition, 1843), accessed online at https://www.gutenberg.org/files/16014/16014-h/16014-h.htm.

This memorial was erected in Andrew Kerins' hometown of Ballymote in 2004 paid for by public donations.

An Gorta Mor memorial at St Mary's church, Calton, Glasgow serves as a permanent tribute to the diasporic community which Andrew Kerins was part of, served in life and continues to inspire more than a century after his death

CHAPTER 2
An Gorta Mor

The local parish priest, Father Tighe had returned to Ballymote with a reputation for advocating and fundraising on behalf of the poor from his previous parish in County Mayo after successive potato crops in Ireland began to fail in 1845. This signalled the onset of *An Gorta Mor*. In a letter, published in January 1847, to the editor of *The Freeman's Journal*, Father Tighe describes 'the awful distress now prevailing' and a lack of government relief contributing to the deaths of at least twenty-six of his parishioners from starvation. With a large readership outside of Ireland, in England and Scotland for example, Father Tighe states his aim 'to advocate the cause of the poor' and appeals for aid to those who may have had the means to offer charity at the time.[1]

Historians such as Nally have been critical of the British government's 'Malthusian'[2] relief policy at the time of the Famine. By 1850, for example, soup kitchen relief had been withdrawn prematurely, there was no provision for outdoor relief in Ireland and to qualify for indoor workhouse relief Irish farmers had to part with any land over one-quarter acre to the state.[3] Father Tighe, writing in the London-based Catholic publication *The Tablet* in August 1849, summed up the severity of the situation in Ballymote:

> Let the Prime Minister of England boast as he may, that
> 'famine is at an end', were his Lordship to visit this parish
> he would be easily convinced that the contrary was the fact;
> he would also be obliged to admit that famine and hunger
> are committing a havoc at this very moment on her
> Majesty's loving people unprecedented in any other
> civilised nation.

I grieve to tell you we have unmistakeable evidence that
the potato blight has returned. It has rapidly developed
itself for the last few days. When I add to this that the
cholera has broken out in the workhouse, and that our poor
are rather determined to die of hunger at home sooner than
go there, you may easily imagine their sad condition.[4]

In the same published letter, Tighe acknowledges financial aid
received from an Irish priest in Boulogne-sur-Mer, Northern France
and from subscribers to *The Tablet* in London.[5] In August 1850, Father
Tighe was present at the inaugural meeting of the Irish Tenant League
in Dublin. The Tenant League – comprised of parish priests and
ministers alike – stated its objective to 'obtain justice and due
protection for the tenant' class across Ireland.[6] By 1854, Tighe seeks
and gains approval from the Bishop of Achonry to begin fundraising
for a new church in Ballymote, the old Catholic Chapel having fallen
into disrepair. In letters published by the *Freeman's Journal*, the priest
explains that financial support would need to be sought as 'the parish
is small and its population much reduced during the famine'.[7] The
new Church of the Immaculate Conception was eventually consecrat-
ed in 1864 following receipt of donations from the Irish diaspora,
including from London, America and continental Europe.[8]

The parish Kerins belonged to was thus outward-looking in its
worldview, as much by necessity as by design. Such techniques of
humanitarian fundraising and advocating on behalf of the poor
exhibited in this period are themes replicated in his later life as Brother
Walfrid: charity is one enduring hallmark.

On the subject Irish migration, Langlan's framework for interpret-
ing the experience of emigration, when applied to the case of Andrew
Kerins, is elucidating in the context of the aftermath of *An Gorta Mor*.
In the 'famine decade', between 1841 and 1851, Kelly and Fotheringham's study finds that 'Connaught was the worst affected province,
losing 28.4% of its population'.[9] By 1861 a further 9.9% of the
population had left the province of Kerins' birth.[10]

Family testimony offers a new insight into the narrative and socioeconomic context surrounding Kerins' own departure from Sligo to Glasgow in 1855, aged just fifteen, amidst the wider phenomenon of mass emigration from Ireland.[11]

By this time the worst effects of *An Gorta Mor*, in terms of successive potato crop failures and excess deaths due to lack of sustenance, had passed. Smyth summarises the devastation wrought in the west of Ireland farming communities:

> . . . as many men, women and children died of famine-related causes in *rural* Connacht as might have died if the cities of Cork, Dublin and Waterford with a combined population of 336,662, had disappeared off the map.[12]

Additionally, outflow migration continued into the twentieth century as Irish people sought 'opportunities to escape' the economic ruin.[13] 'So began the great exodus from the west', continues Smyth, highlighting the importance of geography for those living in Ireland at the time. The major port of Sligo offered escape and the hope of survival for many thousands in the surrounding region.[14]

As second-born son, Andrew Kerins would have been aware of his position in the rural family unit from an early age. Fitzgerald and McCullough describe how following An *Gorta Mor* 'there was a gradual but clearly perceptible transition to impartible inheritance, as primogeniture became increasingly established as the norm'.[15] The land holding would pass to his older sibling Peter, as is shown in the later census returns for 1901 and 1911.[16] Furthermore, Kelly and Fotheringham note 'Irish agriculture had been gradually moving towards extensive types of farming involving grazing and livestock production and away from traditional labour-intensive tillage farming'. This process was expedited by *An Gorta Mor*, which in turn accelerated emigration in the subsequent decades.[17]

It increasingly became the case that 'non-inheriting siblings with few alternative income streams in Ireland looked out towards the Diaspora for their futures, and having gone overseas, they had limited reason to return to the home place'.[18] That Andrew Kerins, aged just fifteen, was compelled to leave behind his family, community and homeland demonstrates the stark reality of diminished prospects as a result of the wider *An Gorta Mor* period.

The testimonies in 2019 of Alison Healy and Professor Bart McGettrick shed new light on Kerins' crossing to Glasgow in 1855. Alison's mother, Mary Healy – a grand niece of Kerins and granddaughter of Andrew's brother Peter – recorded that Andrew and a friend of the same age left Sligo harbour aboard a coal boat, as per recollections passed down through the Kerins family.[19] The friend was one Bart McGettrick from a neighbouring townland in Ballymote. Professor Bart McGettrick, retired principal for Catholic teacher training at Glasgow University, is a direct descendant of his namesake who embarked on the journey with Andrew Kerins. Professor McGettrick confirms the crossing of family members from Ballymote to Glasgow, as well as some details which also feature in Healy's narrative of events.[20]

It is recorded that the two boys sold a 'weanling' – or calf – at the Ballymote Fair to raise the funds required for the passage to Glasgow. Such a substantial financial sacrifice would have been one of the only ways at the time of raising the monies required for a one-off payment for passage across the Irish Sea.[21] The Irish Schools' Collection of folklore memories records a Ballymote man born in the 1850s recalling that 'the great fairs of the year locally' were traditionally held following the spring and summer harvests.[22]

Examination of the Clyde bill of entry and shipping list for 1855 illustrates the established trade route between the port of Sligo and the Broomielaw harbour in Glasgow.[23] Passenger lists, unfortunately, were rarely recorded for this period as Ireland remained under colonial British rule throughout the nineteenth century. However, the bill of entry shows that agents such as J. Wright Co. and Raeburn & Middleton in Glasgow were engaged in importing foodstuffs – particularly oatmeal and barley, but sometimes livestock – from Sligo. In return, these same companies facilitated large shipments of coal from the coalfields of Lanarkshire surrounding Glasgow to the port of Sligo.

Shipments of coal usually exceeded one hundred tonnes, peaking in the summer months and again in November and December when seven shipments of coal from Glasgow to Sligo were completed.[24]

The desperation of the young Kerins to seek a new life is evident from the nature of his crossing aboard one such cattle and coal-carrying vessel. Smyth details how, for the poorest Irish emigrants who could not afford the voyage to the New World, by the 1850s, new steam technology meant that:

> For passage money of a few shillings, they could cross by steamer to land in ports in England and Scotland or cross (as did some 'emaciated, ragged men and children') as ballast in the coal ships.[25]

'Steerage' fares were advertised as the lowest cost, below-deck option for those most desperate to embark on what was reportedly 'a rough passage'. An edition of *The Glasgow Free Press* from October 1858 described how a standard crossing between Sligo and Glasgow aboard a cargo steamer ship took at least twenty-four hours. The overnight crossings were often delayed due to severity of weather and could be treacherous. [26]

Upon arrival in Scotland, Andrew Kerins joined a community of an estimated 100,000 Irish-born refugees who fled their homeland during and immediately after *An Gorta Mor*. Like Kerins, the vast majority of the Irish arriving in mid-century were Catholic and settled in Glasgow or the surrounding Lanarkshire region in the industrialised west of Scotland.[27] Having survived the famine and left his immediate family behind at Ballymote aged just fifteen, Kerins would face the challenges associated with what Collins terms 'rural Irish – urban British migration' which prevailed for those who settled in Britain's Victorian cities in the hope of a better life.[28] In many ways his early life was typical of that migratory process, and its illuminates 'the relationship between social forces and personal character'.[29]

Negotiating these abrupt changes in circumstances involved drawing on his formative experiences and his subsequent life offers a singular insight into immigrant Irish Catholicism in nineteenth century Britain. Even by this stage in his young life, having experienced poverty and hunger in rural Ireland, the self-defining reduced role of second son, child labour, the all too close effects of landlordism and life under British colonial rule, not to mention the trauma of famine and effectively forced migration, it is likely that in his own developing mind, young Andrew Kerins had already formed an outlook and attitude to the world as he found it. Certainly themes and motifs that were to recur and dominate his later adult life were evident – hunger, poverty, education, charity, and insofar as it helped alleviate and assist these, sport. A child, whose tenant farmer father, just as so many at the time, was likely incarcerated in 1848 for debt, takes on the mindset and awarweness of life's injustices.

Before moving on to the greeting and challenges the young Kerins would encounter in his chosen destination and new life in Scotland, it is important to acknoweldge and recount the fact that this breach from the land of his birth was by no means just his own. This was encountered by generations of the youngest and fittest Irish citizens before and since. These historical and political forces were traumatic and impactful.

Cormac O'Grada concluded that 'the Irish famine was much more murderous, relatively speaking, than most historical and most modern famines'.[30] Emigration was, in fact, a continuous feature of nineteenth century Irish society, during and after *An Gorta Mor*.[31] Various 'push and pull' factors influenced decisions on emigration during this period. For example, seasonal workers left Ireland in the early part of the century to fill short term labour demand in Britain, attracted by the promise of summer employment.[32]

But the humanitarian disaster of the 1840s and 1850s was trans-formational in Ireland's demographic history in that it arrested the steady population growth experienced during prior decades. This forced unprecedented numbers to flee their homeland permanently amidst the suffering and starvation triggered by the 'tragic' and deadly failure of the potato crop.[33] Thus, although the years of *An Gorta Mor* represent a watershed moment in Irish history, the experience of emigration before and after the period of successive crop failures between 1845 and 1852 is also critical.

Mary Daly contests that 'Famine emigration is now largely seen as a continuum from the immediate pre-Famine pattern of the early 1840s. O'Grada, on the other hand, writes that 'it was push migration with a vengeance'. [34] It is clear from scholarship that Irish emigration during the nineteenth century has been a contentious and enduring source of debate for historians, often with more modern revisionist explanations in one camp and 'nationalist' perspectives in the other.[35] Analysis of key themes which also influenced emigration during the period – such as the decisions of the British colonial government, the Industrial Revolution and traditional folk narratives – contributes to a more nuanced understanding of why people left Ireland in the nineteenth century.

Graham Davis described how the population of Ireland rose steeply during the first half of the nineteenth century until the onset of the 'Famine'. During the period between 1785 and 1841 the number of people in Ireland more than doubled from an estimated 4 million to 8.2 million.[36] K.H. Connell argues that 'overpopulation arose through a combination of universally early marriage and high fertility', allied to a number of mediating factors.[37] A trend towards subdivision of farm holdings due to increased demand from England for Irish produce during the Napoleonic Wars saw a growing rural workforce reliant on the highly-nutritious potato crop.[38] However, Davis also explains that 'a pattern of continuous emigration' from the island also emerged at this time.[39]

Kerby Miller, for example, states that around one million people left the island of Ireland for foreign shores in the thirty years preceding *An Gorta Mor* – and , for the first time, people from all levels of the social spectrum were moving overseas rather than a number of more wealthy Ulster-Scots Protestants who could traditionally afford to travel.[40] In terms of Irish movement to Scotland, Collins demonstrated how 'seasonal migration fitted well into the agrarian structures of both islands'. For example, summer employment for the Irish rural worker between 'potato planting and harvesting' meant Scottish employers had short term labour shortages met.[41] This mutually-beneficial arrangement meant that by 1841 a summer census counted 57,000 people leaving Irish ports for Britain – 'almost all were men and the majority were aged 16-35, the group likely to be the most physically fit'.[42] J. E. Handley [Brother Clare, ex-headmaster of St. Mungo's in Glasgow] found 'reciprocal immigration' between Ireland and Scotland to be a continuous feature of the two nations throughout the nineteenth century.[43]

Davis explains that the burgeoning Industrial Revolution also encouraged established migratory patterns by bringing with it advances in transport – rail travel and steamships by the mid-century in particular – while competition meant 'cheapness of fares both assisted and encouraged the flow of seasonal and permanent emigration to Britain'.[44] Collins found that 'steam boats began on the routes from Derry and Belfast to Glasgow in the early 1820s': and ships would carry 'people as well as freight' before the 1820s.[45] By the 1840s there were said to be as many Irish 'navvies' as indigenous Scots working on the construction of the Caledonian railway line as competition between the steamboat companies facilitated cheaper migration.[46]

Furthermore, a National Schools system had been established in Ireland in 1831 which assisted in providing more people with the ability and desire to seek better living conditions elsewhere. For Davis, the nascent education system 'had the indirect effect of equipping a substantial section of the Irish people for leaving the country'.[47]

Collins asserts that emigration was so commonplace in Irish society – even before the Famine – that it 'became part of the expected cycle of life'.[48] Indeed 'by 1841 there were 126,000 Irish-born people in Scotland' for example, by far the biggest immigrant community. This was especially the case in the West-Central region surrounding Glasgow.[49]

Of the typical Irish immigrant, Handley wrote that 'self-improve-ment was the impulse that transported him to Scotland in pre-famine days' and that 'self-preservation was the urge that drove him onwards in the black night of pestilence' with the rupture of *An Gorta Mor* after 1845.[50] The event is held as a 'watershed' moment in Irish history, with Mokyr arguing 'had there been no Famine, Ireland's population would have continued to grow like any other European country in the second half of the nineteenth century'. Today, Ireland remains the only European nation to have a population now smaller than at the mid-point of the nineteenth century.[51]

The *Freeman's Journal* of September 1845 reported that the potato crop had been perfectly conditioned one week, then 'unfit for the use of man or beast' the next, thus demonstrating the sudden onset of the emergency.[52] Davis calculated that at least 1.5 million people emigrated due to the impact. At least another 1 million people died as a result of *An Gorta Mor.* Comparing the census of 1841 with that of 1851, Davis shows that the population of Ireland was reduced by around 20%.[53]

The shock of the disaster was felt acutely by contemporary commentators, and the impact in addition to the response of colonial government officials has been a source of historical dispute since. Modern revisionist historians such as Daly have argued that 'Famine emigration is now largely seen as a continuum from the immediate pre-Famine pattern of the early 1840s'.[54] Kinealy explained the argument that 'in view of Ireland's large population and under-developed agricultural sector, a subsistence crisis was inevitable'.[55] Boyce and O'Day concluded that widespread death 'could not have been solved by closing the ports', for example.[56] Indeed, amongst other prominent Irish nationalists Land League leader Michael Davitt 'denounced Irish politicians for failing to prevent food exports by organising popular resistance' against the British government.[57] Kinealy though, concludes that 'the revisionist interpretation, which has so long dominated academic writing, is clearly being overtaken by interpretations which have more in common with the traditional nationalist perspective on the Famine'. [58, 59]

John Mitchell's 'The Last Conquest of Ireland ' was written a decade after the event and is viewed as the original source of the nationalist historical image of the Great Hunger. Mitchell concluded that 'British policy' was to blame for the scale of death and emigration caused by the crisis of the 1840s and 1850s.[60] Mitchell had been convicted of treason and was incarcerated in the United States from where his writing was published in the *Southern Citizen*, a Washington newspaper which he used as a platform to hold Britain to account for 'a deliberate act of genocide'.[61] Stating that 'The Almighty indeed sent the potato blight, but the English created the Famine', Mitchell's work 'became an article of faith with many nationalists' of the time and since.[62]

More recently, O'Grada's historiography of the time agreed with Mitchell that 'Ireland died of political economy' and suggests the scale of people who left Ireland had been 'under-recorded' given that port officials were overwhelmed by the numbers. Providing a philosophical context to the decisions taken by politicians at the time, O'Grada described how 'people in high places in both London and Dublin in the 1840s believed that the famine was nature's response to Irish demographic irresponsibility'.[63]

Sir Charles Trevelyan produced the only written account of the Great Hunger by a British official in his role in charge of government relief, describing 'the judgement of God on an indolent and unself-reliant people'.[64] According to Mitchell, the opportunity presented by the failure of the potato crop in 1845 was seized upon by the British government, who devised 'a blueprint for sweeping land clearances', including relief schemes and workhouses.[65] While Ireland was 'exporting sufficient corn to England to feed 2 million people' – contemporary accounts described Ireland as 'the granary of Britain'. Kinealy noted that Britain's initial response to the Famine was to dictate that 'relief was dependent on undertaking hard, physical labour'. Kinealy is critical of the public work schemes as the system meant those most in need received the least owing to their diminished physical capability.[66] Soup kitchens were introduced by the British government in Ireland in January 1847, an act representing:

... the first and only time during these years, the government tackled the problem of hunger directly, without imposing a test of destitution on the people, thus giving practical considerations priority over ideological ones.[67]

Three million people were accessing food aid per day at the height of the scheme which Kinealy argued further illustrated Britain's capacity to provide effective relief if it chose to.[68] Nationalist polemics have focussed on the position that 'Malthusian doctrine offered a seductively simple explanation of the poverty of Ireland'. In terms of British government policies, Malthus's theory remained influential throughout the nineteenth century and held that 'checks' such as famine and disease would act to correct 'overpopulation' when it occurred.[69] Mokyr, however, points to the fact that Ireland was less densely populated than Belgium – also affected by potato blight – which was able to sustain a growing population. Furthermore, the Irish diet included fish, milk and oatmeal – 'luxury' items typically sold at market to make rent payments. The typical rural Irish diet had potential to be diverse as well as self-sustaining, but has been described as disastrously dependent on the potato as the staple food.[70] The Poor Law Amendment Act of June 1847 brought a return to the prevailing *laissez-faire* response of Britain as the tax burden for relief was shifted entirely on to Irish shoulders. After just six months of a humanitarian crisis which would last over seven years, soup kitchen relief was withdrawn. Kinealy concluded that:

> ... the ruling elite saw it as a chance for the economy (belatedly) to achieve its natural balance: to do any more than the minimum to alleviate the starvation would deprive Ireland of the opportunity to achieve the right balance and to modernise.[71]

Handley sums up the nationalist perspective stating 'All the Irishman asked for was the use of his own; but that was reserved by the government for the markets of England'.[72] Indeed, Handley found that 'between September 1845, the first month of the "famine", and New Year's Day, 1846, the country exported 3,250,000 quarters of grain' – enough to feed the Irish population twice. Handley stated that the

Irish were 'starving in the midst of plenty'.[73] Davis concludes that 'the people of Ireland did not starve for want of food but for want of the means to pay for it from the lack of employment' brought about by failed potato harvests.[74]

A report to Parliament in 1847 by Commander Caffin focussed on Skibbereen, emphasising the scale of suffering brought about by the Great Hunger in Ireland, and the extent of government knowledge of the situation in worst affected localities. He describes how 16,000 of the estimated 18,000 inhabitants of the towns were 'in a state of utter destitution', adding, 'In no house that I entered was there not to be found the dead or dying'.[75]

Suffering did not cease for many of the estimated 310,000 Irish migrants who fled to Britain between 1841 and 1851. For example, in Glasgow, burials doubled in 1847 and this has been ascribed to the influx of the famished fleeing Ireland with associated health problems.[76] In Scotland, mortality rose to 50% higher than normal rates between 1846 and 1848 as people fled their famine-ravaged homeland.[77] Many died on the journey. Robert Scully described the 'coffin ships' in the same vein as 'the trains of the Holocaust, as an icon in Ireland's oppression'.[78]

Another by-product left in the wake of the Great Hunger was the social and economic reorganisation of the population on the island. The Irish census of 1851 reported the 'disorganisation of society became marked and memorable by the exodus of above 1 million people, who deserted their homes and hearths to seek food and shelter in foreign lands'.[79] Collins shows that between 1851 and 1911 the total population of Ireland fell from 6.5 million to 3.2 million.[80] In short, the population of Ireland was reduced by over 50% as the outflow of emigration continued apace throughout the second half of the nineteenth century. Collins also ascribes this to a fall in the birth rate which was 33 per 1,000 in 1841. By 1870 this had reduced to 26 per 1,000.[81] Daly states 'emigration and deaths proved largely complementary: the young and the old died, those in active age groups emigrated'.

Notes

1 *The Freeman's Journal*, January 27th 1847.

2 Malthusianism is the idea deriving from the work of nineteenth century English economist and clergyman Thomas Robert Malthus.

3 Nally, D., '"That Coming Storm": The Irish Poor Law, Colonial Biopolitics, and the Great Famine', *Annals of the Association of American Geographers*, Vol. 98, No. 3 (2008), p. 730.

4 *The Tablet*, August 25th 1849.

5 *Ibid.*

6 *The Freeman's Journal*, August 10th 1850.

7 *The Freeman's Journal*, February 28th 1854.

8 Rogers, *Ballymote Aspects Through Time*, p. 23.

9 Kelly, M., and Fotheringham, A.S, 'The online atlas of Irish population change 1841–2002: A new resource for analysing national trends and local variations in Irish population dynamics', *Irish Geography*, Vol. 44, No. 2-3 (2011), p. 221.

10 Kelly, and Fotheringham, 'The online atlas of Irish population change 1841–2002: A new resource for analysing national trends and local variations in Irish population dynamics', p. 222.

11 Healy, A., *The Man Who Started Celtic* (as yet unpublished), p. 2.

12 Smyth, W.J., 'The province of Connacht and the Great Famine' in Crowley, J., Smyth, W. J. and Murphy, M., (eds), *Atlas of the Great Irish Famine* (Cork: University Press, 2012) p. 286.

13 Kelly, and Fotheringham, 'The online atlas of Irish population change 1841–2002: A new resource for analysing national trends and local variations in Irish population dynamics', p. 224.

14 Smyth, W.J., 'The province of Connacht and the Great Famine', p. 289.

15 Fitzgerald, P, and McCullough, C., '"Derry mountains no more": Irish migrant departures in a historical context', *AEMI Journal*, Vol. 17-18 (Slovenia: ZRC, 2020), p. 47.

16 Census of Ireland 1901 and 1911, accessed online at http://www.census.nationalarchives.ie/

17 Kelly, and Fotheringham, 'The online atlas of Irish population change 1841–2002: A new resource for analysing national trends and local variations in Irish population dynamics', p. 224.

18 Fitzgerald and McCullough, '"Derry mountains no more": Irish migrant departures in a historical context', p. 47.

19 Healy, A., *The Man Who Started Celtic* (as yet unpublished), p. 2.

20 McGettrick, B., 'From Portinch to Glasgow', *Corran Herald*, Vol. 29 (1996), p. 13. *The Sligo Champion*, October 27th 2004.

21 Healy, A., *The Man Who Started Celtic* (as yet unpublished), p. 2. *The Sligo Champion*, October 27th 2004.

22 The Schools' Collection, Vol. 0183, p. 323. Accessed online at https://www.duchas.ie/en/cbes/4701745/4698597.

23 *Clyde Bill of Entry and Shipping List 1855*, Glasgow City Archives, FCN 26.9.

24 *Ibid.*

25 Smyth, W.J., 'Exodus from Ireland - patterns of emigration', in Crowley, J., Smyth, W. J. and Murphy, M., (eds), *Atlas of the Great Irish Famine* (Cork: University Press, 2012) p. 494.

26 *The Glasgow Free Press*, October 9th 1858.

27 Reid, J., 'Irish Famine refugees and the emergence of Glasgow Celtic Football Club', in Smyth, W.J., 'The province of Connacht and the Great Famine' in Crowley, J., Smyth, W. J. and Murphy, M., (eds), *Atlas of the Great Irish Famine* (Cork: University Press, 2012) pp. 513-516.

28 Collins, B., 'Early evidence of Irish immigration to Scotland: a note on a Catholic parish register', *Local Population Studies*, Vol. 32 (1984), p. 28.

29 Erben, M., 'The purposes and processes of biographical method', p. 159.

30 O'Grada, C., *Black '47 and Beyond: The Great Irish Famine* (Princeton: Princeton University Press, 2000) p. 232.

31 O'Grada, C., *Black '47 and Beyond: The Great Irish Famine*, p. 228.

32 Collins, B., 'The Origins of Irish Immigration to Scotland in the Nineteenth and Twentieth Centuries', in Devine, T.M. (et al), *Irish Immigrants and Scottish Society in the Nineteenth and Twentieth Centuries* (Edinburgh: John Donald Publishers, 1991) p. 6.

33 O'Grada, C., *Black '47 and Beyond: The Great Irish Famine*, p. 105.

34 O'Grada, C., *Black '47 and Beyond: The Great Irish Famine*, p. 105.

35 Davis, G., *The Irish in Britain, 1815-1914* (Dublin: Gill and Macmillan, 1991) p. 50.

36 Davis, G., *The Irish in Britain, 1815-1914* (Dublin: Gill and Macmillan, 1991) p. 10.

37 Collins, B., 'The Origins of Irish Immigration to Scotland in the Nineteenth and Twentieth Centuries', in Devine, T.M. (et al), *Irish Immigrants and Scottish Society in the Nineteenth and Twentieth Centuries* (Edinburgh: John Donald Publishers, 1991) p. 2.

38 Collins, 'The Origins of Irish Immigration to Scotland in the Nineteenth and Twentieth Centuries', p. 3.

39 Davis, *The Irish in Britain, 1815-1914* p. 10.

40 Davis, *The Irish in Britain, 1815-1914*, p. 13.

41 Collins, 'The Origins of Irish Immigration to Scotland in the Nineteenth and Twentieth Centuries', p. 6.

42 Collins, 'The Origins of Irish Immigration to Scotland in the Nineteenth and Twentieth Centuries', p. 7.

43 Handley, J.E., *The Irish in Modern Scotland* (Cork: Cork University Press, 1938) p. 1.

44 Davis, *The Irish in Britain, 1815-1914*, p. 42.

45 Collins, 'The Origins of Irish Immigration to Scotland in the Nineteenth and Twentieth Centuries', p. 8.

46 Collins, 'The Origins of Irish Immigration to Scotland in the Nineteenth and Twentieth Centuries', p. 7.

47 Davis, *The Irish in Britain, 1815-1914*, p. 41.

48 Collins, 'The Origins of Irish Immigration to Scotland in the Nineteenth and Twentieth Centuries', p. 1.

49 Collins, 'The Origins of Irish Immigration to Scotland in the Nineteenth and Twentieth Centuries', p. 8.

50 Handley, *The Irish in Modern Scotland*, p. 1.

51 Daly, M., 'Revisionism and Irish History: The Great Famine', in Boyce, G.D. and O'Day, A., *The Making of Modern Irish History: Revisionism and The Revisionist Controversy* (London: Routledge, 1996) p. 82.

52 Swift, R., *Irish Migrants in Britain, 1815-1914* (Cork: Cork University Press, 2002) p. 15.

53 Davis, *The Irish in Britain, 1815-1914*, p. 10.

54 Daly,'Revisionism and Irish History: The Great Famine', p. 80.

55 Kinealy, C., *A Death-Dealing Famine: The Great Hunger in Ireland* (Chicago: Pluto Press, 1997) p. 3.

56 Boyce, G.D. and O'Day, A., *The Making of Modern Irish History: Revisionism and The Revisionist Controversy* (London: Routledge, 1996) p. 85.

57 Boyce, G.D. and O'Day, A., *The Making of Modern Irish History: Revisionism and The Revisionist Controversy*, p. 73.

58 Kinealy, C., *A Death-Dealing Famine: The Great Hunger in Ireland*, p. 3.

59 Kinealy, C., *A Death-Dealing Famine: The Great Hunger in Ireland*, p. 15.

60 Davis, *The Irish in Britain, 1815-1914*, p. 21.

61 Quinn, J., 'Reviewed Work(s): The Last Conquest of Ireland (Perhaps) by John Mitchel and Patrick Maume', *Irish Historical Studies*, Vol. 35, No. 138 (Nov., 2006), p. 256.

62 Quinn, 'Reviewed Work(s): The Last Conquest of Ireland (Perhaps) by John Mitchel and Patrick Maume', p. 257.

63 O'Grada, C., *Black '47 and Beyond: The Great Irish Famine* (Princeton: Princeton University Press, 2000) p. 6/ p. 10.

64 Kinealy, C., *A Death-Dealing Famine: The Great Hunger in Ireland*, p. 4.

65 Quinn, J., 'Reviewed Work(s): The Last Conquest of Ireland (Perhaps) by John Mitchel and Patrick Maume', *Irish Historical Studies*, Vol. 35, No. 138 (Nov., 2006), p. 256.

66 Kinealy, *A Death-Dealing Famine: The Great Hunger in Ireland*, p. 5/9.

67 Kinealy, *A Death-Dealing Famine: The Great Hunger in Ireland*, p. 9.

68 *Ibid.*

69 Davis, *The Irish in Britain, 1815-1914*, p. 11.

70 Davis, *The Irish in Britain, 1815-1914*, p. 12.

71 Kinealy, *A Death-Dealing Famine: The Great Hunger in Ireland*, p. 10/11.

72 Handley, *The Irish in Modern Scotland*, p. 17.

73 Handley, *The Irish in Modern Scotland*, p. 1/2.

74 Davis, *The Irish in Britain, 1815-1914*, p. 14.

75 Swift, *Irish Migrants in Britain, 1815-1914* p. 16.

76 O'Grada, C., Black '47 and Beyond: The Great Irish Famine (Princeton: Princeton University Press, 2000) p. 6/ p. 111.

77 O'Grada, C., Black '47 and Beyond: The Great Irish Famine (Princeton: Princeton University Press, 2000) *ibid.*

78 O'Grada, C., *Black '47 and Beyond: The Great Irish Famine* (Princeton: Princeton University Press, 2000) p. 6/ p. 105.

79 Handley, The Irish in Modern Scotland, p. 17.

80 Collins, 'The Origins of Irish Immigration to Scotland in the Nineteenth and Twentieth Centuries', p. 10.

81 Collins, 'The Origins of Irish Immigration to Scotland in the Nineteenth and Twentieth Centuries', p. 10.

An Gorta Mor

Walfrid

Glasgow City Archives

Glasgow's Broomielaw in the nineteenth century.
Note the mixture of sail and steamships and the teeming wharfside.

CHAPTER 3
Glasgow 1855

The annals of the poor are not often recorded. They do not own property and, if literate, their letters are generally not handed down through family. The child, Andrew Kerins travelling in the company of his friend Bart McGettrick – and most probably a number of dozens of other souls, refugees from famine and hopelessness – arrived in Scotland's largest city likely cold, hungry, tired and vulnerable. There is no way of knowing where and when they dismbarked in this foreign city and who, if anyone, would be on the Broomielaw wharfside to meet them. Light tonnage steamships at that time would sail up river into the centre of the city. They would deposit their cargo, first human then cattle before re-loading with Lanarkshire coal for the return journey. Having spent up to twenty-four hours below decks, the modern reader can only speculate on the state of the human cargo.

The boys may have been forewarned to 'clear the dockside as soon as you can' for fear of crime and the risk of kidnap for child labour. They may have had a scribbled address of a family or church contact who might provide shelter and safety for a few nights at least. As refugees they were entering a land that was in some respects a classic 'hostile environment'.

Stereotypical hostility in British newspapers towards the Irish during the famine crisis stoked native fears of arriving Irish immigrants. One report stated that, 'If some restraint be not imposed on the Irish immigration into this country, we will soon be reduced to the condition of the miserable beings who fly to our shores'. Davis argues this was symptomatic of dominant xenophobic views on the part of the British establishment, and contemporary reportage 'exemplifies how a tragedy can be interpreted to fit predisposed prejudice, in which everything is explained in terms of the moral degeneracy of the Irish'.[1]

Bernard Aspinwall, in a famous article titled 'Children of the Dead End' discusses the 'shock of an alien culture' which met the young Kerins on arrival in heavily industrialised Glasgow, described as the 'Second City of the Empire' at the height of the Industrial Revolution but nonetheless featuring abject urban poverty, especially in the places where Irish Catholics could afford to settle.

Life in the Scotland of the mid-nineteenth century at the height of the Industrial Revolution was considered 'competitive, unprotected, brutal and, for many, vile'. For much of the urban working class, life was routinely abject. Prostitution, drink and disease went unchecked and Scots had an average life expectancy of around 40 years. The 1842 *Reports on the Sanitary Condition of the Labouring Population of Scotland* recorded housing 'of the lowest grade consisting of only one small apartment, always ill-ventilated. . . densely peopled. . . and damp.'[2] Immigrants from rural Scotland and from Ireland would join this miserable ladder on the bottom rung.

The narrative of Andrew Kerins' individual experience helps to breathe life into a larger phenomenon of outmigration from Ireland to Britain that was accelerating by the mid-point of the nineteenth century, with unprecedented numbers fleeing the horrors of famine. And of course, as well as the unprecendented numbers of Irish, mixed in with Highland and Lowland clearances from the land to the urban centres, there was another obstructive factor in the arrival process. Religion presented an obstacle which may astonish the modern reader in a secular age. Until well into the twentieth century, with some remants still evident in contemporary Scottish society, religious belief was the cornerstone of behaviour at every level in employment practices, housing and social life. 'No Catholics or Irish need apply' was common currency in Scotland well into the twentieth century.

The Reformation, dated from 1560, and reputed to have been led by John Knox against the then Catholic Stuart monarchy, introduced a brand of reformed, Protestant beliefs based heavily on the precepts of the Swiss theologian, John Calvin. It was a dramatic shift from the beliefs of the Roman Church and life in Scotland and other European countries would never be the same. The change came with an attitude of contempt for what had gone before and anti-Catholicism was rife.

In Scotland, the Presbyterian version of Protestantism 'was not just a state religion but, for more that three centuries, defined the Scots to one another and to the rest of the world'.[3] An indicator of the prevalence of anti-Catholicism in post-Reformation Scotland long before the Irish immigration are the rarely quoted statistics from the 1790s when there were no more than 39 Catholics living in Glasgow. At this time in the city there were 43 anti-Catholic societies [Devine notes 60 anti-Catholic societies in 1791].[4]

Anti-Irish sentiment – particularly targeting Irish Catholics – was prevalent and enduring in post-Reformation Scotland, culminating in the General Assembly of the Church of Scotland's approval of an infamous 1923 report. Titled 'The Menace of the Irish Race to Our Scottish Nationality', the extraordinary text describes in negative racial terms 'alarm and anxiety' prompted by 'the incursion into Scotland of a large Irish Roman Catholic population'. Laying the blame for crime, drunkenness and vice principally at the feet of Catholics of Irish origin in Scotland, the report suggests deportation to the Irish Free State as one possible solution to protecting 'the destruction of the unity and homogeneity' of Scotland's population. In 2002, the Church of Scotland issued an apology, expressing regret for endorsing the report some seventy-nine years prior.

Maver's history of Glasgow describes the origins and roots of the Irish Catholic community in the city. She finds that 'by 1851, the Irish-born presence in Glasgow constituted over 18% of the population, with obvious ramifications for the social and cultural direction of the city'.[6] The Irish Catholic community Andrew Kerins joined in Glasgow, by then numbering over 100,000 people, embodied the biggest ethno-religious minority group in the country. Irish immigration numbers peaked at over one thousand per week in the late 1840s. The proximity of Scotland, with established shipping routes offering the cheapest escape from Ireland, made Glasgow a prime recipient of refugees to Britain from *An Gorta Mor*. For those without substantive means, such as the fifteen-year-old Kerins, Glasgow offered a more feasible alternative to the long-haul voyage to North America taken by a greater number of emigrants fleeing Ireland at the time.[7]

Given the desperate conditions in Ireland, for many the exodus from their homeland was a chaotic process of departure, driven as much by necessity as by design. From family testimony it certainly seems that Kerins' voyage, aboard a coal boat from Sligo harbour to Scotland, speaks more of a journey of desperation rather than a planned departure for a new life.

It is likely that Kerins, as was the case with the vast majority of the Irish diaspora in Scotland, settled close to the point of arrival. The cohort that followed a similar route to Scotland became most prominent in the East End of Glasgow, particularly in the Garngad and Calton districts with which Kerins himself became associated certainly in later years. Bradley argues 'the figure of 332,000 [Irish immigrants] by 1878' gives an indication of the size of the multi-generational Irish community growing in Scotland, many of whom also settled in the broader West of Scotland region, in and around the industrial towns and villages of Lanarkshire. Smaller numbers travelled East and settled in communities such as Dundee's Lochee and in Edinburgh's Cowgate and Old Town.[8]

It has been shown that although Irish immigration following *An Gorta Mor* had slowed significantly by the 1871 census, the majority of Glasgow's Irish Catholics remained housed in the poorest areas throughout the nineteenth century.[9] The poverty endured by Andrew Kerins in his formative years, exacerbated by *An Gorta Mor* humanitarian crisis in Ireland, in many senses persisted for him and the thousands of other Irish Catholic refugees who settled in Glasgow.

For young males like Kerins, the promise of employment in Glasgow's booming manufacturing works associated with the Industrial Revolution swelled the population of the city over the course

of the nineteenth century. Correspondence with surviving descend-
ants of Andrew Kerins has helped substantiate his earliest experience
of arrival. Another great grand-neice Alison Healy's family record of
Andrew Kerins' earliest activity in Glasgow shows he 'started working
on the railways' soon after arriving from Sligo. Healy also states that
the family 'don't know a lot about his life at this time, because it was
so long ago': although subsequent historians have corroborated this
version of events.[10]

A smaller Catholic community of Scots Highlanders had earlier
settled in Glasgow after being dispossessed of their land during the
Clearances starting in the latter part of the eighteenth century into
the first decades of the nineteenth century.[11] By 1800, Mitchell states
'there were only 30,000 Catholics in Scotland, accounting for 2% of a
population of around 1.5 million'.[12] Johnson finds that although some
Highlanders shared the same Catholic faith as the vast majority of
the Irish, Irish-born Catholics outnumbered indigenous Catholics in
Scotland as early as 1829, when the Catholic Emancipation Bill was
passed by the British Parliament.[13] The number of Roman Catholics
of Irish birth in Glasgow alone was estimated at 19,333 in 1831.[14] By
the time of the 1851 census, the number of Irish-born seeking refuge
in Scotland following *An Gorta* Mor had swelled to 207,367, comprising
7.2% of the total population. Although a minority of that number were
Protestant, Mitchell estimates that over 100,000 Irish Catholics were
residing in the West of Scotland by the time of Kerins' arrival from
Sligo in 1855.[15] The community Andrew Kerins joined represented the
largest ethnic minority group in Scotland, and the city of Glasgow.
The revival of Catholicism in Scotland during the nineteenth century
is inextricably linked to the arrival of that diaspora community from
Ireland.

Despite the unprecedented economic growth and output of
Glasgow, the endemic poverty of its Victorian slums – with its
associated problems of overcrowding and disease – began to demand
attention at a civic level. Alongside grinding poverty, prejudice was
also experienced by the immigrant Irish Catholic minority in Scotland.
Whether through negative stereotyping in newspaper reportage or

from influential societal figures, contemporary evidence shows the genesis of an anti-Irish discourse in response to Irish immigration to Scotland during the nineteenth century. Maver shows that indigenous discrimination encountered at the time extended to significant politicians like the Glasgow City Chamberlain, Dr John Strang. Strang served as Glasgow's City Chamberlain for thirty years from 1834, producing a series of public health reports on the 'Statistics of Glasgow' between 1841 and his death in 1863. Two years after the arrival of Andrew Kerins, Strang found in his study of 1857 figures that 405 Glasgow residents died of smallpox, 350 of whom were infants under the age of five. His report concludes:

> The great bulk of this endemic is, we feared, to be traced to the Celtic race who inhabit this City, in short, to the low and labouring Highlanders and Irish, who, through neglect or prejudice, allow hundreds of the most innocent of our citizens to be destroyed, blinded or deformed by this cruel distemper.[16]

During a cholera epidemic in 1849, Strang had previously campaigned for 'the growing evil' of Irish immigration to be checked, arguing, 'otherwise Glasgow will become a city of paupers and of the plague'.[17] Bradley's work on representations of the Irish in Scotland cites the *North British Daily Mail* as but one newspaper with a similar tendency to produce particularly negative coverage of Irish Catholics resident in Scotland. Bradley also notes that publications such as *The Scotsman*, published in Edinburgh, was fairer in its portrayal of the immigrant community during this period.[18] It is, however, agreed that discourse surrounding the Irish, and often their co-religionist Highlander migrants, was coloured by a 'native animosity' within the established Scottish printing press and civic society – at times, representing 'a form of racism', given the context of Victorian obsession with racial classification.[19] 'Racialism', argues Kidd, 'added a gloss of scientific respectability to nativist and sectarian opposition to Irish Catholic immigration' following *An Gorta Mor.*[20]

Kerins and the Irish Catholic immigrant minority to which he belonged, therefore, faced impoverished living conditions, discrimination, and prejudice during its integration into Glaswegian life. It is from within this socioeconomic and cultural context that Kerins' developed a moral and ethical consciousness that would make a difference to many lives in years to come. This was achieved primarily through engagement in the wider promotion of Catholic education and charity during the second half of the nineteenth century.

Discrimination and marginalisation of the newly arrived Irish was not confined to elements outside of their Catholic faith. The huge influx of Irish Catholics to Scotland at the time also gave rise to a period of 'conflict between the Scottish clergy who ran the Church and sections of the Irish laity: conflict over politics, and over the governance and identity of the Church in the region'.[21] The Catholic Church in Scotland remained a mission territory in Vatican terms until the restoration of the hierarchy in 1878, which was previously swept away by the Scottish Reformation beginning in the sixteenth-century.[22]

Prior to the arrival of a large Irish diaspora community, senior clergy positions were dominated by recusant Scottish priests who retained their faith despite persecution in the centuries which followed the Reformation. Influential figures such as Bishop Murdoch were drawn from the North-East of Scotland, where small-scale practising of the Catholic faith had endured during penal times.[23] Murdoch's tenure as head of the Catholic Church in Glasgow, between 1845 and 1865, coincided with a charitable drive to establish a new school system which would be heavily reliant on monies donated from a largely impoverished laity, enhanced by the personal contributions of wealthy benefactors such as the Third Marquess of Bute, and from overseas. The *Glasgow Free Press*, first published in 1851 by Irish Catholics and aimed at the diaspora community growing in the city, carried an article in October 1856 on 'Catholic Charity in Scotland'. The article emphasises the role of Bishop Murdoch as patron of the network of new Saint Vincent de Paul Society branches establishing around Glasgow, stating:

The active and beneficent efforts of which would soon be

able to realise in these localities the desirable establishments of Catholic schools, and means for alleviating, in some measure, the miseries of the necessitous.[24]

At the time of Kerins' arrival in Glasgow there was no state provision for Catholic education in Scotland. Prior to the Education Act for Scotland of 1872, Catholic education lay outside the national system, which by definition was Protestant in character and did not provide for religious instruction in the Catholic faith. This meant that Catholics seeking to have their children instructed in their own faith had to, in effect, 'pay twice' – paying for the national school system through taxation as well as funding their own Catholic schools. To this end, McDermid shows how the Scots joined with the bishops of England and Wales who had established the Catholic Poor School Committee 'with the purpose of negotiating with the Government for a share' in educational grants to ameliorate the burden placed on an already impoverished laity.[25]

The senior clergy sought to ease the financial burden by appealing outside Scotland to willing religious teaching orders to build up an embryonic Catholic education system. This was to be based on sound pupil teacher training, whilst working for lower salaries than their state counterparts.

The first post-Reformation religious teaching communities to arrive in Glasgow were female; the Franciscan Sisters of the Immaculate Conception arriving from France in 1847, followed by the Sisters of Mercy who came from Ireland in 1849. McDermid states 'it appears that Catholic girls in Glasgow had a better (relatively speaking) education than Catholic boys, because of the earlier arrival of female religious orders' which pre-dated the arrival of male religious by around a decade.[26] Kehoe similarly finds 'communities, whose origins were French and Irish, worked with Church and community leaders to construct a Catholic parochial education system that would reach working-class girls and young women'.[27] Building upon McDermid's view that provision of female Catholic education was initially superior to that of boys in Scotland, Kehoe explains that greater availability of female religious teachers, compared to their male counterparts at the time, was the main reason why this was initially the case.[28]

Letters published in the *Glasgow Free Press* emphasise the anxiety for equivalent institutions for boys to be established and carried forward by similar male religious educationalists, at a time when separate male and female schooling was the norm in Britain.[29] The same Irish immigrant newspaper reported in 1856 that 'the Right Rev. Dr Gillis, Bishop of Edinburgh, will preach a charity sermon at St. Mungo's Chapel, in aid of the building fund of the new Catholic schools in St. Mungo's Parish'.[30] Construction of an education system equipped for the substantial Irish Catholic diaspora community in Scotland's most populous city emerged as a priority for laity and senior clergy alike.

Notes

1 Davis, *The Irish in Britain, 1815-1914*, p. 45.

2 Smout, T.C. *A Century of the Scottish People 1830–1950*

3 Gallagher T. 'The Catholic Irish in Scotland: in Search of Identity' in Devine T. M. (ed) 1991.

4 Murray B, 1984 p.93 and Devine T. 1998 p.154

5 New footnote

6 Maver, I,£*Glasgow* (2000), p. 84.

7 *Ibid.*

8 Bradley, J.M., *Celtic Minded: Essays on Religion, Politics, Society, Identity and Football* (2004), p. 19.

9 Pooley, C., 'Segregation or integration? The residential experience of the Irish in mid-Victorian Britain', in Swift, R. (ed), *The Irish in Britain 1815-1939* (1989), pp. 60-84.

10 Healy, A., *The Man Who Started Celtic* (as yet unpublished), p.3. Sweeney, B., *Celtic, The Early Years: 1887-1892* (Scotland: CQN Books, 2015), p. 20.

11 MacDonald, R., 'The Catholic Gaidhealtachd', *The Innes Review*, Vol. 29, No. 1 (1978), pp. 60-62.

12 Mitchell, M.J., 'Anti-Catholicism and the Scottish Middle Class 1800-1914' in C. Gheeraert-Graffeuille, G. Vaughan (eds.), Anti-Catholicism in Britain and Ireland, 1600–2000, Practices, Representations and Ideas (London: Pallgrave MacMillan, 2020), p. 219.

13 See Chapter 1, p 21.

14 Johnson, C., *Development in the Roman Catholic Church in Scotland, 1789 – 1829* (University of Strathclyde: unpublished thesis, 1980), p. 419.

15 Mitchell, M.J., 'Anti-Catholicism and the Scottish Middle Class 1800-1914', pp. 219-220.

16 Strang, J., 'Statistics of Glasgow 1841-62', DTC 7.5.3A held at Glasgow City Archives, the Mitchell Library.

17 Maver, *Glasgow*, p. 85.

18 Bradley, J.M., *Celtic Minded: Essays on Religion, Politics, Society, Identity and Football*, p.21.

19 Brown, S.J., ''Outside the Covenant': The Scottish Presbyterian Churches and Irish Immigration, 1922-1938', *The Innes Review*, Vol. 42, No. 1 (Spring, 1991), pp. 19-45.

Finn, G.P.T., 'Racism, Religion and Social Prejudice: Irish Catholic Clubs, Soccer and Scottish Society - I The Historical Roots of Prejudice', *The International Journal of the History of Sport*, Vol. 8, No. 1 (1991), pp. 72-95.

Kelly, E., 'Challenging Sectarianism in Scotland: The Prism of Racism', *Scottish Affairs*, No. 42 (Winter, 2003), pp. 32-56.

Kidd, 'Race, Empire and the Limits of Nineteenth-Century Scottish Nationhood', pp. 873-892.

20 Kidd, 'Race, Empire and the Limits of Nineteenth-Century Scottish Nationhood', pp. 883.

21 Mitchell, M. J. (et al), *New Perspectives on The Irish in Scotland* (Edinburgh: Birlinn, 2008), p.11.

22 Bradley, J.M., *Ethnic and Religious Identity in Modern Scotland: Culture, politics and football* (Aldershot: Avebury, 1995), p. 9.

23 MacDonald, 'The Catholic Gaidhealtachd', pp. 56-72.

24 *Glasgow Free Press*, October 4th 1856.

25 McDermid, J., 'Catholic women teachers and Scottish education in the nineteenth and early twentieth centuries', *History of Education*, Vol. 38, No. 5 (2009), pp. 608-609.

26 McDermid, 'Catholic women teachers and Scottish education in the nineteenth and early twentieth centuries', p. 610.

27 Kehoe, S. K., 'Women Religious and the Development of Scottish Education', in McKinney, S.J. and McCluskey, R., A History of Catholic Education and Schooling in Scotland: New Perspectives (London: Palgrave Macmillan, 2019) p. 61.

28 Ibid. p. 66.

29 *Glasgow Free Press*, December 13th 1856.

30 *Glasgow Free Press*, October 25th 1856.

CHAPTER 4

Glasgow: the Marist Mission 1858 – 1874

Post-Reformation Scotland, for over three centuries, remained distinctly Protestant in terms of its national religion, education system, laws and cultural outlook as part of the United Kingdom.[1] The Catholic Church in Scotland remained a mission territory in Vatican terms prior to the mass arrival of Irish Catholic immigrants fleeing *An Gorta Mor*, and as such was required to embark on a programme of community building to cater for and integrate the spiritual needs of the thousands who fled from Ireland.

The revival of the Catholic Church in nineteenth century Scotland has largely been attributed to this process, which was primarily facilitated through the work of Catholic charitable organisations, religious orders enlisted from Europe and the development of a distinct system of education.

Andrew Kerins' childhood experiences and influences in Ireland equipped him with a 'self-confidence, based on literacy, moral purpose, social responsibility and a cohesive community' focus: qualities which inspired and characterised his subsequent life's work and legacy in Glasgow, as Brother Walfrid.[2] Kerins' formative years and early experience of hardship – most likely in the form of hunger – in Ireland clearly influenced the path he would embark on in adult-hood. In Glasgow, as evidenced in his late teenage years, we begin to witness how faith and education became the vocational focus for the life of Andrew Kerins.

Glasgow had been separated into seven geographical parishes in 1849, each with its own central church and presbytery.[3] Alongside

59

construction of new church facilities to cater for the spiritual needs of huge numbers arriving from Ireland, the development of parochial schools became a priority for the Catholic Church in Scotland in the wake of *An Gorta Mor* immigration.[4] While Catholic education remained outside the jurisdiction of the state until the 1872 Education Act in Scotland, religious authorities were forced to simultaneously fund and train teachers for the early schools. To this end, the Marists answered the call of Bishop Murdoch in Glasgow – aided by the charitable French linen merchant Charles Thiebault's financing and religious contacts in France – to provide much-needed teaching experience for a nascent Catholic school system. The church in Scotland was in dire need of help from elsewhere.

The arrival of the first Marist Brothers to Scotland's most populous city in 1858 closely followed Kerins' own arrival in Glasgow. As the first male religious order to embark on a new mission in Scotland since the Reformation, it was a significant help in meeting what must have seemed overwhelming needs in establishing the first Marist house in the city.

At the time of Andrew Kerins' arrival in Glasgow and first engagement with the Marists, the role of senior Brothers centred on identifying candidates potentially suitable for religious vocation and eventually facilitating their novitiate at the Beaucamps base of the Marist Order. Given the lack of Catholic religious training centres in Scotland at the time – both in terms of preparing young men for the priesthood or religious teaching life – access to the established Marist Brothers novitiate and established educational tradition appealed greatly to the senior clergy in Glasgow.

Given the proximity of Glasgow's major railway works and the location of this first Marist bridgehead, Andrew Kerins most likely settled in the St. Mungo's parish in the north of Glasgow, encompassing both the Townhead and Garngad districts, in 1855.[5] It appears that it was here that Kerins would live during the initial years of his time in Glasgow.

Contemporary postal records highlight that Garngad Hill was also host to major rail works in Glasgow, including the St. Rollox locomotive works established in 1854: this at the time of Kerins' arrival from Sligo.[6] The St. Rollox works were by then the major employer of young male labourers in the Garngad area, which had a high concentration of Irish Catholic immigrants. This supports the view passed down within the family that Kerins found employment 'working on the railways' with the largest employers sited in the north of the city,

An advertisement held by the Scottish Catholic Archives shows the earliest details of lessons conducted by the Marist 'French Academy' at 96 Garngad Hill, Glasgow.[7] Published in the late 1850s, the commercial describes the opening of a French class to be held on Monday, Wednesday, and Friday evenings at the first Marist Brothers residence in Scotland. These lessons were offered alongside a private day school for children along with night school classes for adults, all under the direction of the Brothers. On January 6th 1859, the entry for the St. Mungo's expenses book, kept by the Brothers, reads, 'paid 1000 circulars of private school'.[8] Figures from the Scottish Catholic Directory printed in 1856 show that St. Mungo's had seating accommodation for just seven hundred parishioners.[9] Clearly the Marist Brothers were intent on garnering interest in their teaching abilities as widely as possible in the local area, possibly also across the city within neighbouring parishes.

In addition to promoting the newly opened French language classes, the advertisement appeals to 'Adults desirous of improving themselves in Reading, Writing, Arithmetic, Book-keeping'.[10] Kerins first travelled to the Marist base at Beaucamps in France as a postulant in 1864, so it is most likely that he first became engaged in the late 1850s with the Marist Brothers at such night classes in the Garngad area of Glasgow. Young candidates at this time traditionally spent a six-year apprenticeship period working as a pupil teacher under the guidance of more senior Brothers before being funded to travel and begin the formation process in France.[11]

The St. Mungo's parish church served as a social hub for immigrant Irish Catholics and, for Kerins, having left his family behind in Ireland,

St. Mungo's and parish priest, Father Small would have held prime spiritual significance for a young man in unfamiliar urban surroundings. Knowledge of the newly arrived teaching Brothers would likely have been acquired through these parish connections, whether by word of mouth or the circular itself. Father Small is mentioned in a report on St. Mungo's parish and schools by the *Glasgow Herald* in the year of Kerins' arriving from Sligo, highlighting the close relationship between clergy and education within individual parishes. Parish priests would act as 'school managers' overseeing regular inspections of their local Catholic schools throughout the nineteenth century in Scotland. The report comments favourably on the work of the Sisters of Mercy at the 'educational institution connected with St. Mungo's Catholic Church'. They were acclaimed for 'accomplishing incalculable benefits for society by training up a vast number of female children in the paths of industry, virtue, and religion'.[12]

Three years later the *Glasgow Free Press* described how Small joined Father Forbes, parish priest of nearby St. Mary's in the eastern district of Calton, in an inspection of the local schools under the management of Forbes. The article again praises the impact and 'proficiency' of the Sisters of Mercy who had come from Ireland, concluding that a 'similar Institution for boys is a great desideratum in Glasgow'.[13] Within a matter of months of the same year, 1858, the first Marist Brothers began teaching in Father Small's St. Mungo's parish from their residence in Garngad.

Accommodation for the first small community of Brothers had been arranged by Bishop Murdoch in 1855 and Charles Thiebault financed the annual rent for at least the first six years of the school residence coming under the ownership of the church. As recorded by Handley, delays in the availability of suitable Brothers meant 'it was not until July 1858 that three Brothers, Brothers Procope, Tatianus and Faust, were sent from London to take charge of the school'.[14]

Amongst the first items purchased by Brothers in Glasgow for teaching purposes in the latter months of 1858 were copies of 'Robertson's Method of Learning French', 'Keenan's Catechism of the

Christian Religion' bought from Ireland, as well as 'Chamber's Atlas'. Funds were also used to buy 'one globe for the parlour' of the French Academy at 96 Garngad Hill.[15] No registers of pupils survive for this time, but the diversity and breadth of materials used for lessons illustrates attempts at a superior method of instruction not merely geared towards attainment of aptitude in 'the three Rs' of reading, writing and arithmetic.

The night classes, likely attended by Kerins as a young adult, can be characterised as an outward-looking, international initiative. The opportunities for self-improvement offered at such night classes would have piqued the interest of an individual already versed in the virtues of education given his bilingual upbringing in an Irish speaking home as well as English lessons in the Ballymote National Schools system.

The 1861 census of Scotland places the English-born Brother Faust (Joseph James Wincott) together with a Brother Oswald (Patrick Crawley) at the Garngad house.[16] By this time Brother Tatianus had departed Glasgow in 1860 to help establish the first Marist school in Dundee based below St. Andrew's church building in Nethergate. Tatianus was working alongside fellow Irishmen Brother Columba (Hugh O'Neil) and Brother Anthony (Daniel Dougherty) under a French Brother Superior, Brother Chumald (Claude Descombes).[17] The Frenchman Brother Procope – of the original three Brothers who arrived in Glasgow – was by then engaged in the direction of a separate school for boys in St. Mungo's Street connected to the parish church in Glasgow.[18]

The early communities of Marist Brothers were multi-lingual, diverse, and pious groups of men engaged in the work of building up Catholic education – qualities which held obvious appeal to Kerins. At this time, senior Brothers tended to be French-speakers from France or Belgium, while younger postulants in Scotland were largely drawn from the recently arrived Irish Catholic communities of the major industrialised cities.[19]

The death of a young Irish Marist, Brother Laurence (James Joseph

Judge), in 1861 in Glasgow was one such event which profoundly
impacted the St. Mungo's community of teaching Brothers and was
widely reported in the city newspapers. Brother Laurence was born
in Dublin on August 15th 1840 – the same year as Andrew Kerins.
Named in religion after the twelfth century Archbishop of Dublin,
Saint Laurence O'Toole, he began teaching at St. Mungo's after
completing his novitiate from the winter of 1858 'and thus dedicate
the remainder of his life to the education of the poor'. Whilst in charge
of the Middle School boys of St. Mungo's, Handley states that Brother
Laurence was 'carried off rapidly by typhoid', dying on 30th March
1861 aged 21.[20] Keenan has traced distinctive aspects of Marist funeral
traditions since the beginnings of the teaching Brothers Institute.[21]
The reportage of the funeral of Brother Laurence in Glasgow illustrates
some of these characteristic Marian devotional practices:

> At the conclusion of the service, the body was taken outside
> the church, where the funeral procession was formed by
> the Marist Brothers – some of whom had come from other
> towns to be present at the funeral of their much lamented
> brother. The procession was headed by St. Mungo's brass
> band, preceded by Mr Gillies as Drum-major. The band
> were in full uniform, with crape on their left arms.
> Immediately behind was carried the coffin, resting on a bier
> and covered with a large black pall, on which was stitched
> in broad white outline, a large latin cross. Immediately
> behind the coffin marched the Marist Brothers in their long
> dark cloaks, and succeeding them came three of the
> Catholic clergy, followed by the scholars attending St.
> Mungo's schools in rank and file, four deep. The coffin was
> flanked on either side by a single file of the boys attending
> the middle school, where Brother Lawrence [sic] had
> laboured so assiduously and with so much effect. The
> mournful cortege was followed by a very large number of
> gentlemen from all parts of the city, who, in different
> successive relays carried the body to its last resting place,
> Dalbeth.[22]

The unprecedented public nature of the funeral procession – with
accompanying band and distinctive religious dress and imagery on

display – is testament to the growing self-confidence of Glasgow's Catholic community, so recently burgeoned by unprecedented numbers from Ireland. The 'very large number' in attendance coupled with the fact that the 'novel scene created quite a sensation in those parts of the city through which the funeral passed' is also indicative of the impact and public awareness of the first male Catholic teaching order in post-Reformation Scotland.[23]

It is highly likely that Andrew Kerins would have been in attendance. Given the similar age of Kerins and Brother Laurence in all probability the two were contemporaries of both the St. Mungo's parish and the connected Marist schools. Both shared a background of growing up during, and surviving, *An Gorta Mor,* before departing Ireland for Glasgow. Thus, the sense of loss was in all likelihood particularly keenly felt by Kerins. Whereas Kerins was forced to leave his family behind in Sligo, census records show that Brother Laurence fled Ireland accompanied by his parents Jones and Eliza Judge and siblings. He was the oldest of two brothers with three younger sisters residing at 76 King Street in the East End of the city in 1851.

The loss of Brother Laurence – the first death of a Marist Brother in Scotland – to typhoid disease, speaks of the grave public health conditions in heavily industrial cities in Victorian Britain. Epidemic outbreaks of diseases such as typhoid, scarlet fever, and cholera were regularly reported in the later school log books of the schools run by the Marist Brothers. Canning finds that many priests and teaching Brothers succumbed to infection during the nineteenth century, especially in urban areas, during the carrying out of religious duties. The precarious nature of daily life as a Marist Brother, teaching in close quarters to the children of impoverished slum areas in Glasgow in poorly-ventilated, often damp conditions, would have been known to Kerins before deciding to undertake novitiate in France. O'Donoghue concludes 'teaching was not a job; it was a vocation – a call to serve God' in the case of the Marist Brothers.[24]

The sacred vows of poverty, chastity and obedience taken by some of those joining the Marist Brothers exacted the highest price. Two junior colleagues, Brother Sennanus (born Luke O'Brien in London, 1842) and Brother William (Henry Banham born in Suffolk, 1845) both died whilst teaching at Dundee within months of one another following an outbreak of illness in late 1866. This was just one year after taking first vows on the same day as Brother Walfrid in Glasgow. They would also be known to Kerins and had been transfered to Dundee and died shortly after of an unspecified illness. Apart from the necessary physical contact with contagious diseases like typhoid, cholera and other infection, living conditions for the Brothers themselves were not conducive to health and reflected the value of self-sacrifice evidenced by religious men and women of the day. Living arrangements were inspected by electoral officials in Glasgow and even as late as 1894 it was found Brothers 'living in little dormitories partitioned off by curtains, and that about twelve of them occupied one room'.

By the summer of 1861, the Marist Brothers had moved from 96 Garngad Hill to a more permanent base adjacent to the St. Mungo's parish school at 16 and 18 St. Mungo's Street.[25] Watters finds that 'St. Mungo Academy house-school in St. Mungo Street opened in April 1861 with 40 pupils, and by 1867, 100 boys attended'.[26] The Marist Brothers of St. Mungo would remain at St. Mungo's Street until 1882, but an additional community was opened in Glasgow based in Bishop Murdoch's former residence at 71 Charlotte Street, close to Glasgow Green, in 1863. By this time the Brothers were expanding further in Glasgow and now also directing St. Andrew's School (later St. Alphonsus) as well as St. Mary's in the Calton district, at the invitation of Father Forbes, from their new community residence towards the East End of the city.

By the time of Kerins' journey to France in 1864, over twenty postulants had passed from Britain and Ireland through the Beaucamps novitiate to mitigate the increasing burden on the Marist Brothers in the new Province of the North. As the Institute expanded, the number of Marist Brothers, as well as schools under the charge of the Brothers, continued to increase throughout Kerins' lifetime.[27]

The first mention of the name 'Brother Walfrid' in Scotland – the name in religion given to Andrew Kerins by his superiors in France – appears in expenses entries for the St. Mungo's junior school after his return from France. Handley explains that school log books were not kept for the Marist schools by the Brothers until 1864 when it became a legal requirement for schools open to government inspection in Scotland.[28] However, the St. Mungo's expenses record written in Glasgow on September 16th 1865 reads 'paid shoes for Br. Wilfrid [sic]' costing 10 shillings 6 pence.[29] It is therefore clear that Kerins was based at the St. Mungo's Marist residence and engaged as an apprenticed pupil teacher at the parish school prior to departing Glasgow for France, where he spent his period of postulancy between January and September 1864.

Andrew Kerins' formation as Brother Walfrid occurred in Beaucamps, near Lille in the north of France near the end of this period spent there as a postulant.[30]

Before moving on to the start of Brother Walfrid's life and work at St. Mary's Calton in late 1864, it is instructive to learn of the Marist Brothers' French origins and the mission of the teaching Brothers, as distinct from traditional Catholic priests, 'to labour for the education of youth' which should be achieved by living out the Christian values of obedience, charity, humility, simplicity, poverty and detachment.

France had been de-Christianised by the anti-clerical movements resulting from the Revolution at the end of the 1700s. In the early 1800s it began to experience a renewal of religious fervour which brought about the creation of numerous congregations and religious orders. A lively enthusiasm for the religious cause soon made France the principal home of Catholic missions.[31]

The 'Society of Mary' was founded in Lyon on July 23rd 1816 and comprised three separate branches: priests, and both teaching Brothers and Sisters 'bonded together by the same spiritual ideal – to be like Mary at the service of the Church through efficacious but discreet work'.[32] Father Champagnat – later canonised as Saint Marcellin in 1999 by Pope John Paul II and described as an 'Apostle for Youth' – began training the first Marist Brothers as teachers instructed in these values on January 2nd 1817 at La Valla, the first house of the Marist Brothers located just east of Saint-Étienne.[33] The Brothers received approval from the Vatican in 1836 from Pope Gregory XVI and 'committed themselves to assist the poor, the young and the foreign missions'.[34] As part of these foreign missions, Britain, and later Ireland, became the main focus for Marist expansion to the English-speaking world from the mid-nineteenth century onwards.

Pioneering historian of the Irish in Scotland, Marist Brother James Edmund Handley (Brother Clare FMS) produced the first history in English of the Brothers' expansion from France to Britain in 1858. That same year, Marian apparitions occurred in Lourdes, southern France, capturing the attention of the Catholic and mainstream press in Europe as well as the United Kingdom. The doctrine of the Immaculate Conception had been defined in Papal law in 1854, while Pope Pius IX officially recognised the event experienced by Bernadette Soubirous at Lourdes in 1862, leading to her canonisation in 1925.[35] These events stimulated a reinvigoration of Marian devotion amongst the Marist Institute itself as well as in the wider lay public.[36]

Following the reinstatement of the Catholic hierarchy in England in 1850, London saw the establishment of the first Marist community outside of France in 1852 at St. Anne's Spitalfields, upon the invitation of Cardinal Wiseman.[37] Scotland, by comparison, did not see the reinstatement of its Catholic hierarchy until 1878. The role played by an influx of new religious orders, including the Marist Brothers, helped expedite the shift from missionary territory to full, post-Reformation reinstatement of the Catholic hierarchy by contributing to the development of educational and parochial life in Scotland.

On the occasion of the Brothers' fiftieth anniversary of arriving in Scotland in 1908, the Marist *Bulletin De L'Institut* recalls the pivotal role of French linen merchant Charles Thiebault in facilitating its subsequent establishment in Glasgow.[38] Thiebault's will and testament shows that he bequeathed a sizeable amount of his fortune to the Brothers, including his personal library of literary books for use in the Marists' Dundee schools. Throughout his life he remained a significant benefactor to the development of Marist education and the wider development of Catholicism in Scotland.[39]

Thiebault was born in Arras, close to Lille in northern France, and such personal connections with the region and knowledge of developments in religious life in his homeland were key to the first Marist Brothers arriving in Scotland. It was decided that it was Glasgow – with the greatest number of immigrant Catholic Irish in Scotland – where the most pressing need for Catholic schools was to be found.

Handley's *A History of the Marist Brothers Province of the British Isles* tells us that the first three Brothers to arrive were named Procope (Charles Darou b. 1834), Faust (Joseph Wincott b. 1840) and Tatianus (Jeremiah O'Donoghue b. 1834). Brother Procope was a native of France whereas Faust and Tatianus were amongst the first young postulants to be sent from London to the Marist novitiate in Beaucamps, France, under the patronage of Madame la Contesse de la Granville, Caroline de Beaufort.[40] From the early 1840s, De Beaufort along with her husband Henri Julien Leon Bide, Count de la Granville, were instrumental in establishing a 'Province of the North' for the Marist Brothers attached to their castle grounds in Beaucamps, close to Lille.[41] Between her founding of a Marist school to be run by the Brothers in 1842 and her passing in late 1865, de Beaufort's role as benefactor earns her the title of 'Mother of the Brothers' in the Institute's own historiography of its early expansion from France to Britain and Ireland.[42]

A historical timeline of the development of the Marist Brothers from its beginnings in 1817 sketches out the international growth of the infrastructure of the Institute from its roots in France by 1858. Brother Louis-Marie, a pupil of St. Marcellin Champagnat who founded the Marist Brothers, became the third 'Superior General' of the Brothers in 1860, following St. Marcellin Champagnat and Venerable Brother François. The number of Brothers worldwide now under the charge of Louis-Marie exceeded one thousand, with Marist communities based in various parts of the world. In administrative terms this required a separation of layers of hierarchical governance across geographic zones which were changing as the Brothers grew in number. For the 'North', which included Britain and Ireland, Brother Théophane was made 'Provincial' in 1860, with Brother Alphonsus becoming 'Visitor' to those communities on behalf of Théophane.[43]

Notes

1 Aspinwall, B., 'Children of the Dead End: the Formation of the Modern Archdiocese of Glasgow, 1815-1914', The Innes Review, Vol. 43, No. 2 (Autumn, 1992) p. 119.

2 Aspinwall, B., *Portable Utopia: Glasgow and the United States 1820-1920*, p. 186.

3 *Scottish Catholic Directory* (1854), p. 85.

4 Watters, D.M., "Our Catholic school': themes and patterns in early Catholic school buildings and architecture before 1872', *The Innes Review*, Vol. 71, No. 1 (2020), p. 65.

5 Healy, A., *The Man Who Started Celtic* (as yet unpublished), p.3.

6 Post Office annual Glasgow directory (1859-1860), p. 337, held online at: https://digital.nls.uk/directories/browse/archive/83895844

7 *Extract on French Academy opened at 96 Garngad Hill by Marist Brothers*, SCA/MB/6/2/9/7, (1850s).

8 *School expenses book 1858 - 1890*, January 6th 1859, SCA/MB/6/2/2.

9 The Catholic Directory, Ecclesiastical Register, and Almanac (London, Burns and Lambert, 1856), p. 88.

10 *Extract on French Academy opened at 96 Garngad Hill by Marist Brothers*, SCA/MB/6/2/9/7, (1850s).

11 Microfiche of Brother Walfrid, No. 2998 held at the General Archive for The Institute of Marist Brothers, Rome.

12 *The Glasgow Herald*, August 20th 1855.

13 *The Glasgow Free Press*, May 22nd 1858.

14 Handley, J.E., *The History of St Mungo's Academy* (Paisley, 1958), p. 15.

15 *School expenses book 1858 - 1890*, SCA/MB/6/2/2.

16 1861 England, Wales and Scotland Census, accessed online at findmypast.co.uk.

17 *The Free Press*, October 13th 1860. 1861 England, Wales and Scotland Census, accessed online at findmypast.co.uk.

18 Handley, *A History of the Marist Brothers Province of the British Isles*, p. 60.

19 Beaucamps Admissions Register, SGL/01-0702/02 held at held at Archives of the Marist Brothers of France, St Genis Laval.

20 *The Free Press*, April 13th 1861. Handley, *A History of the Marist Brothers Province of the British Isles*, p. 60.

21 Keenan, W.J.F., 'Death figures in religious life: Components of Marist death culture 1817-1997', *Mortality*, Vol. 3, No. 1 (1998), pp. 7-26.

22 *The Free Press*, April 13th 1861.

23 *Ibid.*

24 O'Donoghue, T., *Catholic Teaching Brothers: Their Life in the English-Speaking World, 1891-1965* (New York: Pallgrave, 2012), p. 1.

25 Handley, *A History of the Marist Brothers Province of the British Isles*, p. 60.

26 Watters, "Our Catholic school': themes and patterns in early Catholic school buildings and architecture before 1872', p. 36.

27 Fitzpatrick, T.A., 'The Marist Brothers in Scotland before 1918', *The Innes Review*, Vol. 49, No. 1 (1998), pp. 1-10.

28 Handley, *A History of the Marist Brothers Province of the British Isles*, p. 59.

29 *School expenses book 1858 - 1890*, SCA/MB/6/2/2. N.B. 'Walfrid' was often misspelt in the Marist's own record-keeping as well as in other publications (for example, Wilfrid, Wolfred and Walfred have all been noted as different variations of spelling, but Walfrid is correct). As there was no 'Brother Wilfrid' at this time we can assume this is Walfrid.

30 Microfiche of Brother Walfrid, No. 2998 held at the General Archive for The Institute of Marist Brothers, Rome.

31 Le Chevallier, I., *Rendez-vous Leicester Square: The History of Notre Dame de France 1865-2015*, (Notre Dame de France: London, 2015), p. 21.

32 Le Chevallier, *Rendez-vous Leicester Square: The History of Notre Dame de France 1865-2015*, p. 22.

33 Taylor, *Jean-Claude Colin: Reluctant Founder*, p. 100.

34 Le Chevallier, *Rendez-vous Leicester Square: The History of Notre Dame de France 1865-2015*, p. 22.

35 Available online at https://www.thetablet.co.uk/news/14735/relic-of-st-bernadette-of-lourdes-to-tour-britain accessed November 2021.

36 Taylor, J., *Jean-Claude Colin: Reluctant Founder*, p. 1004.

37 Handley, J.E., *A History of the Marist Brothers Province of the British Isles* (1968), p. 13.

38 *Bulletin of the Institute*, Vol. I, No. 6 (November, 1909), pp. 299-305.

39 '*Photocopy extracts of Thiebault's will*', SCA/MB/7/1/12, (1873).

40 Handley, *A History of the Marist Brothers Province of the British Isles*, p. 57.

41 *Bulletin of the Institute*, Vol. 26, No. 199, (July, 1965), pp. 615-620.

42 *Bulletin of the Institute*, Vol. 26, n. 200, (October, 1965), pp. 707-712.

43 Brother Colin Chalmers, 'Administrative History of Marist Brothers of Great Britain', information received from the General Archives of the Marist Brothers in Rome, 2018.

A dinner table as used by St. Marcellin at the birthplace of the Marist Brothers near Lyon, France. The image evokes the practice set up by Brother Walfrid of Penny Dinners for poor children in Glasgow's East End.

CHAPTER 5

Beaucamps 1864 –
St. Mary's, Calton 1869

On 9th January 1863, the Marist Brothers received formal recognition from Pope Pius IX as the 'Marist Brothers of the Schools' under Canon Law. Official endorsement from Rome for the teaching Institute began by Marcellin Champagnat in 1817 brought with it access to more sources of funding and a prestige which in turn increased interest in the service of the Brothers.

Andrew Kerins was received into the Marist provincial house at Beaucamps in France as a postulant on 29th January 1864.[1] Kerins' own journey is not logged in the expenses record but an earlier entry for 10th July 1859 reads: 'Received from Mr Thiebault for Novice's voyage £10'.[2] Figures from the St. Mungo's expenses log show that the cost of his journey was around £10 (about £1,300 in today's values). The Marist Brothers therefore relied on the generosity of certain wealthy benefactors, such as the Dundee-based Thiebault, to enable those deemed capable of undertaking their novitiate of going to France. In Beaucamps, the Madame Countess, Caroline de Beaufort, had agreed with the Brothers that pupils and novices who were unable to pay would have accommodation and expenses covered during their stay.[3] At this point, the 'voyage' to Beaucamps was the only option for prospective young Brothers based in Scotland who were intent on undertaking their formation as a Marist Brother.

It was not until 1874, when Irishman Brother Alphonsus (John O'Hara b. 1830) opened a dedicated novitiate in Dumfries, Scotland, that a training centre was available to the Brothers in the United Kingdom.[4] Thus, twenty-four-year-old Andrew Kerins joined a select group of early Marist Brothers born in Ireland or Britain who received their religious habit at Beaucamps between 1853 and 1874.[5]

Andrew Kerins was the eighteenth postulant born in Britain or Ireland to be sent to Beaucamps who subsequently lived out his life in community with the Marist Brothers. Of the seventeen who journeyed before to France, twelve were Irish-born. Four were born in England, with one from Scotland. The same trend – of a sizeable majority of Brothers hailing from Ireland – is borne out over the twenty-year period when Beaucamps was used by the Marist Brothers of Britain and Ireland. Of the total number of thirty-six young men – including Kerins – who came to northern France before embarking on a life of Marist service, twenty-five were Irish-born (almost 70%).[7] Seven were English and five Scots.

Even amongst those born in England or Scotland, Irish surnames predominate: McHugh, Gallagher, McCarran, O'Brien, McCann and Hayes are all featured in the Beaucamps admissions register for Brothers born to Irish parents in Britain.[8] Familiar faces – many were received in France from Glasgow – and accents would no doubt have eased the shock for Kerins of moving, albeit for a short period of nine months, to a country foreign in language and custom. One such familiar face to be found on arrival was that of Irish Brother Tatianus who, along with Brother Procope and Brother Faust, helped establish the St. Mungo's Marist school Kerins had been sent from as a postulant. Brother Tatianus had departed Glasgow in July 1862 after being appointed Master of English-language novices at Beaucamps.[9] Six years senior to Kerins, Tatianus was born in Killarney, County Kerry in 1834 and completed his own novitiate at Beaucamps in 1857.[10] His knowledge and experience of the process of formation as a Marist Brother would have served as a source of support and inspiration for the younger postulant.

The average age for postulants entering the Beaucamps novitiate from Britain or Ireland during this period was nineteen. Kerins was twenty-three when he arrived from Glasgow, the same age as Tatianus had been in 1857 when joining the Brothers in France.[11] Both men had the advantage of being senior to other young men who undertook their spiritual formation (some were as young as sixteen), as well as having had experience working as a pupil teacher prior to making the journey to France. The admissions register and subsequent research by Brother John Parker shows that the older a postulant entered the training system in France, the more likely they were to commit themselves to the Institute for life, although there are many notable exceptions.[12] As master of the novices, the role of Tatianus was to ensure the spiritual welfare and educational development of the English-speaking postulants under his charge. The master of novices also directed the curriculum of the younger candidates.

A later prospectus for Beaucamps states that the 'English course of instruction embraces all the branches necessary for a first-class commercial education', delivered in the style of preparatory schools for university learning or employment in the professions. The advert also describes how 'acquisition of the French language is rendered easy and agreeable by the constant intercourse which exists between the French and English boys during recreations. . . as well as by the superior system of study adopted by the French Professors'.[13]

Having learned and worked alongside fluent French-speaking Marist Brothers at St. Mungo's, Kerins likely already had some basic command of the French language. The annals also show that young postulants were required to complete manual farm labour – after breakfast and before afternoon instruction – Beaucamps 'being situated in the open country amidst the richest scenery in the North of France'.[14]

The overall experience of postulants at Beaucamps was primarily geared towards preparation to sit and achieve the French 'brevet' teaching qualification before formally 'taking the habit' – the distinctive black cloak dress of the Marist Brothers – during their period in northern France. As well as representing an opportunity to develop and test himself academically, these months in France would also have seen Kerins work to prove himself worthy of becoming a religious Brother. The rural upbringing in Ireland of Brother Tatianus, similar to that of Kerins and several other postulants he taught, likely made the senior Irish Brother well suited to performing the role of mentor and confidante to those seeking to achieve full status as a Marist Brother.

The vocational nature of entering into the Marist Brothers is outlined in the Institute's own published material as follows:

> A boy may feel a great desire to serve God, he may have a particular attention for prayer, he may come to the conclusion that the world has little to offer to satisfy the glowing aspirations of his soul; it may be that God enkindles in his heart a great zeal for helping other souls and leading them to their true destiny – all these and similar motives may be the dawn of a Religious Vocation that will light the pathway of youth on the way to true happiness in Christ.[15]

On 'Postulantship', the prospectus reads,

> ... that is to say, he is asking earnestly to be accepted as a member of the Institute. During this period the Postulant examines more closely the life he hopes to lead and, at the end of six months, if he still persists in his request for admission and is acceptable, he is clothed with the Religious Habit and takes a Religious name.[16]

For Andrew Kerins, the date of his 'Vêture' ('Clothing' in English) came at the end of his period of training at Beaucamps on 11th September 1864 as part of the closing of the annual summer retreat for Brothers in the north of France. Alongside eight other postulants, Kerins received his religious habit in the presence of the Countess Caroline de Beaufort as well as the Assistant General responsible for the Province of the North, including Britain and Ireland, Brother Théophane. Brother Aidant, director of the Beaucamps schools and novitiate, also signed the register to formalise the ceremony, along with Théophane.[17] Brother Aidant had been instructed and formed as a Marist by the founder of the order, [later] Saint Marcellin Champagnat.[18] Andrew Kerins' formation as a Marist Brother therefore drew inspiration from, and links directly back to, the Marist teaching Institute's founder and patron Saint.

Kerins was the only non-native French speaker of the eight postulants taking part in the September ceremony, which at the time occurred twice annually.[19] On 19th March 1864, Kerins witnessed six fellow postulants from Britain and Ireland take the habit in the presence of the director, Brother Aidant.[20] Two of those Brothers – Brother William (Henry Banham b. 1845) and Brother Sennanus (Luke O'Brien b. 1842) – were living in community with Kerins in Glasgow after returning from France.

In this era, candidates were required to take the name of a Saint in order to become a Brother. Saint Galfrido of Pisa in Italy founded a Benedictine monastery and lived out his life as the abbot of the house until his death in 765. Galfrido, or Walfrid as the Saint became known in France, was canonised in 1861 by Pope Pius IX: just as Andrew Kerins was beginning his own spiritual vocation with the Marist Brothers.[21] It is important to note that individual Brothers did not choose their name in religion at this time, rather it would have been given to Kerins by one of the superior Brothers. Given that Saint Walfrid became canonised just three years prior to Kerins taking the habit, the name would have been prominent in the thinking of those in charge of directing the postulants at Beaucamps. His given name of Andrew Kerins continued to feature on civil records such as voter registers and school inspection reports. Henceforth, however, Kerins would become known as Brother Walfrid internally within the Institute, by his pupils and the wider communities in which he lived and worked after taking the habit as a Marist Brother.

Interestingly, the religious name is written 'Wolfred' on the Beaucamps record of the ceremony, perhaps a Francophone version of the spelling which became more widely used in Scotland and England.[22]

The annals of Beaucamps offers further insight into the activities and achievements of Andrew Kerins in the months between his arrival in France and his accepting the Brother Walfrid name in religion.

Towards the close of February 1864, a matter of weeks after arriving at Beaucamps, Kerins took part in the 'Forty Hours' prayers in preparation for the beginning of Lent along with the other Brothers resident at the provincial house: an ancient practice of French Catholicism. The next entry for March in the annals records the 'opening of the month of St. Joseph', patron Saint of workers and husband of the Blessed Virgin.[23] By taking part in these religious ceremonies, Kerins becomes imbued in the spirit of the Marist Institute in its native French tongue, as well as a cultural style of devotion quite distinct from that to which he had been accustomed.

Success of several candidates in gaining the 'brevet' qualification, which served as proof of an individual's ability to teach, is recorded on 27th July 1864. A total of three qualifications were gained at Lille, while two more individuals presented at the nearby town of Arras for their 'first tests'.[24] It is entirely possible that Andrew Kerins was amongst those sent to take exams at this time, although none of the individuals are named in the annals. No record of Kerins gaining a teaching qualification in Britain exists – neither at the Glasgow Normal College used by some Brothers based in Scotland, or at St. Mary's, the Hammersmith Catholic Training College in west London used by some London-based teaching Brothers. Given that Brother Walfrid is recorded by the Institute as teaching in London and Glasgow immediately after leaving Beaucamps does, nevertheless, increase the likelihood that some elementary form of teaching qualification may have been gained in France, either at Lille or Arras.[25]

The 4th of September saw a local Jesuit priest Father Berthon of Lille open the annual retreat at Beaucamps.[26] The retreat offered an opportunity for professed Marist Brothers to renew their sacred vows and participate in one week of spiritual renewal through prayer, meditation and discussion. In the absence of the Superior General of the Institute, Brother Louis Marie, who was unable to attend, Brother Pascal travelled to Beaucamps to lead the retreat for three days.[27] Brother Pascal was previously responsible for the first Marist schools in Britain and was instrumental in the establishment and supply of Brothers for St. Mungo's in Glasgow.[28] Pascal spoke with 'fire' to the

Brothers and hopeful postulants, including Kerins, before departing for St. Genis, Lyon. The week took on particular significance for Kerins as he and seven other young postulants prepared to take their religious habit in the presence of the Countess and superiors. The admission of eight postulants is recorded on 11th September on the final day of the annual retreat. Brother Walfrid departed Beaucamps on 12th September 1864.[29] His first *enseignment* – teaching assignment – would be in London.[30]

One notable peculiarity from the Beaucamps register is the suddenness with which the newly admitted Irish and British Brothers left to return to their schools and begin teaching. Traditionally, postulants would immediately begin their novitiate, which lasted one year, after being clothed with the Marist habit and taking a religious name before then embarking on their teaching duties in community.[31] For the French-speaking postulants this meant staying at Beaucamps after taking the habit and undertaking further study and spiritual formation in preparation for making religious vows the following year.

Brother Walfrid, like several other British or Irish Brothers at this time, was instead immediately assigned back to the schools in Britain to begin teaching.[32] It is known that, in this early stage in the development of the Marist Brothers in Britain, there was a shortage of English-speaking teachers of requisite experience and formation in the charism of the Institute.[33] Brother Walfrid, having gained experience learning and working in France with senior Brothers within the Institute, therefore fitted the profile to begin his novitiate period alongside his teaching vocation in the Marist schools of Britain. He is recorded as teaching briefly in London until returning to Glasgow by April 1865.[34]

Handley's history of the province describes how St. Patrick's in Soho was taken on by the Brothers in London to complement their original house at St. Anne's, Spitalfields in the East End of the capital. Both Soho and Spitalfields were home to large communities of Irish Catholics who sought refuge in the metropole following *An Gorta Mor*. One such individual was Cork-born Brother Stephen (William Cotter

b. 1837) who was charged with establishing the new residence close to Euston station and the St. Patrick's parish school. It is most likely that, returning to Euston in central London by rail following his voyage from France, Brother Walfrid was instructed to report to the new residence at 9 Polygon Square to assist Brother Stephen in the new venture.[35]

By April 1865, Andrew Kerins returned to the St. Mungo's school in the Townhead area of Glasgow as Brother Walfrid: a school where he had sought refuge and self-improvement as a young man amidst the often-hostile reception met elsewhere by immigrant Irish Catholics in the city. Study of the school log books from this time illustrates the two most pressing issues of the day – the desperate need for children from acutely impoverished families to contribute financially, and the pervading threat of proselytising from native dominant Protestant churches. An entry by the principal teacher Brother Procope in August 1867 read:

> Some boys absent as usual on Fridays. They are kept at home by their parents to run messages or to mind the child while the mother is washing; this seems to be the washing day with many and may account for the small attendance at school.[36]

Simply put, the level of poverty in Glasgow at the time excluded a large proportion of Catholic children from participating in basic education. Many were 'admitted free' with small fees covered by chapel collections and the work of charities, such as the Saint Vincent de Paul Society. The fact that many remained unable to attend – often owing to 'slacking in trade' and loss of employment in the family home – conveys the size of the task facing Catholic schools in the city throughout the Victorian era. In August 1868, Walfrid's superior Brother Procope, headmaster and director of the St. Mungo's community, also lamented the proselytising influence which tested the faith of those most desperate:

> A number of our boys are now working in the pottery and

are compelled to attend a Protestant school half time.[37]

A month later, Brother Procope explained discriminatory employment practices further:

> Some of the pottery boys attend the night school, but they dare not attend our day school half time through fear of being expelled from their work.[38]

Aspinwall estimates that fewer than one third of Catholic children in Glasgow were able to avail of basic education during the 1860s.[39] Community-building through the development of a new parochial system of education became a priority for senior Catholic Church figures in the wake of the arrival of unprecedented numbers of refugees from Ireland.[40] The leading role Brother Walfrid performed in the East End parishes is representative of such community-building on behalf of first and second generation Irish Catholics in Scotland.

After taking the habit in France, Kerins returned to take his first vow of Obedience as Brother Walfrid on August 3rd 1865 in Glasgow, in the presence of Archbishop Eyre. The presence of the city's most senior Catholic clergyman, along with the Superior General of the Marist Brothers, Brother Louis Marie, who travelled from Lyon, conveys the significance of the occasion for the progress of Catholic education in Glasgow.[41]

In 1868, Brother Walfrid's work at St. Mungo's is punctuated by a brief return to Beaucamps, this time engaged as a teacher of the English-speaking novices in northern France.[42] Walfrid was thereafter formally enrolled as an assistant teacher at St. Mungo's on April 12th 1869, having excelled in his teaching duties at the day school for boys and evening classes provided for adults by the Marists at the same school.[43] A recording of the timetable for the night school (designed for adult pupils who would have been required to work during the day) shows weekly lessons in Catechism, French, Algebra, Grammar, Geography and History.[44] Led by dedicated Marist Brothers, such diverse tutoring aimed to deliver much-needed teachers for overcrowded classrooms while also facilitating a forum for self-improvement: this for 'many adults who seem most anxious to get on'.[45] Irish Catholics may have been ghettoised in numerous ways but many were also pro-active in terms of their self-improvement.[46]

The recordings of the school log books illustrate this. In the example of St. Mungo's, where Walfrid first received his religious instruction, the school and church ran by the Marists appears as a cultural centre for the community. For example, an entry on October 8th 1866 describes how the school was given over to a brass band who played a charity concert that night.[47] Similarly, on February 12th 1870, it is recorded that 'the children of St. Mungo's schools, about 300, went to see the Christmas pantomime at the Prince's Theatre'.[48] Such events serve as evidence that Brother Walfrid worked as part of an outward-looking and innovative social enterprise which sought to take full part in the civic life of their new surroundings. Aspinwall stresses that 'teachers provided local families with a sense of continuity: theirs was a community-building vocation'.[49]

Notes

1 Beaucamps Admissions Register, SGL/01-0702/02: Freres Renseignements - 1854-1877: Liste des Freres, p. 69 held at held at Archives of the Marist Brothers of France, St Genis Laval.

2 *School expenses book 1858 - 1890*, SCA/MB/6/2/2.

3 *Bulletin of the Institute*, Vol. 26, No. 199, (July, 1965), pp. 615-620.

4 Brother Colin Chalmers, 'Administrative History of Marist Brothers of Great Britain', information received from the General Archives of the Marist Brothers in Rome, 2018.

5 Brother John Parker, 'Names and Particulars transcribed from the Register of Admission to the Novitiate of Beaucamps', received April 2020.

6 Brother John Parker, 'Names and Particulars transcribed from the Register of Admission to the Novitiate of Beaucamps', received April 2020. N.b. This figure does not include those Marist Brothers who left the Institute at a later date.

7 *Ibid.*

8 Beaucamps Admissions Register, SGL/01-0702/02.

9 Brother Colin Chalmers, 'Administrative History of Marist Brothers

of Great Britain', information received from the General Archives of the Marist Brothers in Rome, 2018.

10 Brother John Parker, 'Names and Particulars transcribed from the Register of Admission to the Novitiate of Beaucamps', received April 2020.

11 *Ibid.*

12 Beaucamps Admissions Register, SGL/01-0702/02.

13 The Catholic Directory, Ecclesiastical Register, and Almanac (London, Burns and Lambert, 1883), p. 207.

14 Beaucamps Vie de la Province, SGL/02-02-09: Annales Maison de Beaucamps et Province, p. 86 held at held at Archives of the Marist Brothers of France, St Genis Laval.
The Catholic Directory, Ecclesiastical Register, and Almanac (London, Burns and Lambert, 1883), p. 207.

15 'The Marist Brothers of the Schools: Their Life and Work' (1955), p. 30 held at Dumfries and Galloway Council Archives, GD517/10.

16 'The Marist Brothers of the Schools: Their Life and Work', p. 23.

17 Beaucamps Vie de la Province, SGL/02-02-09: Annales Maison de Beaucamps et Province, p. 87.
Beaucamps Freres-Communautes, SGL/01-07-03: Registres des Vêtures 1844-1886 (936 in total), No. 42 held at held at Archives of the Marist Brothers of France, St Genis Laval.

18 Delorme, Br. A., *Marvellous Companions of Marcellin Champagnat* (Rome: Institute of the Marist Brothers, 2011), p. 169.

19 Beaucamps Freres-Communautes, SGL/01-07-03: Registres des Vêtures 1844-1886 (936 in total), No. 42. Andrew Kerins received the habit of the Marist Brothers along with Henri Lievin, Arsene Jouillard, Louis Basteur, Sienne Lemine, Achille Equinel, Augustin Charle and Aime Hanoteau.

20 Beaucamps Freres-Communautes, SGL/01-07-03: Registres des Vêtures 1844-1886 (936 in total), No. 41.

21 Accessed online February 2020 at https://catholicsaints.info/book-of-saints-walfrid

22 Beaucamps Freres-Communautes, SGL/01-07-03: Registres des Vêtures 1844-1886 (936 in total), No. 42.

23 Beaucamps Vie de la Province, SGL/02-02-09: Annales Maison de Beaucamps et Province, p. 86.

24 *Ibid.*

25 Microfiche of Brother Walfrid, No. 2998 held at the General Archive for The Institute of Marist Brothers, Rome.

26 Beaucamps Vie de la Province, SGL/02-02-09: Annales Maison de Beaucamps et Province, p. 87.

27 *Ibid.*

28 Handley, *A History of the Marist Brothers Province of the British Isles*, p. 58.

29 Beaucamps Vie de la Province, SGL/02-02-09: Annales Maison de Beaucamps et Province, p. 87.

30 Microfiche of Brother Walfrid, No. 2998 held at the General Archive for The Institute of Marist Brothers, Rome.

31 'The Marist Brothers of the Schools: Their Life and Work', p. 23.

32 Beaucamps Admissions Register, SGL/01-0702/02, p. 69. Brother John Parker, 'Names and Particulars transcribed from the Register of Admission to the Novitiate of Beaucamps', received April 2020.

33 Taylor, *Jean-Claude Colin: Reluctant Founder*, p. 764.

34 Microfiche of Brother Walfrid, No. 2998 held at the General Archive for The Institute of Marist Brothers, Rome.

35 Handley, *A History of the Marist Brothers Province of the British Isles*, p. 26-27.

36 Log Book of St Mungo's R.C. School, Townhead, Glasgow, March 1864 – March 1899. (D-ED7/247/1.1, available at the Mitchell Library, Glasgow).

37 *Ibid.*

38 *Ibid.*

39 Aspinwall, B., 'The Formation of the Catholic Community in the West of Scotland: Some Preliminary Outlines', The Innes Review, Vol. 33, No. 33 (1982) p. 46.

40 *Ibid.*

41 N.B. the first Vow of Obedience then also incorporated Chastity and Poverty – the 'Three Vows' of Obedience, Chastity and Poverty did not become part of Marist life until revisions to Canon Law in 1917.

42 Sweeney, *Celtic. The Early Years: 1887-1892*, p. 23.

43 Microfiche of Brother Walfrid, No. 2998 held at the General Archive for The Institute of Marist Brothers, Rome.

44 Log Book of St Mungo's R.C. School, Townhead, Glasgow, March 1864"– March 1899. (D-ED7/247/1.1, available at the Mitchell Library, Glasgow).

45 *Ibid.*

46 Walker, W.M., 'Irish Immigrants in Scotland: Their Priests, Politics and Parochial Life', The Historical Journal, Vol. 15, No. 4 (Dec., 1972), pp. 649-667.

47 Log Book of St Mungo's R.C. School, Townhead, Glasgow, March 1864 – March 1899. (D-ED7/247/1.1, Mitchell Library, Glasgow).

48 *Ibid.*

49 Aspinwall, 'Children of the Dead End: the Formation of the Modern Archdiocese of Glasgow, 1815-1914', p. 139.

CHAPTER 6
Glasgow: 1870 – 1892

On May 13th 1870 'Mr A. P. Kerins began his duties as assistant teacher' at St. Mary's Boys' school in the Calton area in Glasgow's East End.[1]

It is here that we see the introduction of football as a means of advancement for the children of the East End by the Marists. Principal teacher, Brother James (Thomas McCann, b. 1844), happily reports in September 1872 that:

> Attendance (punctual) much improved by the foot-ball being placed at the disposal of early comers.[2]

Football, and sporting recreation more generally, is first mentioned with reference to the Marist Brothers of Glasgow in September 1866. The St Mungo's 'annual excursion' saw '600 children and about 100 adults' travel by train to Cambuslang for a celebratory day of music, food and games. The *Glasgow Free Press* reports a 'grand procession' was made through the city centre to the railway station whereby:

> The girls marched in front, and were followed by the pupils of St Mungo's Academy, about 100 in number, preceded by the St Mungo's flute band. Then came the boys of the Parish School, all marching three abreast. The scholars were under the guidance of their teachers, the Marist Brothers.[3]

As a professed Brother, Walfrid would have been part of the travelling party of teachers, pupils and parents from the parish. In terms of sport, the article continues:

A great variety of games had been provided on the grounds for the children, in which they all took a hearty part, and it was most amusing to see the efforts of the little fellows to carry off some of the many excellent prizes that were offered to the successful competitors. The football in particular was greatly relished by some of the adult excursionists.

McBrearty dates the formation of the first organised, distinctly Irish Catholic football club in Scotland at 1868 with the creation of an Airdrie Football Club playing out of the Rochsoles estate. McBrearty finds that:

> The Rochsoles estate, two years earlier, had hosted an excursion, which included games of football, involving the sabbath schools associated with St. Margaret's Christian Doctrine Society, a Catholic organisation connected to the local church in Airdrie.[4]

Clearly the Marists and Brother Walfrid of St Mungo's in Glasgow were doing likewise with their own excursion to Cambuslang in the same year. The Marist Brothers were evidently swift to note the growing interest in, and potential of, football amongst their own community. This detail takes on added significance when considering Brother Walfrid's most-renowned legacy during his years in Glasgow: namely his role in the foundation of Celtic Football Club, constituted to raise funds for his Poor Children's Dinner Tables charity attached to the Catholic schools of the East End of Glasgow.[5] The first era of Walfrid's time in Glasgow saw him begin his journey as a Marist Brother and begin to live out his vocation as an educator in the Catholic male religious tradition. The next two chapters demonstrate how Brother Walfrid began to take on an increasingly senior role within the Marist Institute in Glasgow and begin to champion the cause of impoverished children, culminating in his involvement in the early history of Celtic FC.

By the 1870s he begins to take on a leadership role within the Institute of Marist Brothers, beginning with his headmastership of the new Sacred Heart school which he opened in 1874. Walfrid's own progress was reflected by the Marists' wider expansion in Glasgow in terms of teaching Brothers, schools and pupils under their care.

Over the course of the 1860s, the Marist Brothers became fully engaged in the educational life of the city, their aptitude as teachers noted by government officials as the Brothers navigated the regulations of the Scottish education system whilst discharging their roles as Catholic religious teachers. This decade marked an era of increasing scrutiny of the state of education generally in Scotland, with the Argyll Commission established in 1864 under royal patronage taking a 'particular focus' on the schools of Glasgow.[6]

On returning from France to begin life as a teaching Marist Brother at St. Mungo's, these standards were expected to be maintained by Walfrid and his fellow Brothers. Regular inspection of the schools is apparent from the log books, from senior Catholic clergy but perhaps more importantly, in terms of achieving grant funding, from local and national government officials. Brother Procope, as headmaster of St. Mungo's, records in the school log book on 18th May 1865:

> Visit from the Royal Commissioner, Mr Harvey. He examined the children and expressed his satisfaction at their proficiency and especially at the state of discipline in the school. He gave it as his opinion that the elementary Catholic schools of this country have in general better discipline and display greater efficiency than similar schools belonging to other communions.[7]

Procope states that 'several of the biggest boys have gone to work' in May 1864, illustrating the context of voluntary education for children before the 1872 Education Act for Scotland.[8] Partitions had been removed to accommodate more desks and combat over-crowdedness in March of 1864 at the outset of the commission on the inspector's recommendation, records Brother Procope. Despite this, the overall report of May 1865 highlights the 'better discipline' and 'greater efficiency' of St. Mungo's and marks the Marist school out as a notable early success, even compared to better-funded state schools. St. Mungo's was one of only three 'upper' schools for older children offering a more advanced curriculum – the others ran by the Jesuits and Franciscan Sisters.

Close analysis of the log book shows that St. Mungo's was not an exception to McDermid's finding that 'all the city's Catholic schools were plagued by irregular attendance and lack of punctuality'. She also states, 'Catholic education suffered from poor accommodation and lack of resources'.[9] Those boys from the poorest families were required to forego school in order to supplement household income, whether in the urban factories or engaged in seasonal rural work outside Glasgow.[10] Brother Procope explains further that 'pupils that are admitted free on the recommendation of the clergy, are generally the most irregular' in February 1865.[11]

The teaching Brothers themselves were also required to undertake teaching examinations in fulfilment of state regulations, which in Scotland was dominated by the national Protestant religion in the nineteenth century. In order to guarantee funding in the form of government grants, the Brothers and the schools under their charge were required to attain high standards with respect to these external examinations of their progress. 'Pupil Teacher examination' was held for Catholic teachers, including the Marist Brothers, in local parishes, notably including the large St. John's church based in the Gorbals area of Glasgow.[12] Brother Walfrid, as a newly-professed Marist Brother, was engaged in pupil teacher training at this time in St. Mungo's, leading classes whilst also preparing for his own examination to gain full status as an assistant teacher as per Scottish regulations, this against the backdrop of abject poverty amongst the Irish Catholic community which reduced income from voluntary pupil fees, at a time when school attendance was not mandatory for minors. On the Roman Catholic population of Glasgow, the Argyll Commission describes:

> . . . in other public works, such as silk-mills, potteries, foundries, glass-works, papermills, match-works, etc., there does not appear to be any such restriction, and so children are admitted to work very young in them. It is no uncommon thing to see children nine or ten years of age in many of these works. The father, perhaps, is not earning more than

12s. or 13s. a week, and he has a wife and four or five little children to support, and he has the chance of securing 2s. 6d. or 3s. a week more; though this is necessarily at the expense of the child's education. In some instances, not a few, I have seen children sent very early to work.[13]

Sister Martha Skinnider and John Wilson provide an in-depth historical overview of the social and economic context for Catholic education at this time and the conditions Brother Walfrid and the Marist Brothers worked under in their early Glasgow schools. Wilson finds that one of the recommendations of the Argyll Commission at its conclusion in 1867 was 'that all teachers should be trained', whilst also reporting the lack of funding and impoverished conditions Catholic teachers were working under in Glasgow.[14] Apprenticing of pupil teachers, including Brother Walfrid, was henceforth prioritised by the Marist Brothers of Glasgow in accordance with the Commission's recommendations.

Brother Procope, as superior tasked with directing the preparation of pupil teachers under his charge, includes the weekly timetable followed by Walfrid and others on August 30th 1866:

Monday	Grammar, analysis & composition
Tuesday	Arithmetic, Algebra & Geometry
Wednesday	Geography
Thursday	French
Friday	History & map drawing

N.B. Lesson in catechism of Perseverance, by Gaume, every day except Thursday.[15]

Following his return from France in late 1868, Brother Procope records on April 12th 1869 that 'Andrew Kerins & Hugh O'Neill (Br. Columba) were entered as assistants' in support of him as headmaster of St. Mungo's.[16] This represents a significant promotion in Brother Walfrid's teaching career as well as his journey within the Marist Brothers Institute. By graduating from pupil teacher to assistant headmaster, Walfrid is clearly marked out as a Marist Brother of requisite educational proficiency and spiritual character just five years after receiving the religious habit.

Monies raised in grant-aid by participation in the Education Department exams amounts to almost £1000 in today's value, funds desperately required by the Marist Brothers of St. Mungo's as they sought to facilitate the attendance of the poorest of the local community. For example, a letter was written to the Education Department in April 1870 requesting papers for examinations administered by the Science and Art Department, responsible for dispensing grant-aid to successful applicants who passed the set examination. Papers were requested at elementary grade for boys in the upper class and also at 'Second Grade for Assistants' – two papers to be sat on 'Freehand' and 'Geometry'.[17] The log book for 10th May 1870 shows 'drawing examination presided over by Fr. Nicholas who broke the seals & gave out the papers'.[18] The final mention of Brother Walfrid in connection with St Mungo's appears on July 15th 1870 as follows:

> Received the result of the Drawing examination –
> 12 children received prizes – The Pupil Teachers Hackett, McDermott, Wilson & Assistant Teacher A. Kerins also received prizes. The Grant amounted to £8. 10.[19]

The proactive efforts of Brother Walfrid – both in teaching the prizewinning children and successfully completing the examination himself – were to the fore at this time of financial need. For context, Tierney finds that 'between 60 and 70 per cent of Catholic children were paying less than three pence per week or nothing at all' towards school fees owing to prevailing poverty in Glasgow.[20] That the Marist school of St. Mungo's was able to win such a sizeable grant-aid payment towards costs is testament to the foresight and ingenuity of the teaching Brothers, including Brother Walfrid – in fundraising for their first established school in Glasgow.

The next period of Brother Walfrid's life in Glasgow comprised five years from 1870 -1874 spent ministering at St. Mary's in the Calton area in the East End of Glasgow, then the largest Catholic parish in Scotland, having departed St. Mungo's on 13th May 1870.[21]

Glasgow-born Brother James (Thomas McCann), as headmaster of St. Mary's, welcomed Walfrid to his new post in the school log book on the same day his departure from St. Mungo's is recorded, writing 'Mister A Kerins began his duties as Assistant Teacher today'.[22] The two Marist Brothers worked closely together in the direction of the 'Mother Parish' school under the management of Father Peter Forbes who established the school behind St. Mary's church on Abercromby Street in 1850. The church itself was constructed in 1842 and opened by Father Forbes, making it the second oldest parish in the city of Glasgow after St. Andrew's Cathedral, Clyde Street. By 1870, the Marist Brothers were leading a staff of eight at St. Mary's, including pupil teachers, and were in charge of a roll of four hundred boys – the largest roll for a Catholic school in the city at that time.[23]

Overcrowded classrooms comprising upwards of fifty boys were not uncommon in this era and log books show that health problems typical of urban poverty – such as typhus, tuberculosis and cholera – were a recurring theme for pupils and staff alike.[24]

A summary of the status of the Marist Brothers and the other Catholic religious orders' efforts in providing education for the children of the predominatly Irish population of school age makes for a story of perilous existence in the 1860s and 1870s. The pressure from the state to impose teaching and curriculum standards with funding that was in no way adequate was a persistent challenge. The same state authorities, while solicitous of the interests of children in schools, seemed to take little responsibity for children not in schools when economic necessity forced them into precarious employment 'in silk-mills, potteries, foundries, glass-works, papermills, match-works, etc.'

The standard of school buildings too would have left much to be desired and many classrooms were themselves hazardous places to spend time, overcrowded, inadequate and damp. All this left the teaching staff, pressured enough by their daily work to have to give consistent, serious attention to the rasing of necessary funds to keep the whole operation going. Not only attempting to generate income from fees to be paid by parents who could ill-afford them, but the ever present reality of hunger as an obstacle to concentration on learning – growing children were hungry and a school dinner was the least that could be provided both to attract attendance and to enable learning.

Having left St. Mungo's to the north of the city, Brother Walfrid is listed as living at 71 Charlotte Street with Superior of the Charlotte Street community, Brother John, and six other Marist Brothers.[25] It was here in the presence of his Brothers in religion that Walfrid took final vows on the 29th of July 1869, confirming his dedication to the Marist Brothers teaching order.[26]

In preparation for headmastership, he continued to put himself forward for examination aimed at securing the relevant teaching qualification from the Education Department. Brother James records on November 12th 1870 'Assistant teacher allowed to absent himself all week on account of the Examination'.[27] The '*date du brevet obligatoire*' was achieved by Walfrid in December 1870 according to the general archives of the Marist Brothers in Rome. This most likely occurred at the Normal School run by the Free Church in Glasgow as was common custom for Brothers at the time, though no record survives.[28] The St. Mary's log book records another of Brother Walfrid's key duties as a senior member of the teaching Brothers on March 18th 1872 when 71 Charlotte Street is named as the venue for ongoing pupil teacher lessons, held in the evening after school classes. Both Walfrid and headmaster Brother James would have been tasked with delivering these preparatory lessons to aspiring Catholic teachers.[29]

Pupil teacher instruction took on added significance with the coming of the 1872 Education (Scotland) Act, necessitating change all round for the Marist Brothers of Glasgow, as well as Scottish schools in the wider sense. Skinnider finds 'the Act set up the anomalous situation by which the public schools of Scotland were Presbyterian denominational schools, for which Catholics had to pay an education rate, while at the same time they paid for their own schools all deficit not covered by grant, and met the cost of all new buildings' required to accommodate the anticipated increase in numbers. For the first time, education for children was compulsory between the ages of five and thirteen.[30] Grants were now 'given on average attendance' and only children 'with at least 250 attendances' could be examined annually as a source of additional grant-aid from the government. A huge financial burden was thus placed on the Catholic community from 1872 and the Marist Brothers, like the senior clergy school managers, 'had to make constant efforts to bring children to school regularly'.[31]

Apostolic Administrator Charles Eyre, an English recusant Catholic clergyman sent to Glasgow by Pope Pius IX to mediate between quarrelling Scots and Irish Catholic clergy, was tasked with overseeing an immediate programme of school building. Charles Eyre became the first Archbishop of Glasgow since the Reformation and latterly, an early honourable patron of Celtic Football Club. He is recorded visiting St. Mary's school on October 15th 1872 and encouraging 'boys to remonstrate if parents wished to keep them at home'.[32]

Perhaps to offset the admonishment of senior clergy, the Marist Brothers took to providing incentives for good attendance in the form of sweets and fruit, while a 'new foot-ball' was required on November 6th 1872, such was the popularity of the new game amongst the boys attending St. Mary's.[33] For his part, Brother Walfrid is noted as the 'best teacher' of the older class of boys, whom he gives an unusual lesson on coal and iron noted by Brother James on March 13th 1873.[34]

Given the drive to encourage attendance amongst the pupils, the lesson was possibly aimed at preparing the oldest boys for employment in Glasgow's heavy industries after leaving school aged thirteen, when attendance was no longer compelled by law. Until his departure for the newly-built Sacred Heart school located in Bridgeton at the close of 1873, Brother Walfrid was again granted absence in preparing for Science and Art Department examinations by Brother James in the hope of securing much-needed grant funding.[35] On December 22nd 1873 before the break for Christmas holidays, Brother James records simply 'Mr Kerins leaves': to begin his assignment of opening the new Sacred Heart school in Bridgeton.[36] 'Bridgeton opened at last, therefore an almost imperceptible decrease in attendance', reads the entry for the 26th of January 1874, as Brother Walfrid begins his role as headmaster of the Sacred Heart school most closely associated with his life served as a Marist Brother.[37]

Sacred Heart 1874

Brother Walfrid was to remain in post at Sacred Heart from its opening under his leadership in 1874 until his transfer to London by his Superiors in the summer of 1892, making it his longest association with any one parish school over the course of his lifetime.[38] This period is marked by a period of challenge and growth for both the Irish Catholic community in Glasgow, as well as for Brother Walfrid himself as he sought to live out his educational, charitable vocation in the Marist tradition. For the Marist Brothers teaching order in Britain, the General Chapter of 1873 brought about a milestone development with Brother Procope – Walfrid's former Superior and headmaster at St. Mungo's, Glasgow – appointed as an Assistant General of the Institute. The 'Province of the Isles' was made distinct from the 'Province of the North' housed at Beaucamps, giving Procope responsibility for Brothers and schools in Britain, Ireland, Australia and South Africa. The Irishman Brother Alphonsus, in his election as 'Provincial Director' of Britain and Ireland in support of Brother Procope, became the first non-French Brother to hold such a senior position in the Institute.[39]

The Catholic order Brother Walfrid joined in France just a decade prior now represented an international religious teaching institution, with colleagues he knew personally from Glasgow directing its expansion. In the Scottish context in the light of the 1872 Education Act, Fitzpatrick highlights 'the most pressing need for Catholic education was an increased supply of trained teachers'. To this end, he describes how Brother Procope and Brother Alphonsus first secured premises in Dumfries for a novitiate for the new province starting in 1873 which grew to become St. Joseph's College. Additionally, Fitzpatrick cites Brother Alphonsus as a driving force in opening a 'Pupil teacher Centre or Juniorate at 71 Charlotte Street'.[40] Unlike St.

Joseph's in Dumfries, which flourished, Fitzpatrick is less positive about the juniorates established in Britain, who states, 'the idea was not successful, and the comparative failure of it in Glasgow was repeated later in London and Dundee'.[41]

Nonetheless, the house councils from the juniorate house in Glasgow, where Brother Walfrid was resident for the remainder of his time in the city, begin in 1879 and offer an almost daily insight into how the male religious negotiated daily life in community in often cramped and challenging circumstances. Unfortunately, the log book of the Sacred Heart school – which would have been maintained by the hand of headmaster Brother Walfrid – does not survive as part of the Mitchell Library's Glasgow City Archives collection of nineteenth century Catholic school materials. Many such items were simply lost when moving premises, degenerated over time or were sadly thrown out. However, the log books of neighbouring Catholic schools in Glasgow – especially those also directed by Marist Brothers – provide valuable glimpses into the Marist teaching tradition as well as cross-over vignettes in terms of social events and fundraising efforts which Sacred Heart and Brother Walfrid were also part of and contributed wholly to. Personal writings produced by Brother Walfrid, in addition to contemporary newspaper reports, further illuminate his own development and charitable motivation during this period, culminating in his promotion to Brother Superior of the community in Glasgow and what was to become a leading role in the foundation of Celtic Football Club.

In Handley's view, the main upshot of the Education (Scotland) Act of 1872 was that the new regulations 'took under the control of the state the education of the young, hitherto in the hands of the churches'. Preservation of 'the Catholic spirit' within the schools was prioritised over access to greater state funding.[42] Thus, Fitzpatrick describes how Catholics authorities elected to join with their Episcopalian counterparts and other voluntary education bodies in deciding to remain outside the new national system of education in Scotland – perceived to reflect only the majority Protestant religion of the population in practice – to protect a distinct 'denominational character'.[43] Handley and Fitzpatrick agree that this precipitated a period of 'survival' for Catholic education in financial terms, relying heavily on contributions from its own parishioners aided by more wealthy benefactors.

For the schools, this meant maximising those sources of government grant-aid which remained open to them.[44] Initial notice was received and processed by the Education Department for Scotland from the new Sacred Heart in Bridgeton on 29th January 1874. Completed by the school manager and parish priest Father Edward Noonan, in consultation with his curate Father Thomas Heffernan, the document gives a detailed picture of the planned elementary day school. The building itself is described as belonging to 'The Roman Catholic Congregation, Bridgeton' with the premises solely designed 'for use of children attached to [the] mission' in that district of Glasgow.[45] Father Noonan describes 'good' light, drainage and ventilation for the shared building, which housed separate entrances for boys and girls. The school room for boys measured 102 feet in length, 26 feet in breadth and 16 feet in height. These dimensions were replicated for the female department, albeit with a slightly higher roof at 20 feet. A separate classroom is also described – one for boys, one for girls – each measuring 24 feet by 20.[46]

For the Boys Department, headmaster Andrew Kerins (Brother Walfrid) confirms he became 'Certificated' in December 1870 during his time as assistant at St. Mary's in the Calton, making him legally qualified to take on the role of headmaster under the terms of the 1872 Act. It is recorded that Walfrid had been teaching for nine years at this point, dating to his return from Beaucamps as a professed Marist Brother.[47] As previously discussed, it is likely he was engaged in pupil teacher duties prior to this event. Brother Walfrid would be joined by Mary Louis McKenzie who took charge of the Girls Department – McKenzie had a decade of experience in teaching and was previously attached to St. Vincent's, close to the Gallowgate in Glasgow for three years.[48] Both male and female divisions were each anticipating an average daily attendance roll of two hundred pupils at the Sacred Heart school. Father Noonan gives an estimated required annual expenditure of £300 translating to £1. 10 d per boy in the boys division, slightly higher than the £1. 7d factored for girls on account of the lower salaries paid to female teachers. £250 was expected to be paid in salary to male staff, compared to £220 for female teaching staff. £50 to each division would be dedicated to books, running costs and other expenses.[49]

To offset costs, Noonan estimates an annual income of £60 voluntary contributions along with £100 from the 'School Pence' – weekly payments from the families of pupils in attendance who could afford to pay. 75% of places would be at a higher rate of 3d per week with the other 25% available at the lower level of 2d per week. This meant plans were in place for boys and girls to contribute to running costs 'according to the means of the parents', with many in reality admitted free on account of prevailing poverty.[50] The remaining £140 income required to run the school – nearly 47% of the estimated amount required – would be supplied through 'voluntary contributions and church collections' writes Father Noonan.[51] Noonan, in his 'statement of the grounds on which the Managers apply for an Annual Grant', explains:

> A population of 4000 Roman Catholics for whom no other provision exists within a reasonable distance, some of the children formerly attended St. Mary's in which school there was no longer sufficient accommodation.[52]

The school managers and teaching staff under the direction of Brother Walfrid clearly laboured under continually perilous financial conditions from the outset of the newly established Sacred Heart parish school, a fact borne out by the house councils recorded at the Marist Brothers house at 71 Charlotte Street. Brother Walfrid personally appealed to the Archdiocese Catholic hierarchy, restored in 1878, throughout his time as headmaster of Sacred Heart on behalf of the school and others directed by his fellow Marist Brothers in Glasgow.[53] In terms of Sacred Heart, Aspinwall finds that the mission 'was able to call on substantial support at its foundation in 1873'.[54] The church itself was opened by Father Heffernan, assistant priest to Father

Noonan, on the 'Feast of the Nativity of Our Lady, 8th September 1873'.[55] Initial donations pledged towards tackling the church debt of £7,696 began at £2 from parishioners up to '£1,000 from Dr James Scanlan, 62 Buccleugh Street'. £800 came from the Nelis merchant family who specialised in the sale of Irish butter and eggs, while wine and spirit merchant Arthur McHugh gave £500.[56] Alongside what government grants could be secured, Father Noonan and Brother Walfrid could lean on the generosity and faith of a small coterie of individual sources within the local Irish Catholic community to support their endeavours.

Fundraising drives were a regular occurrence within the Sacred Heart parish, evidenced at the formal opening of the church building by famed Irish Dominican preacher Father Tom Burke on 27th April 1874. 'An unpretending wooden edifice' is described by the *Glasgow Herald*, while in his charity sermon Father Burke 'spoke of the humble structure as one which did not realise his ideal of the house of God, although they must accept it gratefully as the promise of better things to come'.[57] Tickets were sold for the fundraising ceremony conducted by Burke from the offices of the influential Catholic publisher Hugh Margey – responsible for the annual Catholic Directory – in 14 Great Clyde Street, Glasgow.[58] Father Tom Burke achieved international renown speaking in his native Ireland and amongst the diaspora in Britain and North America. Pope Pius IX aptly styled him 'prince of preachers' and his attendance at the opening of Sacred Heart secured a turnout in excess of the capacity of the church building itself.[59] Similar charity sermons, Christmas concerts given by the pupils of Sacred Heart and lecture events were features of parochial life during Brother Walfrid's time at Sacred Heart.[60]

Funds raised were used by the Marist Brothers to reward regular attenders of their schools with trips to notable events occurring in the city such as 'Buffalo Bill's Wild West' show in the winter of 1891.[61] Brother Walfrid even managed to secure a donation for the Poor Children's Dinner Tables from the North American travelling show.[62]

Likewise, monies were received from Sir George Trevelyan,

Member of Parliament for Bridgeton while Walfrid was headmaster of Sacred Heart.[63] Trevelyan was the only son of Sir Charles Trevelyan, infamous for his *laissez-faire* response to the humanitarian crisis in Ireland engendered by the failure of the potato crop. It is right and just that Walfrid availed of donations from the Trevelyan family to feed the children of those forced to leave Ireland as a direct result of his failure to adequately intervene as the colonial British government's treasurer in charge of relief in Ireland at the time.

Aspinwall finds that parochial income peaked in Walfrid's final year in Glasgow, 1892-93, at £4,018. 11s 5d, while the Catholic congregation of Bridgeton rose from 4300 in 1874 to 6350 by 1893.[64] This enabled the associated growth of the parish school under Brother Walfrid's charge. By 1886, the annual roll for Sacred Heart rose to 1045 with an average attendance of 819. This was sustained by the achievement of annual grant aid of £723. 9s.[65]

In a more general sense outside of his daily duties at Sacred Heart, Brother Walfrid began utilising his increasingly senior role within the Marist Brothers community in Glasgow to advocate on behalf of the poorest amongst the Irish Catholic population in the city – especially children. One striking example of his advocacy on behalf of the least fortunate of his own community, living and working amongst the Irish Catholic diaspora of Glasgow, is a handwritten letter of appeal to the Marquess of Bute, written by Walfrid in 1885. Brother Walfrid displays awareness of the wider economic and social factors afflicting Irish Catholics at the time, referring to the 'depressed state of Trade in and around the City' at the onset of winter in 1885.[66] Walfrid, by way of explanation in his letter of appeal to the Third Marquess of Bute, continues:

> Nearly a year ago, with the kind assistance of the Brotherhood of St. Vin. de Paul, we were enabled to put into shape the 'Penny Dinner' system, in a Room adjoining the School. Since then, we have been giving a good bowl of Soup and a slice of Bread for a penny, and when the parents send bread with the children they can have the soup for a halfpenny.
>
> This did well enough as long as they could patronise it

and till our funds went down. There are also about 150
adults, who have, I may safely say, almost nothing to subsist
on, and who receive daily, what the Society of St. Vin de
Paul can afford to give them.

I know the Society have very little money on hand, and I
am therefore not inclined to ask their ever ready assistance,
for our poor children just now. Hence I am compelled to
apply, to those who are always willing to assist the Poor and
the Orphan, for some help.[67]

In making representation on behalf of the most vulnerable in his
community, Brother Walfrid demonstrates the non-judgemental,
universal mode of charity favoured throughout his life. Biographer
Rosemary Hannah characterised John Charles Patrick Stuart – the
Third Marquess and recipient of the above letter – as a man of
extraordinary wealth and charity in the second half of the nineteenth
century. Hannah wrote that the Marquess – a high-profile convert to
Catholicism in 1868 – became a patron of British Catholic revivalism
and supported 'many charities with an open hand, especially
educational ones'.[68] Crucially, Walfrid's letter refers to the dual purpose
of the Penny Dinners scheme:

I may state that since the 'Dinners' were started, last
January, our school attendance has gone up considerably.[69]

With the help of his fellow Marist Brother Dorotheus, Walfrid had
expanded the feeding programme from St. Mary's Calton to his own
Sacred Heart parish in Bridgeton. The 'Dinners' had the twin intention
of providing physical sustenance to local Irish Catholic children, as
well as enabling them to receive education in the tradition of their
own faith.[70] Clearly, this innovation would be a cause which would
appeal to the wealthy Marquess. The Marquess himself had written
to Rev. Alexander Munro, Provost of the Glasgow Cathedral, in October
1885 to express concern over the physical and spiritual condition of
the city's Catholic boys following regular visits to Glasgow.[71] Less than
a fortnight later, the Marquess received his letter of appeal from
Brother Walfrid [see text and copy of letter in Appendix].

Correspondence in early 1886 between Rev. Munro and the Marquess shows that funds were received for Catholic soup kitchens in the city. Hannah wrote that the Third Marquess of Bute was 'dogged once his sympathy had been roused'.[72] A refuge centre was established in the East End of Glasgow one year after Walfrid's appeal to Bute, where a copy of the letter penned by Walfrid is privately archived. 'St. Vincent's Shelter for Newsboys and Newsgirls' was founded in 1887 in Market Street 'chiefly through the benevolence of the Marquess of Bute' in order to 'provide a day shelter with warm meals, and provision for evening recreation' in a religious setting. Brother Walfrid, in his prominent position at the head of the Marist teaching order in Glasgow, was clearly willing and able to avail of a wider network of influence to aid his community.

Brother Walfrid also found forum for expression of his charitable instincts with the Saint Vincent de Paul Society, of whom he remained a member until his passing in 1915. John Burns Bryson, an Edinburgh solicitor who joined the SVDP, was responsible for establishing the first Glasgow conference, St Andrew's, when he returned to Glasgow in 1848. Aspinwall emphasises the impact of mass Irish Catholic immigration to the city, in bolstering the patronage of such Catholic self-help sodalities, during the proceeding years as a result of *An Gorta Mor*. He concludes that the SVDP, along with the League of the Cross, were examples of Catholic Action which 'reinforced domestic devotional discipline within the locality, neighbourhood and city'.[73]

Continuing in that same tradition of Catholic self-help, the League of the Cross would also play an integral role in Glaswegian life. Created by Cardinal Manning in London in 1873, the League was a Catholic confraternity based around the pledge of total abstinence.[74] It was of course the St Mary's League of the Cross parish hall (67 East Rose Street, off Abercrombie Street) which played host to the meeting coordinated by Brother Walfrid resulting in the institution of Celtic FC on November 6th 1887.[75] From first contact with the Marist teaching order at St Mungo's parish as a young man, Walfrid rose considerably within the institution. As Superior of the Marist Brothers of Glasgow Green, Brother Walfrid was willing and able to utilise his position as a leader within the Irish Catholic community of Glasgow to organise the foundation of a flagship football club. For Walfrid, football became a unique vehicle and expression of the distinctive Marist charism of charity.

Notes

1 Log Book of St Mary's R.C. Boys School, Calton, Glasgow, May 1864 – June 1876. (D-ED7, Mitchell Library, Glasgow).

2 *Ibid.*

3 *Glasgow Free Press*, September 15th 1866.

4 McBrearty, R., 'Glasgow Before The Explosion: the role of migration and immigration in the development of football cultures in the city prior to 1873', article published online at https://scottishfootballorigins.org/2021/08/26/glasgow-before-the-explosion-the-role-ofmigration-and-immigration-in-the-development-of-football-cultures-in-the-city-prior-to-1873/ accessed August 26th 2021.

5 Maley, W., *The Story of the Celtic, 1888-1938* (1939) pp.14-15.

6 McDermid, J., 'Gender, National Identity and the Royal (Argyll) Commission of Inquiry into Scottish Education (1864-1867)', *Journal of Educational Administration and History*, Vol. 38, No. 3 (December, 2006), pp. 249-262.

7 Log Book of St Mungo's R.C. School, Townhead, Glasgow, March 1864 – March 1899. (D-ED7/247/1.1, available at the Mitchell Library, Glasgow).

8 Log Book of St Mungo's R.C. School, Townhead, Glasgow, March 1864 – March 1899.

9 *Ibid.*
  McDermid, 'Gender, National Identity and the Royal (Argyll) Commission of Inquiry into Scottish Education (1864-1867)', pp. 256-257.

10 Log Book of St Mungo's R.C. School, Townhead, Glasgow, March 1864 – March 1899.

11 *Ibid.*

12 Log Book of St Mungo's R.C. School, Townhead, Glasgow, March 1864 – March 1899. Entries for February and March of 1865.

13 Report by Her Majesty's Commissioners Appointed to Inquire Into Schools in Scotland (1867), p. 118. Accessed online at https://archive.org/details/reportbyhermaje01scogoog.

14 Bone, (Ed.), Studies in the History of Scottish Education 1872-1939, p. 24-27.

15 Log Book of St Mungo's R.C. School, Townhead, Glasgow, March 1864 – March 1899.

16 *Ibid.*

17 January 28th 1868. Log Book of St Mungo's R.C. School, Townhead, Glasgow, March 1864 – March 1899.

18 April 13th 1870. Log Book of St Mungo's R.C. School, Townhead, Glasgow, March 1864'– March 1899.

19 Log Book of St Mungo's R.C. School, Townhead, Glasgow, March 1864 – March 1899.

20 Tierney, D., *Financing the Faith: Scottish Catholicism 1772-c.1890* (Aberdeen University thesis submitted May 2014), p. 166-167.

21 Log Book of St Mungo's R.C. School, Townhead, Glasgow, March 1864 – March 1899.

22 *Ibid.*

23 May 13th 1870. Log Book of St Mary's R.C. Boys School, Calton, Glasgow, May 1864 – June 1876. (D-ED7, Mitchell Library, Glasgow).

24 'Schools History - Marist Brothers'. Accessed online at http://saintmarycalton.org.uk/marist-brothers.

25 1871 England, Wales and Scotland Census, accessed online.

26 Parker, Br. J., *Remembering the Marist Brothers* (2009), p. 112-114. Brother Colin Chalmers, 'Administrative History of Marist Brothers of Great Britain', information received from the General Archives of the Marist Brothers in Rome, 2018.

27 Log Book of St Mary's R.C. Boys School, Calton, Glasgow, May 1864 – June 1876.

28 Brother Colin Chalmers, 'Administrative History of Marist Brothers of Great Britain', information received from the General Archives of the Marist Brothers in Rome, 2018.

29 *Ibid.*

30 Bone, (Ed.), *Studies in the History of Scottish Education 1872-1939*, p. 24-27.

31 Gallagher, T., *Glasgow the Uneasy Peace: Religious Tension in Modern Scotland, 1819-1914* (Manchester: University Press, 1987), pp. 43-46.

32 Log Book of St Mary's R.C. Boys School, Calton, Glasgow, May 1864 – June 1876.

33 *Ibid.*

34 Entries for May 7th 1873, November 13th 1873 and December 16th 1873. Log Book of St Mary's R.C. Boys School, Calton, Glasgow, May 1864 – June 1876.

35 December 22nd 1873. Log Book of St Mary's R.C. Boys School, Calton, Glasgow, May 1864 – June 1876.

36 Log Book of St Mary's R.C. Boys School, Calton, Glasgow, May 1864 – June 1876.

37 *Ibid.*

38 Brother Colin Chalmers, 'Administrative History of Marist Brothers of Great Britain', information received from the General Archives of the Marist Brothers in Rome, 2018.

39 *Ibid.*

40 Fitzpatrick, T.A., 'The Marist Brothers in Scotland before 1918', *The Innes Review,* Vol. 49, No. 1 (1998), p. 7.

41 Fitzpatrick, T.A., 'The Marist Brothers in Scotland before 1918', p. 8.

42 Handley, J.E., 'Scotland' in Corish, P.J. (Ed.), *A History of Irish Catholicism* (Dublin: Cahill and Co. Limited, 1968), p. 21-22.

43 Fitzpatrick, T.A., *Catholic Secondary Education in South-West Scotland before 1972: its contribution to the change in status of the Catholic community* (Aberdeen: University Press, 1986), p. 31.

44 Handley, J.E., 'Scotland', p. 22.
Fitzpatrick, T.A., *Catholic Secondary Education in South-West Scotland before 1972*, p. 32.

45 'School Inspectors' Reports - Glasgow: Primary Schools Sacred Heart Boys' R.C.', National Records of Scotland, ED18/3406, 29th January 1874.

46 'School Inspectors' Reports - Glasgow: Primary Schools Sacred Heart Boys' R.C.', 29th January 1874, p. 2.

47 'School Inspectors' Reports - Glasgow: Primary Schools Sacred Heart Boys' R.C.', 29th January 1874, p. 3.

48 *Ibid.*

49 'School Inspectors' Reports - Glasgow: Primary Schools Sacred Heart Boys' R.C.', 29th January 1874, p. 2.

50 *Ibid.*

51 'School Inspectors' Reports - Glasgow: Primary Schools Sacred Heart Boys' R.C.', 29th January 1874, p. 3.

52 'School Inspectors' Reports - Glasgow: Primary Schools Sacred Heart Boys' R.C.', 29th January 1874, p. 4.

53 'Annals of (St Andrews) St Josephs Monastery 71 Charlotte Street Glasgow', SCA/MB/6/8/1/2 held at Scottish Catholic Archives, p. 80.

54 Aspinwall, B., 'Children of the Dead End: the Formation of the Modern Archdiocese of Glasgow, 1815-1914', *The Innes Review*, Vol. 43, No. 2 (Autumn, 1992) p. 131.

55 8th September 1923, *Glasgow Observer.*

56 Aspinwall, B., 'Children of the Dead End: the Formation of the Modern Archdiocese of Glasgow, 1815-1914', p. 131.

57 *Glasgow Herald*, 27th April 1874.

58 *North British Daily Mail*, 23rd April 1874.

59 Joyce, G., 'Father Tom Burke, O.P.', *Dominicana*, Vol. 16, No. 3 (September, 1931), p. 229.

60 December 14th 1881, *North British Daily Mail*. Pupils of Walfrid's Sacred Heart conclude the annual Christmas concert with a customary rendition of 'God Save Ireland' which became a traditional way of ending such social events.

61 Log Book of St Mary's R.C. Boys School, Calton, Glasgow, November 1891 - January 1892.

62 Annual reports of the Society of St. Vincent de Paul (Glasgow: Patrick Donegan & Co., 1890-1892).

63 *Ibid.*

64 Aspinwall, B., 'Children of the Dead End: the Formation of the Modern Archdiocese of Glasgow, 1815-1914', p. 132.

65 'Report of the Committee of Council on Education in Scotland (1885-1886), pp. 364-365.

66 Walfrid, Rev. Brother, Letter of Appeal to the Third Marquess of Bute 26th October 1885, Glasgow Archdiocese Archive BU/21/214/101.

67 *Ibid.* For images of the handwritten letter and a full transcript see Appendix B.

68 Hannah, Rosemary, *The Grand Designer: Third Marquess of Bute* (Edinburgh: Birlinn, 2012) p. 256.

69 Walfrid, Rev. Brother, Letter of Appeal to the Third Marquess of Bute 26th October 1885, Glasgow Archdiocese Archive BU/21/214/101.

70 Celtic Graves Society, 'In Memory of the Founding Fathers of Celtic Football Club' (2013), p. 25.

71 Hannah, Rosemary, *The Grand Designer: Third Marquess of Bute* (Edinburgh: Birlinn, 2012) p. 257.

72 *Ibid.*

73 Aspinwall, B., 'The Child as Maker of the Ultramone', *Studies in Church History*, vol. 31 (1994), pp. 427-445.

74 Dingle, A.E., and Harrison, B.H., 'Cardinal Manning as Temperance Reformer', *The Historical Journal*, Vol. 12, No. 3 (1969), pp. 485–510.

75 Sweeney, B., *Celtic, The Early Years: 1887-1892* (Scotland: CQN Books, 2015), p. 73.

The statue of Brother Walfrid stands at the top of the Celtic Way, at the main entrance to Celtic Park. Unveiled on 5th November 2005 and funded through monies raised by supporters of the Club, it was created by sculptor Kate Robinson.

CHAPTER 7

The Celtic FC Connection: 1887 – 1892

The name of Brother Walfrid is indelibly associated with, and most-recognised in relation to his leading role in the founding of Celtic Football Club under his greater purpose of fundraising for charity. Certainly Walfrid's position and legacy within the Club's history, along with his individual influence on the formation and first years of operation are assured. Alongside his role as headmaster of the Sacred Heart school in Glasgow's Bridgeton, his connection with Celtic FC played out entirely in conjunction with his vocation as a senior Marist Brother and indeed was an extension of it. O'Hagan explains that the approach of the Marist Brothers to Christian charity was 'strongly based on community effort' and sought to be 'practical' and interventionist in its missionary application.[1] In this vein, the charitable origins of Celtic Football Club can be traced back to the religious influence of the Marist ethos, and an extension of the vow of poverty taken by Walfrid.

With football enjoying an increasingly prominent position in Scottish life, as both the most popular spectator game as well as the most widely practised sport by the late nineteenth century, an opportunity was noted by Brother Walfrid.[2] The Brother Superior of the Marist community close to Glasgow Green envisaged the prospect of harnessing the potential of Glasgow's Irish Catholic diaspora through the vehicle of a football club. This had been achieved by friends in Edinburgh with Hibernian FC, which arose out of the concentration of Irish immigrants chiefly in the areas of the Cowgate and Old Town.[3] This endeavour could in turn provide monies which could be used charitably to ameliorate the situation of the neediest members of the community, particularly the children of St. Mary's, Sacred Heart and St. Michael's parishes.

That founding principle – to provide for the poor children of the East End – is made explicit in the circular heralding the creation of Celtic FC in January 1888, in a written statement which bears all the hallmarks of Brother Walfrid's tone and style of writing. The request for volunteer labour also illustrates the implicit centrality of 'community-building' to the Celtic project from its inception.[4] Morris concludes that such voluntary Catholic charity can be viewed as part of a distinct network of similar organised initiatives including children's refuge homes and industrial schools which also sprang up in Victorian Glasgow. In this sense, the early charity of Celtic FC was part of a progressive philanthropic movement amongst the largest immigrant community in the city which allowed Irish Catholics to take 'pride in the achievements of the group'.[5]

Both McDowell and Tranter agree that the early patrons and administrators of football clubs in Scotland were aware of the wider potential of 'Scotland's working-class pastime' as a vehicle for socialisation and philanthropy.[6] Walfrid himself had tapped into the original 'spirit of folk football', which endured from the first half of the nineteenth century, by introducing football to the pupils of Glasgow's schools opened by the Marist Brothers in the city.[7] In Glasgow especially, football captured the imagination of the paying and playing public like no other sport. McDowell finds:

> Within the space of twenty-five years in the late nineteenth century, football went from being perceived as a gentleman's amusement to becoming a booming entertainment trade that inspired the working class to take up its practice.[8]

Tranter traces the dramatic rise in interest surrounding the sport from the 1867 establishment of Scotland's first association football club, Queen's Park of Glasgow. By 1906, less than forty years later, the number of clubs had risen to 116, the majority of which were based in Glasgow or the surrounding west central belt.[9] Tranter explains that leading figures at football clubs during the period sought to evoke a 'sense of community identity' to supplement the physical side of the activity.[10] Celtic, born out of the Irish Catholic immigrant community in Glasgow to which Brother Walfrid belonged, came to symbolise a club sympathetic to the needs of its community. For McDowell, the role of Walfrid in the creation of a charitable sporting organisation 'was part of a wider Catholic programme in Glasgow to emulate the Protestant social welfare network during the depression of the 1880s'.[11] The Club's community origins gave rise to its enduring association with Irishness, Catholicism and charity.[12]

Brother Walfrid, at forty-seven years of age at the Club's inception, was the eldest of a group of Irish Catholic individuals identified as playing key roles in establishing Celtic FC in its earliest, amateur phase. Brendan Sweeney, author of *Celtic: The Early Years*, highlights an article published in 1893 in the *Glasgow Observer* by vocal Irish nationalist writer John McAdam, a former pupil of Brother Walfrid at St. Mungo's in the 1860s.[13] McAdam found his vocation in Ireland founding and editing newspapers supportive of Michael Davitt's Land League movement, a cause closely associated with the early charitable giving of Celtic FC. Writing from Donegal, McAdam recalls with fondness 'those days when we sat in front of the well-polished desks under the tuition of dear, quick tempered, lovable Brother Walfrid'.[14]

In his 'Reminiscence of St. Mungo's Academy', McAdam goes on to mention notable classmates enabling Sweeney to conclude that 'Brother Walfrid taught Founding Fathers Joseph Nelis, Michael Cairns, Joseph McGroary, John McCreadie and Doctor John Conway' – five of those most closely associated with the foundation of Celtic FC.[15] Indeed both Nelis and Conway feature in reporting of the July 1867 annual exhibition and prize-giving at St. Mungo's. Their roles in performance of the 'Lady of the Lake' and Shakespeare's 'Julius Caesar', respectively, 'gained merited applause'.[16] McAdam's 'Reminiscence' concludes:

... bless them all and bless the good Brothers and their
noble work. Some day I will go and see them and ask
permission to sit at the desk and write upon an exercise.
Perhaps I could live it all over again, if only Brother Walfrid
could be induced to come cautiously behind in the way I
remember so well, and with an accompanying slap behind
the ear, say 'Hold your pen straight', might be eagerly
welcomed.[17]

J.A. Magnan highlights the role of 'missing men' in terms of
educators like Brother Walfrid and their impact on early association
football.[18] Brother Walfrid clearly represented a memorable and
influential figure in the lives of those former pupils who went on to
relative success amongst the Irish Catholic community of Glasgow;
young men schooled in the Marist ethos who answered Walfrid's call
as he sought to organise a football club formed in the spirit of charity.

That call was also answered by individuals who worked on the
construction of the first incarnation of Celtic Park in the winter of
1887 into the spring of 1888.[19] Tom Campbell and Pat Woods consider
the religious influence at the foundation of the Club stating 'it was
manifestly clear that Celtic was a Catholic Club', with Charles Eyre,
Archbishop of Glasgow, becoming the first honorary patron. Reports
from the *Glasgow Observer* show that senior figures from the Catholic
Church were present at Celtic's first fixture on 28th May 1888, a victory
against city rivals Rangers FC at Celtic Park. Campbell and Woods
discuss the notion that by funding a school feeding programme,
Brother Walfrid and the founders of Celtic FC were seeking to reaffirm
the faith and identity of Glasgow's impoverished Catholics by
providing an alternative to Protestant missionary soup kitchens.[20]

Bradley explains that 'Celtic then were founded by and for Irish
Catholics, though never exclusively so'.[21] Absolute poverty, lack of
access to education and anti-Catholic discrimination had relegated
Glasgow's Irish Catholic immigrant community to a disadvantaged
social position from the outset.[22] Brother Walfrid's legacy of Celtic FC
came to represent a beacon of hope, both in terms of strengthening
the communal identity of Glasgow's multi-generational Irish as well

as by providing for that community through the proliferation of an enduring ethos of charity.

The Glasgow Charity Cup tournament, for example, only began including Catholic charitable causes in its list of beneficiaries after Celtic first entered the tournament in 1888. Bradley reinforces this view in concluding 'the Club came into existence as the focus for much Catholic and Irish community activity, a setting for that community's broad social and political aspirations'.[23]

For the purpose of analysis, the first phase of Celtic FC's early development can be dated from its founding in November 1887 until the professionalisation of Scottish football in 1893. It was during these initial years, while Brother Walfrid was the senior Marist in Glasgow, that the Club was most closely devoted to its founding charitable principles, whilst making swift progress on and off the field. Campbell and Woods agree that the 'distribution of funds to local Catholic charities and a fostering of pride within Glasgow's Irish community were being realised'. They note as a portent of the move to professionalism during the 1890s, 'change was inevitable and natural'.[24]

The most obvious change came in 1893 with the legalisation of player payments and the break with amateurism within Scottish football. It is also clear, however, that a number of other factors contributed to Celtic's perceived later shift away from Brother Walfrid's original charitable aims.

Willie Maley – one of the original Celtic players who became the Club's first manager – later wrote that 'the period of the start of the Club was what is now known as the day of the paid amateur'.[25] The uncertainty brought about by 'shamateurism' caused much internal strife and soul-searching within the Club as reported by contemporary newspapers.

Additionally, some have suggested that Brother Walfrid's departure from Glasgow to London in the summer of 1892 marked a major turning point in the outlook of Celtic in terms of its commitment to charity.[26] The move to a larger, more modern stadium in 1892 has also been viewed as indicative of the Celtic committee's commercial plans for the Club.[27] However, newspaper reportage of the time coupled with a closer analysis of donations facilitated by the Saint Vincent de Paul Society, in particular, help to shed new light on the extent and nature of the charitable activity of Celtic FC during these years. The Club's early involvement in the Glasgow Charity Cup and hosting of annual sports day competitions provides further significant examples of the positive impact of Celtic and Brother Walfrid's charitable sporting endeavour. But the reality was that Celtic's relationship with its original ideals as set out by Walfrid was a complex one influenced by several internal and external factors.

Maley's jubilee history of Celtic FC charts the early development of the Club from its birth in 1887 until 1938, arguably offering the most comprehensive contemporary account of the first decades of its progress. He describes the factors which shaped the Club in its early phase; and places the era of Scottish football in context as Celtic rapidly grew from 'humble origins in the amateur age'. Maley's book represents a rare account of the period – his was one of only a few histories of football clubs produced in the United Kingdom before World War Two.[28] As former Celtic player, secretary and manager from 1887 until 1940, Maley offers a unique insight into the Club's inner-workings at all levels from its earliest days. The individuality of the source, however, is tempered by the fact that his official history was commissioned by the Club and is therefore less likely to be critical of positions and policies adopted by Celtic. The book is designed to appeal to Celtic supporters and as an employee of the organisation, Maley's sources could be accused of originating from a biased perspective. Nevertheless, the possibility of bias countered by the first-hand experience recorded by Maley makes for an important contemp-orary source which allows for informed conclusions to be drawn on the early period of Celtic's existence.

Maley acclaimed the role of Brother Walfrid when reflecting on his 'Celtic Memories' in retirement, describing the Marist Brother as 'the Guide, Philosopher and Friend of the movement' behind the Club's foundation. He wrote:

The formation of the new club found in him the right man for the job and by his heroic efforts he found the cash and personal assistants who actually laid down Celtic Park by hard work after their ordinary work was done.[29]

Handley (Brother Clare FMS) built on Maley's contribution in his own history of Celtic published in 1960. The Glasgow-based Marist Brother found that:

... from its foundation the Celtic Club has been closely associated with Ireland and Catholicism. It was called into being to provide money for Catholic charities.[30]

Handley wrote extensively on the background and impact of Irish immigration to Scotland during the nineteenth century in his career as a published historian. Born in County Cavan in 1900, Handley moved from Ireland to Glasgow with his parents at an early age and was educated by the Marist Brothers in Glasgow before entering the Dumfries novitiate in 1912, the same year Brother Walfrid retired there.[31] It is entirely possible that the two men met, so Handley offers another particularly valuable insight into the inspiration behind Brother Walfrid's work in connection with Celtic and the wider ethos of the Marist mission in Scotland. His foreword records that much of Celtic's original financial records, minutes and photographs were lost as the result of the 1929 fire in the pavilion of the stadium. Contemporary newspaper reports, he explains, were relied on to form the basis for his work for the most part. Given the religious background of Handley and his position within the Marist Brothers in Scotland, his work provides a significant insight into the spiritual origins of the Club and the charitable ethos instilled at its birth by Brother Walfrid.[32] The works of both Maley and Handley are central to understanding the early history of Celtic Football Club.

Handley noted the social potential arising from organised football in late nineteenth century Britain, stating 'soccer provided an absorption for the newly acquired leisure of the working man'. He adds 'football teams, which had not yet developed into companies intent on capitalising into their own interest the fervour of their supporters, were induced to play occasional games for the benefit of that work of charity'. On 'community-building', O'Hagan emphasises the novel take on Marist charism adopted by Brother Walfrid. He sought to fuse the Victorian fascination with football together with the ideals of charity and community central to his own faith.[33]

It was in this spirit that Walfrid held a meeting at the League of the Cross Hall in the St. Mary's parish of the Calton, whereby Celtic FC was formally constituted on 6th November 1887. Indeed, Brother Walfrid previously played an organising role in inviting 'the Irishmen' of Edinburgh to Glengarry Park, Bridgeton, owned by the influential Monteith family of Catholic benefactors, for a hugely successful charity match against Clyde FC in 1886.[34] Brother Walfrid also counted on the support of his confrere, Brother Dorotheus, whose contacts from his native Dundee led the arranging of charity fixtures involving Dundee Harp, for example. A report in the *Glasgow Observer* from July 1885 evidences Brother Walfrid's role in organising football matches on Glengarry Park on behalf of a junior Sacred Heart parish team by the 'name of the Eastern Rovers, which had been raised through the exertions of Brother Walfrid'.[35]

Football was evidently a game which captured the imagination of Brother Walfrid – as well as the Marist Brothers generally – over the course of his years in Glasgow. His Marist colleague, long-serving headmaster of St. Mungo's, Frenchman, Brother Ezechiel (Edmond Luc Decoopman, b. 1856), is credited with suggesting the name 'Celtic' to Brother Walfrid for his new sporting chartable endeavour in 1887.[36] The *Scottish Umpire* sports paper carried the first mention of the new Club in print:

> We learn that the efforts which have lately been made to organise in Glasgow a first-class Catholic football club have been successfully consummated by the formation of the 'Glasgow Celtic Football and Athletic Club'.

Handley characterised the mission of the Marist Brothers in the city, led by Brother Walfrid at this time, as one primarily geared towards providing for the welfare of the children of Irish immigrants who comprised the vast bulk of the Catholic population.[38] Indeed, the circular – most-likely drafted by Brother Walfrid – dispersed to Catholic parishes in Glasgow to herald the arrival of Celtic FC states:

> The main object of the Club is to supply the East End Conferences of the Saint Vincent de Paul (SVDP) Society with the funds for the maintenance of the dinner tables of our needy children.[39]

The school feeding programme created by Brother Walfrid, along with his fellow Marist, Brother Dorotheus (Henry Currie, b. 1855), was to be focussed on three parish schools of the St. Mary's Deanery located in the East End of Glasgow. Brother Dorotheus is noted as 'the right hand man' of Walfrid as Brother Superior of the Marist community at Charlotte Street.[40] Walfrid's own Sacred Heart school, along with St. Mary's where Dorotheus was headmaster and St. Michael's, Parkhead closest to Celtic Park were the three schools named in the original circular who would avail of the charity facilitated by the St. Vincent de Paul Society.[41]

Bradley highlights that:

> ... the St. Vincent de Paul Society was founded in Scotland during the Famine in 1846 amongst the Irish Catholic poor of Edinburgh before rapidly spreading throughout the Catholic population of the urban west central belt. Its aim was to succour the poor in spiritual and materials ways.[42]

The 'Penny Dinner' scheme was first trialled by the Marist Brothers at St. Mary's school – then with the largest roll of the Brothers' Glasgow schools in 1885, before being replicated at Walfrid's Sacred Heart school one year later.

Handley explains that 'the penny was charged only when no hardship was involved to preserve the self-respect of the beneficiaries'. As superior of the Marist Brothers in the city, Handley concludes that Walfrid noted the initial success of the venture and 'threw his net much wider' culminating in the idea of Celtic FC as a fundraising vehicle 'founded in the name of charity' by late 1887.[43]

O'Hagan shows that the Celtic FC committee was able to provide £400 – over £50,000 in terms of today's values – to the local branches of the SVDP Society through match ticket sales in season 1888/89, the year of the Club's first games. Although the Club was formally incepted in 1887 it did not play its first games until May 1888. The SVDP branches were furnished with tickets and able to retain the proceeds for charitable purposes, so the drive to promote games and sell tickets was high from the outset resulting in record crowds.[44] This perhaps partly explains the Club's initial success on the field and financial growth off it, as Celtic won the Scottish league champion-ship just four seasons after its creation and assuming a position of prominence within Scottish football almost immediately.

Vamplew states that, in the Victorian era, 'relatively little money went to charity directly from the Club accounts, on average much less than 1% of net profits'.[45] Between Brother Walfrid's role in establishing the Club and his departure for London in mid-1892, Celtic proved to be an exception to the rule. Celtic's first balance sheet – signed off by Brother Dorotheus – was published accompanied by a circular written by John O'Hara, then honorary secretary, and was released on 12th June 1889.[46] The circular calls the first annual general meeting of the founding committee as well as inviting subscribed members to hear the financial report, choose new office-bearers and discuss Club affairs.[47]

John Herbert McLaughlin states in his treasurer's report that just over £420 was donated to fourteen different charitable causes from an expenditure of just over £3807. The SVDP Society was the biggest recipient (£164) and the majority of the causes which benefitted from the Club's revenue were Irish Catholic in character, such as the Sisters of Mercy convent in Lanark, the Little Sisters of the Poor and the Hibernians movement. However, the report also demonstrates that Celtic's charity was not purely confined to Catholic or Irish organis-ations – £10 was donated to the 'Hand-Loom Weavers of Bridgeton' the part of the city where Brother Walfrid was engaged in his daily headmaster duties.[48] By donating to non-denominational causes in Glasgow it is clear that Celtic's charity was quickly able to supersede its original stated aim of helping poor Irish Catholic children in the East End. Moreover, the fact that the Club reported an 11% commitment of its expenditure to charity via its first balance sheet illustrates how after less than two years, Celtic FC was able to surpass the general level of donation of any other football club based in the United Kingdom at the time.[49]

Newspaper coverage of the annual meeting of 1890 shows that the Celtic committee were again keen to draw 'special attention to the charity donations of the Club'. The *Scottish Sport* reports donations increased to £500 of the Club's total gross income of £3700. Brother Walfrid's own favoured Poor Children's Dinner Table scheme continued to be the leading recipient, receiving £160 of the Celtic revenue. However, the *Sport* article stresses the diversity of Celtic's charity. £20, for example, was given to the Greenhead Disaster Fund for the families of twenty-nine women who lost their lives when Templeton's carpet factory collapsed close to Glasgow Green. This further illustrates the practice of not restricting charitable donations to Irish Catholic causes.[50] The Club's scope had also now surpassed its East End of Glasgow roots with donations extended to Edinburgh charities, while the aid offered to the Matt Harris Fund linked to the Irish Land League movement of Michael Davitt – made honorary patron of the Club in 1893 – exhibited an international link back to the homeland of Brother Walfrid and the vast majority of Celtic's original supporters. At this embryonic stage in the Club's history, the *Sport* report was able to conclude that 'Celtic, we may add, has given more in charity than all the other football clubs of Glasgow'.[51]

In the September of 1890, the *Glasgow Herald* reports on how Celtic FC began to gain prominence in the wider Christian philanthropy movement of the Victorian era at a civic level, whilst also retaining the faith and cultural values of its own distinct commonality. The report provides an account of the opening of the 'Catholic

Children's Refuge' at Whitevale in the East End of Glasgow. Celtic had provided a £70 donation towards the establishment of the children's shelter.[52] The involvement of Brother Walfrid's sporting club in the Whitevale project represents a fulfilment of its stated founding obligation to aid the 'needy children' of the predominantly Irish Catholic populated parishes of the East End.[53]

As with Walfrid's own Poor Children's Dinner Table scheme, the Refuge was directed by the SVDP Society and the 'children came to the institution with a recommendation from the local clergyman'.[54] This of course also chimed with the Marist charism of nurturing the Catholic faith amongst the marginalised of society, especially the younger members of the community, thereby preventing what came to be termed 'leakage of the faith'. Senior members of the Catholic Church in Glasgow were present at the ceremony, including Archbishop Eyre and Monsignor Munro.

Munro gave an address emphasising the fact that the Irish Catholic community remained in relative infancy in the city and alluded to the poverty, discrimination and lack of education suffered by the immigrants who had bolstered the community in Glasgow 'after they had been driven from their own country by the calamities which had fallen upon it'. 'Charity and care of the poor and of the young,' he continued, 'was an absolute doctrine in the Catholic Church' and the opening of the Refuge is heralded as a sign of the continued advancement of the Irish Catholic community. A civic judge present at the event commented that 'irrespective of denomination, the magistrates of Glasgow were very glad to see institutions such as this, which they regarded as necessities for the community'.[55]

The charitable function of Celtic FC occurred as part of a wider philanthropic effort on behalf of the Irish Catholic community to take steps to improve the lot of its most vulnerable members. The education work of the Marist Brothers, including Brother Walfrid's Penny Dinner scheme, can also be seen in this light. At a civic level, the source conveys a positive reflection of these efforts, which would have invigorated the charitable works of Brother Walfrid and others engaged in community building amongst the Irish Catholics of Glasgow at the time.

The following year, 1891, saw a £650 rise in revenue and donations peak in excess of £600, which led the *Sport* to describe the Celtic committee – encouraged by Walfrid – as 'masters of organisation'.[56]

The *Scottish Referee* commenting on the arrival of Celtic FC in 1888 states 'the Club had a phoenix-like origin – it arose from the fading ashes of many another organisation' within Glasgow's Irish Catholic community.[57] Brother Walfrid's leading role in the foundation can be understood as one of chief organiser, able to bring together disparate elements of that community – senior clergy, SVDP officials, Irish Forresters, leading Irish nationalist political figures and business-minded individuals – under the common cause of sporting charity. The Marist Brother's will to live out his vow of poverty and found the Club on those charitable values brought Celtic goodwill and support from within its own Catholic community from which it was founded, but also garnered support across civic society and the Scottish sporting press.

The presence of astute committee men – most of whom had ties to the alcohol trade – also ensured that Celtic remained in the vanguard of commercialisation occurring within Scottish football during the 1890s. It is this juxtaposition of motives at the heart of the Club which provoked strident debate at a time of rampant modern-isation of Scotland's national game.[58]

Maley describes Brother Walfrid, along with the first chairman of Celtic, John Glass, as central to the Club's very existence for the first three years during which they acted as a 'binding force' as they set about establishing Celtic FC as a prominent social and sporting institution in Scotland.[59]

However, O'Hagan contests that 'the coming of professionalism into football put an end to the service of charity' as donations to Brother Walfrid's Poor Children's Dinner Tables disappeared from the Club's balance sheet from 1893.[60] This came the year following Brother

Walfrid's transfer to London in the summer of 1892 by his religious superiors within the Marist Brothers Institute, who required him to provide senior leadership for the Brothers' communities there.

Handley finds 'later, in London, Brother Walfrid continued his school charities in St. Anne's, Whitechapel' where he resided for most of his time in England.[61] Although the *Glasgow Observer* later states in Walfrid's obituary 'he never lost interest in the doings of the Celts', the loss of his influential presence and the charitable conscience he had imbued the Club with at birth would undoubtedly have contributed to the increasingly commercial tone of the Celtic committee meetings after his departure'.[62]

It has been argued that the absence of the Brother Superior's guiding influence led to a power struggle 'for the Club's soul' after 1892 until the Club was incorporated as a limited liability company in 1897.[63] Campbell and Woods conclude that the vacuum was filled by a lengthy debate surrounding the future of Celtic FC, between what they term the 'idealists' – protective of the charitable legacy left by Brother Walfrid – and 'opportunists' who looked to expand commercially.[64]

J.H. McLaughlin, then vice president of the Celtic committee, made reference to the recent professionalisation of footballers in Scotland in his speech at the 1893 annual meeting of the Club. The speech appears as part of a report in the *Scottish Sport* on the 'Limited Liability Question', a topic of much debate at the time. McLaughlin states that professionalisation was 'due in great measure to the influence and efforts of the Celtic Club' and informs members of his belief that the legalisation voted for by the Scottish Football Association would enable Celtic to 'field a team worthy of upholding our past reputation'.[65] Clearly, the ruling was welcomed and viewed as a progressive move by some of those in control of Celtic, one which arguably fitted with their increasingly commercial agenda.

McLaughlin, in addition, commends the success of the Club's new 'business committee' created in 1892 for the 'efficacy and effectiveness' of its work, particularly in overseeing the completion of the new

Celtic Park, which opened in August 1892. The ground was designed to be 'superior in any respect to any field in Great Britain' promised McLaughlin, offering more rhetorical evidence that expansion and speculation was being prioritised by this point.[66]

Indeed, Maley – who was voted in as honorary Club secretary at the 1893 meeting – records that 'various schemes were devised to put the Club on a sound business footing', hinting at financial difficulties afoot.[67] On the one hand, it could be argued that McLaughlin and Maley envisaged Celtic moving with the times, swept on by the tide of payments to professional players and the associated need to financially organise and clear debts linked to construction of the new stadium. However, Campbell and Woods cite the 'Lure of Profits', suggesting the Celtic committee had begun sowing the seeds for incorporation at a time of increasing commercialism in British sport on the whole.[68] Tranter, conversely, argues to that in order to ensure survival in this era, football clubs were required to move with the times in terms of sound business arrangements.[69]

The *Scottish Sport* reports Celtic FC's charitable donations amounted to just £63.3s from a considerable annual revenue of £6696. 2s 9d in 1893 – the lowest contributions since the Club's inception and the first time no monies were forwarded to Brother Walfrid's school feeding schemes.[70] In comparison, the previous year saw the Club report donations of £230 from a revenue of £4468. 10s.[71] The lowly figure of £63. 3s of 1893 continued the negative trend began in 1892 of decreasing charitable contributions in Celtic's yearly financial reports to the public. To put the figure into perspective, nearly as much – £56 – was spent on painting by the Club.[72]

The fact that the spirit of charity Brother Walfrid instilled in the Club at birth was fading from the Celtic committee's conscience was not lost on members on the floor of the annual meeting in May 1893. The *Sport* journalist reports a schism between traditionalist supporters of Walfrid's founding principle, led by prominent Irish nationalist politician Arthur Murphy and ex-pupil of Walfrid Joseph Nelis, against 'dispassionate capitalists' attached to the new business committee. Nelis 'touched a sentimental chord' by promising £500 to bolster charitable donations and carry 'on the work of the Club as constituted'. Members of the opposing business committee extolled the potential 'advantages' of the Club incorporating into a limited liability company.

The *Sport*, however, concludes that 'sentiment played its part, and amidst a scene of terrific enthusiasm and prolonged cheering, the Committee's recommendation was thrown out' and incorporation was to be delayed. The 'sentimentalists' resoundingly won the vote 86 to 31.[73] The article demonstrates that Murphy and a majority of Club members were in favour of protecting Brother Walfrid's original charitable aims. Maley's insight into the episode, on the other hand, illustrates how the idealists among the Club membership had only succeeded in buying time for their cause. He records that the £500 promised by Murphy was never received by the Club, concluding the traditionalists only achieved a delay in the transition of Celtic from an expressed charitable endeavour to a limited company.[74]

The heartfelt debate of the 1893 meeting – just one year after Brother Walfrid departed for London – does indicate a groundswell of support for the charitable ethos Walfrid instilled surrounding Celtic FC, however, and reflects the immediate legacy he left behind in Glasgow. Ten pounds of the 1893 donations was given personally to Brother Walfrid in tribute to his leading role in founding Celtic FC in 1887.[75] This sum would have been gladly received by the Marist Brothers to aid their educational and charitable work, but clearly a crossroads was reached in Glasgow as Celtic FC sought to strike a balance between business and the ideals of community and charity on which Walfrid helped to found the Club. With mounting financial liabilities for committee members, incorporating presented an opportunity to ensure the survival of Celtic amidst the rapidly commercialising landscape of sport in Britain.[76] In this way, the Club's legacy and the charitable ethos instilled by Brother Walfrid was protected in the long term.

The *Sport* again reports a new record revenue of £6956. 13s 7d for Celtic FC in 1898, attributed mainly to the use of the new, larger Celtic Park for lucrative friendly matches (£2326. 6s 1d) and in attracting Scotland international fixtures. For the end-of-season Scotland versus England match, £572 was taken which represented a record gate receipt for a British football game at the time.[77] One week later the *Sport* heralded the success of the new Celtic ground, stating 'the greatest crowd ever drawn together to witness a football match was seen at Celtic Park on April 7th last, when 46,000 people viewed the international between Scotland and England'.[78]

Record crowds and gate receipts are reflected in an unprecedented expenditure by Celtic of £6786 13s 7d, making the Club's financial report conspicuous for its notable lack of any form of charitable donation. £1109 of that figure went towards stadium costs including labour and materials, while the wages of the Celtic playing staff comprised just over £1934.[79] The report communicates that the Club was '£156 better than a year ago' and held a balance in the bank of £170 surplus.[80] The neglect of charitable donations for the first time, however, illustrates the shifting priorities amongst the Celtic FC committee following Walfrid's departure.

Kay and Vamplew cite Celtic FC as a 'prime example' of the changing landscape of football in the wake of professionalisation, stating 'the decline in the Club's charitable donations dates from 1893/4, the season in which professionalism was formally adopted in Scottish football'.[81] Misgivings amongst prominent voices within Scottish football gradually gave way to widespread support for the clarity and equity legalisation of player renumeration brought about. Indeed, the *Sport* comments at the close of season in 1894 'professionalism is now a year old, and its birth has done a lot of good to Scottish football'.

Despite the prominence of wage payments on Celtic's fir ost-professionalism balance sheet, it is clear that liabilities linked to the development of the second iteration of Celtic Park completed in 1892 were an equal strain on finances at this point. The debt stood at £2086 in 1893 and was reduced to £1850 by the 1894 annual meeting, with the Club reporting 'a sound financial condition'. It continues that Celtic 'was instituted on behalf of charity and when the liabilities are cleared away there will not exist an association that will come more to the assistance of the poor and the needy than the Celtic Club'.[82] This sentiment came to represent a focal point for ensuing debate between the 'idealists' in favour of Brother Walfrid's original vision of sporting charity and commercially-minded 'opportunists' seeking to incorporate the Club into limited liability status to ensure a prosperous financial future. This was to be played out in subsequent annual meetings as well as the letters sections of Glasgow's sporting press.

A 'Mr S.J. Henry' – leading member of the SVDP Society – spoke from the floor of the December 1895 general meeting of Celtic FC stating that if incorporation meant that the Club could 'donate £2000 or £3000 to the East End charities he was satisfied that the members of the Club would never stand in the way'.[83] A motion to establish a committee to consider incorporation was then carried by 53 votes to 31.[84] Celtic FC's perceived neglect of charitable giving and Brother Walfrid's legacy amongst the Irish Catholics in Glasgow form the two main themes in a series of protest letters from supporters of the Club published in the *Glasgow Observer* and *Catholic Herald* during the summer of 1895.

Featuring the tagline 'The Catholic Organ for the District', the *Glasgow Observer* has been characterised as the 'paper of the immigrants' who arrived in the city from Ireland during the nineteenth century. A letter to the editor from a 'Kerry' of Shettleston, is printed alongside an account of Celtic's annual meeting for that year on 5th June 1895. It reads: 'I fail to find even a small donation' from Celtic's revenue to charity. The letter expresses disbelief that no donations were made to Brother Walfrid's original Poor Children's Dinner Tables scheme, explicitly mentioned in the founding circular of the Club.[85]

This very issue was raised by Tom Maley – the brother of Willie Maley who was an ex-Celtic player, now committee member and local school teacher – at the annual meeting. The *Observer* reports that the lack of charitable giving – despite such healthy financial reporting – was 'characterised as a gross injustice' by Tom Maley. The account continues that 'Mr Maley's remarks were received with cordial applause', while it is telling that Maley declined to accept the position of vice president at the meeting in Glasgow's Gallowgate.[86] Maley's public stand against dwindling charitable donations from the Club along with Kerry's letter protesting the prioritisation of wages over charity demonstrate that Brother Walfrid's founding principles continued to inform the conscience of debates surrounding Celtic FC.

A further letter to the editor signed 'Mac' written on July 2nd 1895 asks 'when will the East End charities come in?' It highlights the improvements made to Celtic Park and the 'largely increased expenditure' this promised.[87] The letter is published as part of a dedicated 'Celtic Donations' column of the *Observer*, then a regular feature of the newspaper, emphasising the scale of polemics surrounding the charitable function of the Club in the wake of Brother Walfrid's departure.

An anonymous letter from Cork Ireland, in the following week's publication responds directly to Mac. It suggests the stadium upgrade was necessary, inviting the correspondent to 'take a theatrical manager to task for strengthening his company and adding to the sitting room of his pit and gallery'. The Irish response concludes 'surely the Celts' increased receipts gives all the better chance to charity'.[88] All clearly agree on the continued importance of charity to Celtic FC and the ethos Brother Walfrid instilled at its outset in 1887.

Handley retrospectively characterised the period culminating in the incorporation of Celtic FC into a limited liability company in 1897 – a decade after its beginnings as a charitable sporting endeavour – as a process when 'the ideals for which the Club was founded had become sicklied over with the pale cast of gold'.[89] McNee, on the other hand, summarised the process through which the Club became 'The Celtic Football Club and Athletic Company Limited' as one borne of necessity. He finds that an emergency meeting of the business committee of Celtic resolved to incorporate 'on 4th March 1897 in the same St. Mary's Hall which had witnessed the birth of the Club'.[90]

Willie Maley describes the pressing need to secure the Club on 'a real business footing' and states that 'Celtic became such with a capital of £10,000'.[91] Reporting on the outcome, the *Scottish Sport* carried an opinion piece lauding 'Celtic's Wise Decision' to follow Dundee and Clyde in becoming an incorporated football club.[92] By 1897, there was an established precedent in Scotland and England for clubs to pursue a corporate approach against the backdrop of increasing commercialism in sport towards the close of the nineteenth century in Britain.[93] The article describes the decision by the Celtic committee as a 'safeguarding principle', citing large bank liabilities traceable to the construction of the new Celtic Park in 1892. The *Sport* concludes 'it is in present circumstances both a prudent and an enterprising step'.[94]

Despite the formalisation of Celtic FC's new commercial constitution, historians agree that the charitable identity and function of the Club 'has never been lost sight of', enduring in varying ways through to the present day in the form of the Celtic FC Foundation.[95] It has equally been demonstrated that 'Celtic's value and meaning comes from its Catholic, Irish and charitable identities' drawn from the guiding ethos and legacy rooted by Brother Walfrid at its birth.[96]

Reflecting on the achievements of the Poor Children's Dinner Tables charity, which Celtic FC was brought into being to support, Walfrid wrote an article published by the *Glasgow Observer* from London in 1895. It reads:

> In 1884 the good Brothers of St. Vincent de Paul opened the penny dinners for the school children, by which means the children were provided with a good, warm meal for a penny. Should parents prefer they could send the bread and the children could get a large bowl of broth or soup for a half-penny, and those who were not able to pay got a substantial meal free. This has been a very great blessing to the poor children. The expenses for some time were met by subscriptions and collections, sermons, etc, til the Celtic FC was started, the committee of which gave the good

Brothers about thirty-three shillings a week up to a short time since.[97]

Walfrid was evidently concerned with the physical, educational and spiritual wellbeing of the children under his care, particularly those most in need. This is reflected on a return visit to Glasgow in 1897 when he implored members of the Sacred Heart Young Men's Society he instituted to 'make good use of the books in the library, and to pay attention to the advice of those in charge of the society'.[98] Brother Walfrid, in publishing articles in the *Glasgow Observer* and other local newspapers, was clearly attentive to the potential of utilising the printed press to garner support and awareness of the causes close to his heart.

Tom Maley later recalled how it was 'good, dear old Bro. Walfrid' who 'woo'd and won' the Glasgow sports journalist J.W. Mackay to secure a positive press for Celtic at its outset in the face of hostility within the local press for their unashamedly Irish and Catholic endeavour. Mackay was a Rangers-supporting writer who published under the alias 'Milo' and was convinced of the noble intentions of Celtic FC by Walfrid himself. He is recorded as stating 'but oh! Above all, give me Brother Walfrid' as the individual most representative of the Club's original charitable purpose.[99]

Brother Walfrid's role in the establishment of Celtic FC will, for many, represents the culmination of a life's work. However, his service as a senior Marist Brother was required in London and it was there that Walfrid continued to live out his religious vocation. Works of charity and a passionate interest in football were two enuring hallmarks that were to continue to be evident in his life and work in London.

Notes

1 Sweeney, B., *Celtic, The Early Years: 1887-1892* (Scotland: CQN Books, 2015), p. 73.

2 O'Hagan, F.J., *The Contribution of the Religious Orders to Education in Glasgow during the period 1847-1918*, p. 105.

3 Kelly, J., 'Hibernian Football Club: The Forgotten Irish?', *Sport in Society*, Vol. 10, No. 3 (2007), pp. 514-536.

4 Bradley, J.M., *Ethnic and Religious Identity in Modern Scotland: Culture, politics and football*, p. 34.

5 O'Hagan, F.J., *The Contribution of the Religious Orders to Education in Glasgow during the period 1847-1918*, p. 177.

6 Morris, R.J., 'Voluntary Societies and British Urban Elites, 1780-1850: An Analysis, *The Historical Journal*, Vol. 26, No. 1 (March, 1983), pp. 95-118.

7 McDowell, M., 'The origins, patronage and culture of association football in the west of Scotland, c. 1865-1902' (University of Glasgow: PhD Thesis, 2010), p. 3.
Tranter, N., *Sport, Economy and Society in Britain, 1750-1914* (Cambridge: University Press, 1998), pp. 60-77.

8 McDowell, 'The origins, patronage and culture of association football in the west of Scotland, c. 1865-1902', p. 9.

9 *Ibid*, p. 133.

10 Tranter, N., *Sport, Economy and Society in Britain, 1750-1914* (Cambridge: University Press, 1998), p. 23.

11 *Ibid*, p. 54.

12 McDowell, 'The origins, patronage and culture of association football in the west of Scotland, c. 1865-1902', p. 54.

13 McDowell, M., 'Football, migration and industrial patronage in the west of Scotland, c. 1870-1900', *Sport in History*, Vol. 32., No. 3 (2012), p. 412.

14 Sweeney, B., *Celtic, The Early Years: 1887-1892* (Scotland: CQN Books, 2015), p. 24.

15 Sweeney, B., *Celtic, The Early Years: 1887-1892* (Scotland: CQN Books, 2015), p. 25.

16 Sweeney, B., *Celtic, The Early Years: 1887-1892* (Scotland: CQN Books, 2015), p. 26.

17 *The Glasgow Free Press*, July 13th 1867.

18 Sweeney, B., *Celtic, The Early Years: 1887-1892* (Scotland: CQN Books, 2015), p. 25.

19 Mangan, J.A., 'Missing men: schoolmasters and the early years of Association Football', *Soccer & Society*, Vol. 9, No. 2 (2008), pp. 170-188.

20 Bradley, *Ethnic and Religious Identity in Modern Scotland: Culture, politics and football*, p. 35.

21 Campbell, T., and Woods, P., *The Glory and The Dream: The History of Celtic FC 1887-1986*, p. 17.

22 Bradley, *Ethnic and Religious Identity in Modern Scotland: Culture, politics and football*, p. 36.

23 Campbell, T., and Woods, P., *Celtic Football Club 1887-1967* (Stroud: Tempus, 1998), *introduction.*

24 Bradley, *Ethnic and Religious Identity in Modern Scotland: Culture, politics and football,* p. 36.

25 Campbell, and Woods, *The Glory and The Dream: The History of Celtic FC 1887-1986,* p. 44.

26 Maley, W., *The Story of the Celtic, 1888-1938* (Essex: Desert Island Books, 1939), p. 9.

27 McNee, G., *The Story of Celtic: An Official History* (1978), p. 93.

28 Maley, *The Story of Celtic, 1888-1939,* p. 14.

29 Maley, *The Story of Celtic, 1888-1939, preface.*

30 Maley, W., 'Celtic Memories' in *St Peter's College Magazine,* Vol. 20, No. 76 (June, 1951), p. 16.

31 Handley, J.E., *The Celtic Story: A History of the Celtic Football Club* (London: Stanley Paul, 1960), p. 168.

32 Parker, Br. J., *Remembering the Marist Brothers* (2009), p. 24-25.

33 Handley, *The Celtic Story: A History of the Celtic Football Club,* p. 11.

34 O'Hagan, F.J., *The Contribution of the Religious Orders to Education in Glasgow during the period 1847-1918,* p. 177.

35 Sweeney, B., *Celtic, The Early Years: 1887-1892* (Scotland: CQN Books, 2015), pp. 33-35.

36 *Glasgow Observer,* July 11th 1885.

37 Parker, Br. J., *Remembering the Marist Brothers* (2009), pp. 50-51.

38 *Scottish Umpire,* November 29th 1887, p. 11.

39 Handley, *A History of the Marist Brothers Province of the British Isles,* p. 78-79.

40 O'Hagan, F.J., *The Contribution of the Religious Orders to Education in Glasgow during the period 1847-1918,* p. 177. For full transcript of the circular see Appendix A.

41 'Annals of (St Andrews) St Josephs Monastery 71 Charlotte Street Glasgow', 9th August 1887.

42 Handley,£A *History of the Marist Brothers Province of the British Isles,* p. 79.

43 *The Brother Walfrid Memorial* booklet published by the Brother Walfrid Commemoration Committee to mark the unveiling of a statue to Walfrid at Celtic Park on the 5th of November 2005.

44 Handley, *A History of the Marist Brothers Province of the British Isles,* p. 79.

45 O'Hagan, F.J., *The Contribution of the Religious Orders to Education in Glasgow during the period 1847-1918,* p. 177.

46 Vamplew, W., *Pay Up and Play The Game: Professional Sport in Britain 1875-1914* (Cambridge: University Press, 1988), p. 86.

47 Kelly, R., *Celtic* (Glasgow: Hay Nisbet and Miller Ltd., 1971), p. 66-67.

48 'Abstract of Treasurer's Intromissions from 1st December 1887 to 31st May 1889' accessed online at www.celticwiki.com/page/ The+First+Balance+Sheet retrieved February 2021.

49 'Abstract of Treasurer's Intromissions from 1st December 1887 to 31st May 1889'.

50 *Ibid.*

51 *Scottish Sport*, June 24th 1890, p. 5.

52 *Ibid.*

53 *Glasgow Herald*, September 19th 1890, p. 9.

54 O'Hagan, F.J., *The Contribution of the Religious Orders to Education in Glasgow during the period 1847-1918*, p. 177.

55 *Glasgow Herald*, September 19th 1890, p. 9.

56 *Ibid.*

57 *Scottish Sport*, June 19th 1891, p. 6.

58 *Scottish Referee*, December 3rd 1888.

59 *Glasgow Observer*, July 10th 1897, p. 4.

60 Maley, *The Story of Celtic, 1888-1939*, p. 39.

61 O'Hagan, F.J., *The Contribution of the Religious Orders to Education in Glasgow during the period 1847-1918*, p. 178.

62 Handley, *The Celtic Story: A History of the Celtic Football Club*, p. 15.

63 *Glasgow Observer*, April 24th 1915, p. 10.

64 Sweeney, B., *Celtic: The Battle for the Club's Soul 1892-1897*, Vol. 1 and 2 (Scotland: CQN Books, 2015)

65 Campbell, and Woods, *The Glory and The Dream: The History of Celtic FC 1887-1986*, p. 48.

66 *Scottish Sport*, May 19th 1893, p. 11.

67 *Ibid.*

68 Maley, *The Story of Celtic, 1888-1939*, p. 17

69 Campbell, and Woods, *The Glory and The Dream: The History of Celtic FC 1887-1986*, p. 44.

70 Tranter, N., *Sport, Economy and Society in Britain, 1750-1914*, pp. 60-77.

72 *Scottish Sport*, May 19th 1893, p. 11.

71 *Scottish Sport*, May 20th 1892, p. 9.

72

73 *Scottish Sport*, May 19th 1893, p. 11.

74 *Scottish Sport*, May 19th 1893, p. 11.

75 Maley, *The Story of Celtic, 1888-1939*, p. 17.

76 *Scottish Referee*, May 19th 1893, p. 4.

77 Tranter, *Sport, Economy and Society in Britain, 1750-1914*, pp. 60-77.

78 *Scottish Sport*, May 11th 1894, p. 11.

79 *Scottish Sport*, May 18th 1894, p. 10.

80 *Scottish Sport*, May 11th 1894, p. 11.

81 *Ibid.*

82 *Scottish Sport*, May 18th 1894, p. 10.

83 *Ibid.*

84 *Glasgow Evening News*, December 13th 1895, p. 6.

85 *Glasgow Herald*, December 13th 1895, p. 17.

86 *Glasgow Observer*, June 9th 1895, p. 8.

87 *Ibid.*

88 *Glasgow Observer*, July 6th 1895, p. 6.

89 *Glasgow Observer*, July 13th 1895, p. 6.

90 Handley,' *The Celtic Story: A History of the Celtic Football Club*, p. 62.

91 McNee, *The Story of Celtic: An Official History*, p. 95.

92 Maley, *The Story of Celtic, 1888-1939*, p. 17.

93 *Scottish Sport*, March 2nd 1897, p. 9.

94 Tranter, N., *Sport, Economy and Society in Britain, 1750-1914* (Cambridge: University Press, 1998), p. 52.

95 *Ibid.*

96 Handley, *The Celtic Story: A History of the Celtic Football Club*, p. 192.
Bradley, *Ethnic and Religious Identity in Modern Scotland: Culture, politics and football*, p. 36.

97 *The Brother Walfrid Memorial* booklet published by the Brother Walfrid Commemoration Committee to mark the unveiling of a statue to Walfrid at Celtic Park on 5th November 2005.

98 Sweeney, B., *Celtic: The Battle for the Club's Soul 1892-1897*, Vol. 2 (Scotland: CQN Books, 2015), p. 400.

99 *Glasgow Observer*, August 14th 1897.

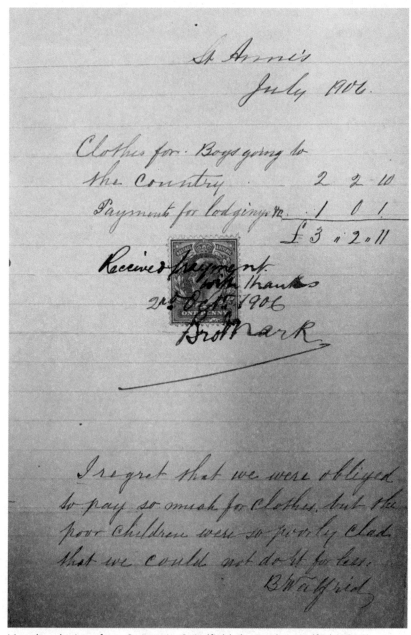

Note handwritten from St Anne's, Spitalfields by Brother Walfrid (1906) The note represents a rare insight into the interior life of the then-elderly Marist Brother. It reflects Brother Walfrid's enduring concern for, and charitable action taken on behalf of, those he affectionately describes as 'the poor children'.

CHAPTER 8
London: 1892 – 1906

The story of Brother Walfrid did not end with the beginning of Celtic FC. His role as a senior Marist Brother endured with further assignments in England, where his endeavours continued to be reflected in the themes of faith, community and an enduring connection with football. The closing two decades of Brother Walfrid's teaching life as a Marist Brother were spent in the south of England, between his transfer to London in 1892 and a final period spent teaching at Grove Ferry, Kent until 1912. This period, which came after thirty years spent in Glasgow, manifest the same themes as distinguished the life and personality of Brother Walfrid – faith, charity and sport.

In his pioneering work on 'The Outcast Irish in the British Victorian City', Roger Swift highlights common perceptions, conditions and problems which Walfrid lived with and worked to ameliorate amongst the Irish Catholic diaspora in both Scotland and England.[1] Swift notes 'it could be argued that the role of Catholic education and charity encouraged social mobility by providing schooling and communal self-help in deprived and poverty-ridden neighbourhoods'.[2] Close analysis of Brother Walfrid's efforts and achievements in London in this vein contributes to knowledge of 'the internal dynamics of Irish communities in terms of leadership, both clerical and lay, community organisations, and cultural and recreational provisions' in Catholic Victorian Britain.[3]

Alongside his educational work as a Marist Brother, one other significant way in which Brother Walfrid sought to serve and find

133

expression for his own distinctive charitable impulse, during his years in England, was through engagement with the St. Vincent De Paul Society. Walfrid also left behind an enduring and tangible legacy in his adopted home city of Glasgow.

In electing to profess the vow of *'stabilité'* on19th August 1886 among the Glasgow community of Marist Brothers, Brother Walfrid stated his intention to commit the rest of his life to the Institute of Catholic religious educators. The vow of stability was reserved for senior members of communities within the Institute and meant committing himself to the Catholic teaching order until death, as well as making himself available for increased responsibilities elsewhere in the province.[4] The 1890s came to represent a significant decade of reorganisation for the Marist order, especially in Britain. Walfrid's standing within the Institute, as Superior of his Marist community in Glasgow and having professed the requisite vow of stability, positioned him as an individual significant to facilitating the reorganisation beginning at the August 1892 annual retreat held at St. Joseph's College, Dumfries.[5] This meeting formalised his transfer from Glasgow to London.

Departing Glasgow: Context and Legacy

Brother Walfrid's achievements in Glasgow, and the reputation he gained for charitable works and organising ability, made him a prime candidate for taking on a senior role in London. Walfrid had first taken on an administrative role within the community of Marist Brothers in Glasgow in 1882, succeeding Brother Vales (Jean Adolphe Verbeke, b. 1850), as recorded by Brother Guerin (Jules Constane Auguste Annias, b. 1852) who served as secretary for council meetings at this time.[6] During his tenure as director, Walfrid's foremost achievements include playing a key role in the foundation of Celtic FC as a source of income for the Penny Dinners scheme, established with the aid of Brother Dorotheus, as well as representing the Marist Brothers at meetings of the Catholic education board for Glasgow.[7]

Brother Walfrid's standing as a senior Brother within the Institute is evidenced by the only documented record of a return to his homeland in the company of Brother Procope – long-serving Assistant General for the province of the British Isles – in 1890 to investigate the possibility of extending the Marist Brothers' establishments in Ireland.[8]

Walfrid's relationship with Procope dates to his first contact with the Marist Brothers at St. Mungo's and Walfrid was able to rely on supporting correspondence from his superior in Lyon to petition the Glasgow Archdiocese for improved accommodation for the Brothers under his charge.[9] Living arrangements were inspected in 1894 by electoral officials in Glasgow who found Brothers 'living in little dormitories partitioned off by curtains, and that about twelve of them occupied one room'.[10] By the summer of 1896 new premises were eventually opened for the Brothers behind St. Mary's church on East Rose Street. Spread over four floors, the new building could comfortably accommodate fifty juniors and included 'a recreation room, for the boys, four private bedrooms for Marist Brothers and a compact neat looking chapel'.[11]

Brother Walfrid had also used his senior position to advocate for better financial and working terms on behalf of those under his charge. A long-running correspondence with one school manager, Father Maginn of St. Alphonsus, centred on the 'burden on the Brothers' – in economic as well as physical terms.[12] Walfrid proved himself a formidable negotiator and a man of practicality in Glasgow who was able to achieve results by recruiting and organising the help of others. This was noted by his superiors who sought to improve the administration of the Institute in Britain during the 1890s.

Fittingly, the house councils from Charlotte Street show that Brother Dorotheus, who as procurator fulfilled the role of 'support and right hand man' to Brother Walfrid, became the new director of the Glasgow community in 1892 when Walfrid departed to London.[13] It has been written that the 'role of Brother Dorotheus in assisting Brother Walfrid and his involvement in Celtic's early formation has often been overlooked'.[14] Under the leadership of Dorotheus, donations continued to be sought and secured from major Glasgow employers on behalf of the Poor Children's Dinner Table operated by the Sacred Heart parish conference of the SVDP Society in Bridgeton. A donation of £3. 2s is acknowledged in the winter of 1895 from Messrs D.&Y. Stewart of the St. Rollox locomotive works, illustrating the enduring nature of the charity first envisaged by Walfrid and Dorotheus in 1884.[15] Annual Christmas donations from the workers of St. Rollox to the 'Children's Dinner Table' also appear in the newspaper reportage after Brother Walfrid's transfer to London.[16] The reorganisation of Marist Brothers in Glasgow was covered in an article – 'The Marist Changes' – appearing in the *Glasgow Observer* on August 20th 1892 and is worth quoting at length:

> Last week the pupils attending several of our largest Catholic Boys Schools, under the charge of the Marist Brothers, were both taking leave of old tried friends, who were starting to other fields of labour, and making the acquaintance of 'new Brothers'. We do not remember hearing so much sober talk among our young folks about the brothers and their whereabouts for an age. We ourselves had so closely allied each Brother with the school in which he was teaching, that we could not dream any change possible.
>
> Brother Walfrid and the Sacred Heart School were one and the same thing; so were St. Mary's and Brother Dorotheus, St. Alphonsus and Brother Ezekiel. These good Brothers, if we remember rightly, have been on an average of twenty years in Glasgow, most of which time was spent by them at the above schools.
>
> Brother Walfrid's arrival in the city dates back some twenty eight years, as already mentioned in a former issue of this papers, he goes as Superior to one of the Marist Brothers' most important houses in Britain, viz, that of Regent Square, London. He leaves behind him in Glasgow a host of the warmest friends. Brother Dorotheus takes his place as Superior of the monastery in Charlotte Street.[17]

The 'former issue' of the *Observer*, a Catholic publication, came a fortnight prior, announcing:

> 'His numerous friends in the city will hear with sorrow of the departure of Brother Walfrid from amongst them. For nearly thirty years he has laboured increasingly for the education of Catholic children. He conducted the schools of the Sacred Heart with singular success. He also assisted in founding in this parish, a branch of the Young Men's Society, by whose members he is held in great respect.

> On Wednesday night this Society met under the presidency of their spiritual director, Father Bird, and presented a farewell address to the good Brother. The address, which was couched in the most affectionate language, expressed the deep sorrow of members at parting with such a trusted friend, and wished him every success in his new duties. The Brother, in reply, thanked the members and exhorted them to continue in the course they had hitherto pursued, to frequent the Sacraments, and obey the injunctions of the spiritual director. In a few days, Brother Walfrid will leave for London, where his order has a large establishment. He leaves Glasgow with the hearty good wishes of all who knew him'.[18]

Sweeney also finds that the parishioners of Sacred Heart announced plans 'to present Brother Walfrid with a testimonial commensurate with his service to the parish', while Celtic FC announced their intention to do likewise during its half-year meeting in December 1892.[19] Indeed, the Club he is credited with bringing to fruition included a £10 donation to Brother Walfrid, towards his vocation in London, in its 1893 financial report.[20] The *Glasgow Observer* records immediately prior to his departure 'Brother Walfrid, before leaving for London, was the recipient of a presentation from the Celtic Football Club'.[21] The house council entry in Glasgow immediately following the annual Marist Brothers retreat at Dumfries reads simply 'Bro. Walfrid changed to 36 Regent Sq. London' as director.[22]

Walfrid maintained links with friends in Glasgow for the remainder of his life, as well as returning to the city at least once from his new assignment in London.

Regent Square 1892 – St. Anne's 1895

Handley writes extensively on 'Difficulties in London' in his history of the province, focusing particularly on the impact of the English Elementary Education Act of 1870. This state legislation caused perennial hardship for the Catholic schools ran by the Marist Brothers in London. The regulations mirrored the financial impact of the 1872 Education Act for Scotland on Catholic education and led, by the time of Walfrid's arrival in London in 1892, to efforts to consolidate its properties and cut costs as far as possible in the metropolis.[23] To this end:

> . . . the Brothers had acquired a large property consisting of four spacious and adjoining houses at 36-39 Regent Square, near King's Cross, to which the staffs of St. Patrick's, St. John's, St. Aloysius's, Corpus Christi and Notre Dame des Victoires (Leicester Square), comprising the community of The Polygon, were transferred.[24]

'The Polygon', explains Handley, was the predecessor community house for the Marist Brothers of central London to the new Regent Square base Brother Walfrid took charge of in 1892. The house at 9 The Polygon had been taken over in 1865 by the Marist Brothers: the second residence owned by the Institute in London purchased to complement its original base at St. Anne's to the east. Situated at Clarendon Square in the Somers Town district, the Polygon house offered close access to Euston Station for visiting Brothers but gradually became outdated and is not fondly recollected in Handley's history. He writes:

> It was an ugly brick erection of the late eighteenth century consisting of a basement and, above it, three storeys surmounted by an attic with dormer windows. The front

was approached by a flight of steps and a railing separated the passer-by from the basement. Water was laid on only in the kitchen and the diminutive scullery. The one water-closet was in the dismal, triangular-shaped backyard diversified with two stunted soot-covered trees, which were just not dead. Number 9 was one of ten or so similar buildings that completed the figure of a polygon.[25]

The combination of unfit-for-purpose lodgings and increased numbers of Marist Brothers engaged in the Institute's schools spread across London forced the administrators in France to restructure arrangements in the city. The man entrusted with facilitating this reorganisation and directing the new establishment, beginning in August 1892, was Brother Walfrid.[26]

Handley offers valuable insight into the practical difficulties and everyday struggles of religious life in community for the Marist Brothers in his description of the assignment facing Brother Walfrid in 1892. The new establishment near King's Cross station in central London was purchased to replace 'the old Polygon' community headed by Brother Stephen, following a period beset by complaints of rationed food, inadequate fixed salaries and 'unnecessarily drab' working conditions.[27] Morale became so low at the Polygon community in Somers Town that a Brother visiting in 1890 (Walfrid's colleague in Glasgow, Brother James) recorded 'uncivil, ill-mannered and disrespectful conduct into which some have fallen through want of sense'.[28]

Handley draws attention to how demand for Catholic teachers in the wake of compulsory education for children in Scotland and England meant 'subjects were hustled into community life after probationary periods of only three or six months; and while the sink-or-swim method may have certain beneficial results in the classroom, for community life' it often proved inadequate.[29] Handley's contention is borne out by statistics: from 'the first forty members of this Province – the pioneering band' to which Brother Walfrid belonged, just seven (17.5%) elected to leave the Institute. He continues that 'of the first

150 Brothers 92 fell away' (61%) by the turn of the twentieth century in Britain and Ireland.[30] Handley concludes that, coinciding Brother Walfrid's arrival in London, Regent Square with its dedicated oratory and unprecedented spaciousness offered an opportunity for a fresh start and a return to what was right and proper in the routine of religious life, but the opportunity was not accepted'.[31] Old problems amongst the Marist Brothers based in the metropole resurfaced during Walfrid's time in central London as head of the new community.

Brother John, a formative figure in Walfrid's early teaching career with the Marist Brothers, was elected to the position of Provincial Director of Britain, Ireland and South Africa at the general chapter of the Institute on 2nd May 1893.[32] In his role assisting Brother Procope in overseeing the administration of the establishments based in these territories, the Irishman Brother John immediately set about addressing the problems afflicting communities in Britain, especially in London. The situation encountered by Brother Walfrid during his comparatively short tenure at Regent Square is described by Handley as follows:

> . . . disedifying conduct of some members of the community remained unchanged. Murmuring and criticism became common. Slackness did not extend to classwork. A high standard of efficiency was maintained in school all through that period of storm and stress; but bickering and dissatisfaction began again when the Brothers came home from school in the evening. One fruitful source of this was the fact that the house contained about twenty Brothers of different nationalities teaching in half a dozen schools. This barracks system encouraged the formation of cliques on the basis of nationality or school staff for wordy battles on the superiority of their respective charges. Religious discipline was shot.[33]

Marist Brothers from countries such as France, Belgium, Germany, England, Scotland and – most-commonly – Ireland were all represented in London. Similarly diverse conditions existed in Glasgow during Brother Walfrid's time there, although the pre-dominance of

Irish-born Brothers there perhaps leant itself to a more agreeable community ambience.

The *Notre Dame des Victoires* parish school located in Leicester Square, for example, was French-speaking and designed to cater for a small immigrant community settled there who left France exiled as a result of the revolutionary period.[34] Walfrid, therefore, encountered a set of circumstances far removed to those he found in Glasgow where Catholicism – as reflected by the teaching Brothers there – was largely Irish in national character. Additionally, the sudden amalgamation of five separate teaching staffs of different nationalities, cultures and outlooks under one roof at Regent Square in 1891 was perhaps doomed to failure from the outset, prior to Walfrid's arrival.

Brother John, as Provincial Director, acted decisively in 1896 when twelve Brothers were dismissed from Regent Square and three London schools – St. Aloysius, St. Patrick's and Corpus Christi – were closed.[35] Brother Walfrid was changed to the East End parish of St. Anne's, Spitalfields in 1895 to take on directorship of the first Marist Brothers community to be established outside France, dating back to 1852.[36] Regent Square represented an expensive failure for the Institute and by 1897 the remaining Brothers removed to a smaller residence at 7 Duncan Terrace, Islington. The following testimony from a former member of the community paints a bleak picture of financial conditions and provides some explanation for the closure of Regent Square:

> In August 1896 I was sent as a pupil teacher to St. John's, Islington. Our residence was at Regent Square. The great exodus had just been completed. . . There was a paying school at the Square, which, however, did not pay. We experienced real want here. . . The food at the Square was not sufficient and not good. There were fourteen Brothers residing in the house. The income for the three Brothers teaching in the 'paying school' was not enough. . . The paid cook had to be dismissed – no money to pay him. . . We took it in turns to wash the outside stairs after dark on a Saturday night in a fashionable residential locality. Daily

Mass in the chapel had to be discontinued. Mass was said only once a week.[37]

The 'great exodus' saw a 'purge' of around forty Marist Brothers between 1890 and 1897 during Brother John's administration of the province. Handley finds 'most of whom were sent away or left the Institute'.[38] After a period of rapid expansion since their arrival in Britain in 1852, by the close of the century the Marist Brothers – guided by the pragmatism of Brother John – sought to consolidate the progress it had made under senior Brothers like Walfrid.

One distraction from the difficulties of community life experienced at Regent Square for Brother Walfrid is evidenced by his enduring passion for sport and a continued connection with members of Celtic FC in Glasgow. Handley states that the proximity of the new Marist headquarters in central London to Regent's Park meant that casual games of football were regularly arranged on Saturday afternoons for the boys of the Brothers' various schools in the capital. Brother Walfrid began his new assignment at St. Anne's in the impoverished East End in April 1895.[39]

St. Anne's 1895 – Grove Ferry, Kent 1906

Salmon, in his centenary history of St. Anne's in Spitalfields, shows that three hundred and six baptisms were conducted in the parish in 1895, the year of Brother Walfrid's arrival as headteacher of the school for boys and director of the community of Marist Brothers. An average of three hundred baptisms was maintained annually throughout Walfrid's assignment there until 1906, making the parish comparable in size to the Sacred Heart, Bridgeton community he left in Glasgow.[40] The parish church and residence at Underwood Road bore particular historic significance for the Society of Mary – the Marist Fathers as well as the teaching Brothers and Sisters – in that it was the first establishment made in Britain, or indeed anywhere in the world outside France. Taylor dates its genesis back to September 1850 when 'the Marists opened a house in London, at Spitalfields in the East End, where they worked among the newly arrived Irish immigrants' made refugees by *An Gorta Mor*.[41] The parish was served by Marist Fathers, two of whom – Irishmen Father Michael Watters and Father Peter Murphy – were significant figures during Walfrid's time spent working closely with the clergy as director of the schools. Brother Walfrid proved himself to be a valuable and dedicated fundraiser for the Spitalfields parish during his work there.

The Catholic press of London had previously noted the success of Walfrid's 'Penny Dinners' in Glasgow. *The Tablet* published a report on Brother Walfrid's Sacred Heart schools feeding programme in 1886 titled 'Children's Dinners at Glasgow':

> At the schools attached to the Mission of the Sacred Heart, Bridgeton, from January 10th, 1885, to January 10th, 1886, the number of 36,360 dinners have been supplied free to the poor children, as well as 1,250 breakfasts. The dinners paid for by the children at a halfpenny or a penny each were 12,200 in number. Thus, no less than 49,810 meals have been given or provided at a very low rate. Of the funds from which these meals were provided, the St. Vincent de Paul Conference contributed £62. 13s 5.25d; £36. 17s. 1.75d. came from children who paid; donations amounted to £5. 11s. 3d.; and 8s. 8.75d. was realised by the sale of bones, &c., making in all an income of £105 10s. 6.75d. The expenditure for food was £69. 14s. 10.75d.; for fittings and utensils, £21. 1s. 7d.; for the wages of the cook, £13. 15s.; and for fuel, £1. 19s. 1d.; making in all a total of exactly the same amount as the income. At present some 167 children are being supplied with breakfast and dinner. On Sunday an appeal will be made at the Church of the Sacred Heart for funds to continue this good work.[42]

The new parish of St. Anne's where Brother Walfrid now found himself had in place a system of school feeding and fundraising facilitated by the SVDP, though not on the scale of that which was attempted in Glasgow. Feheny describes the historic mistrust of the London Catholic clergy of secular state intervention in both education and tackling poverty among its parish communities.[43] Alongside his teaching duties, Brother Walfrid engaged himself in the weekly meetings of the St. Anne's conference of the SVDP in efforts to replicate and continue his charitable work as part of his assignment in Spitalfields.[44] A researcher representing Charles Booth's influential survey and classification of poverty in Victorian London reported on the parish of St. Anne's on March 3rd 1898:

> . . . a large and beautiful building in which I found a considerable congregation of mixed class but especially the poor. . . The congregation was very devout and joined in the responses very genuinely.[45]

In Maynard's history of the parish of St. Anne's, she describes community efforts to aid the poor, especially the children belonging to the schools and Brother Walfrid's integral role within these local community efforts:

> While education provision for the masses had continued to improve, a lot of children still came to school too hungry to learn, public funding for meals had not yet been approved and feeding projects were still *ad hoc* and dependent on charitable donations and willing volunteers. Although the projects were, as a general rule, not run on school premises, they were usually school-specific, and Catholic schools had to organise their own. So each winter, the usual appeal went out for money to feed the St. Anne's schoolchildren: it was an issue very close to Bro. Walfrid's heart. In January 1904 around 400 were receiving free breakfasts.[46]

Local Education Authority of London reports are available only for the years 1904, 1905 and 1906 during Brother Walfrid's headmastership of the St. Anne's boys school. Average attendance was found to total just over 500 children including boys, girls and infants; around 80% were therefore availing of free school breakfasts.[47] The official remarked that teaching 'is very successfully conducted, and the boys are well trained in habits of order and industry'.[48] As with the inspector reports for the Marist schools of Glasgow and reminiscences of Walfrid's own teaching style there, discipline and dedication were common values upon which the daily lessons were founded.

The school of St. Anne's under Brother Walfrid's charge was evidently forthright in expounding the distinct Catholic ethos of the Marist Brothers. Maynard also finds that Walfrid was recurrently involved, along with the St. Anne's clergy, in rallying political support for the Tower Hamlets Catholic League which sought to 'defend the Catholic school system' and encourage 'the Catholic vote in School Board election'.[49] However, evidence demonstrates that the advocacy and charity of Brother Walfrid was not confined to the local Catholic congregation. Donations totalling £1. 1s were collected and made to the non-denominational 'Philanthropic Society' in November 1896.[50]

In this ecumenical spirit, just over £3 was collected by Walfrid and his SVDP confreres towards the 'Indian Famine Fund' the following February. This action displays an international awareness of the suffering of other communities among the British colonies.[51] Brother Walfrid's own experience of the privations of *An Gorta Mor* in his youth in Ireland must surely have had a bearing on his endeavours to assist those who found themselves in a similarly desperate situation elsewhere under the rule of British Empire.

Brother Walfrid's enduring association with sport is further exemplified by the clubs which sprang up in his St. Anne's parish in London during his tenure there. Both a cricket team and an amateur football side bearing the name 'Celtic' appear in the London Catholic press from 1897, just two years after Walfrid's arrival in Whitechapel. Displaying an awareness on the part of Brother Walfrid of the popular interest in the traditionally English game of cricket, the Celtic cricket team from St. Anne's played matches against local Catholic outfits such as Newman House and St. Mary's College in Hammersmith.[52] Similarly, the football team, led by former St. Anne's pupil Stephen Parker, also engaged in local non-denominational tournaments as well as games with other Catholic organisations from its home ground on Hackney Marshes.[53] The utilisation of sport as an expression of Irish Catholic identity is a theme which recurs throughout the life of Walfrid.

Finally, an unarchived letter penned by Brother Walfrid dated 1906 refers to a collection organised in aid of a children's summer excursion to the country. He wrote:

> I regret that we were obliged to pay so much for clothes, but the poor children were so poorly clad that we could not do it for less.[54] [see facing page of this chapter]

In terms of material handwritten by Walfrid, the note represents a rare insight into the interior life of the then elderly Marist Brother. It reflects Brother Walfrid's enduring concern for, and charitable action taken on behalf of, those he affectionately describes as 'the poor children'.

In this sense, Walfrid's words and charitable action reflect the Catholic Church's 'Preferential Option for the Poor', a doctrine outlined for the first time in an 1891 encyclical decreed by Pope Leo XIII titled *Rerum Novarum* (Latin for 'of revolutionary change').[55] Thus, the same spirit in which Brother Walfrid began the Poor Children's Dinner Tables charity in Glasgow – and Celtic FC – is in evidence in the Marist Brother's endeavours later in London. The outing Walfrid referred to in the note was most likely to the Brothers' newest establishment in England: Grove Ferry in Kent which opened in 1903. This was where Brother Walfrid was placed soon after passing the official retirement age of 65 in 1906.[56] Walfrid would continue his role as a senior educator within the Institute, drawing on his previous experience spent living in diverse religious communities and teaching young people in Glasgow, Beaucamps and London.

Notes

1 *Glasgow Observer*, May 6th 1911.

2 Swift, Rodger 'The Outcast Irish in the British Victorian City: Problems and Perspectives', *Irish Historical Studies* Vol. 25, No. 99 (May, 1987), pp.264-276.

3 Swift, 'The Outcast Irish in the British Victorian City: Problems and Perspectives', p. 274.

4 *Ibid*, p. 276.

5 'Annals of (St Andrews) St Josephs Monastery 71 Charlotte Street Glasgow', Microfiche of Brother Walfrid, No. 2998 held at the General Archive for The Institute of Marist Brothers, Rome.

6 *The Weekly Freeman*, August 5th 1892.

7 'Annals of (St Andrews) St Josephs Monastery 71 Charlotte Street Glasgow'.
Parker, Br. J., *Remembering the Marist Brothers* (2009), pp. 333-336.

8 *The Glasgow Herald*, April 11th 1885.

9 *The Freeman's Journal*, September 11th 1890.
Handley, J.E., *A History of the Marist Brothers Province of the British Isles* (1968), p. 136.

10 'Annals of (St Andrews) St Josephs Monastery 71 Charlotte Street Glasgow', October 16th 1883.

11 *The Glasgow Herald*, October 9th 1896.

12 *The Glasgow Observer*, March 21st 1896.

13 'Annals of (St Andrews) St Josephs Monastery 71 Charlotte Street Glasgow', December 27th 1884.

14 'Annals of (St Andrews) St Josephs Monastery 71 Charlotte Street Glasgow', August 9th 1887, 8th August 1892.

15 Celtic Graves Society, 'In Memory of the Founding Fathers of Celtic Football Club' (2013), p. 25.

16 *Glasgow Evening News*, January 3rd 1895.

17 *The Glasgow Herald*, December 30th 1892.

18 *The Glasgow Observer*, August 20th 1892.

19 *The Glasgow Observer*, August 6th 1892.

20 Sweeney, B. *Celtic, The Early Years: 1887-1892* (Scotland: CQN Books, 2015), p. 444.

21 *The Scottish Referee*, May 19th 1893.

22 *The Glasgow Observer*, August 13th 1892.

23 'Annals of (St Andrews) St Josephs Monastery 71 Charlotte Street Glasgow', 8th August 1892.

24 Handley, A. *History of the Marist Brothers Province of the British Isles*, pp. 30-43.

25 *Ibid*, p. 32.

26 *Ibid*, p. 32.

27 Microfiche of Brother Walfrid, No. 2998 held at the General Archive for The Institute of Marist Brothers, Rome.

28 Handley, A. *History of the Marist Brothers Province of the British Isles*, pp. 46-48.

29 *Ibid*, p. 48

30 *Ibid*, p. 43

31 *Ibid.*

32 *Ibid*, pp. 48-49

33 Chalmers, Br. C. 'Administrative History of Marist Brothers of Great Britain', information received from the General Archives of the Marist Brothers in Rome, 2018.

34 Handley, A. *History of the Marist Brothers Province of the British Isles*, p. 49.

35 Microfiche of Brother Walfrid, No. 2998 held at the General Archive for The Institute of Marist Brothers, Rome.

36 Handley, *A History of the Marist Brothers Province of the British Isles*, p. 50.

37 Chalmers, Br. C. 'Administrative History of Marist Brothers of Great Britain', information received from the General Archives of the Marist Brothers in Rome, 2018.
Microfiche of Brother Walfrid, No. 2998 held at the General Archive for The Institute of Marist Brothers, Rome.

38 Handley, A. *History of the Marist Brothers Province of the British Isles*, pp. 50-51.

39 *Ibid*, pp 38039

40 Microfiche of Brother Walfrid, No. 2998 held at the General Archive for The Institute of Marist Brothers, Rome.

41 Salmon, Rev. D.*A. Short History of the Parish of St Anne's, Underwood Road* (London: Salesian Press, 1950), p. 11.
Aspinwall, B., 'Children of the Dead End: the Formation of the Modern Archdiocese of Glasgow, 1815-1914', The Innes Review, Vol. 43, No. 2 (Autumn, 1992) p. 132.

42 Salmon, Rev. D.*A. Short History of the Parish of St Anne's, Underwood Road* (London: Salesian Press, 1950), p. 19.

43 *The Tablet*, February 13th 1886.

44 Feheny, J.M., 'Delinquency among Irish Catholic Children in Victorian London', *Irish Historical Studies*, Vol. 23, No. 92 (Nov., 1983), pp. 319-329.
Feheny, J.M., 'The London Catholic Ragged School: An Experiment in Education for Irish Destitute Children', *Archivium Hibernicum*, Vol. 39 (1984), pp. 32-44.

45 St Anne's log books of the Saint Vincent de Paul Society, accessed at St Anne's R.C. Church, London.

46 Charles Booth Survey B221; B223; B224; B3181; B387.
The London School of Economics website, which holds copies of the inquiry reports, states, 'Charles Booth's Inquiry into the Life and Labour of the People in London, undertaken between 1886 and 1903, was one of several surveys of working class life carried out in the 19th century. It is the only survey for which the original

notes and data have survived and therefore provides a unique insight into the development of the philosophy and methodology of social investigation in the United Kingdom'. Available online at https://booth.lse.ac.uk/learn-more/what-was-the-inquiry accessed March 2021.

47 Maynard, J. O., History of the parish of St Anne's Underwood Road Volumes III, accessed at Tower Hamlets Local History Library and Archives, LC13903/024, pp. 56-57.

48 St Anne's School Inspector Reports 1904 - 1908, accessed at London Metropolitan Archives, LCC/EO/ PS/ IZ/ NP/ S/ 23/ 1-7.

49 *Ibid.*

50 Maynard, J. O., History of the parish of St Anne's Underwood Road Volumes III, accessed at Tower Hamlets Local History Library and Archives, LC13903/024, p. 44.

51 Expenses Book 1896-1901 for St Anne's, Underwood Road, accessed at St Anne's R.C. Church, London, November 3rd 1896.

52 Expenses Book 1896-1901 for St Anne's, Underwood Road, accessed at St Anne's R.C. Church, London, February 14th 1897.

53 *London Monitor,* July 23rd 1897, p. 1.

54 *The East London Advertiser,* March 18th 1899, p. 3.

55 Note July 1906 to Brother Mark.
Expenses Book 1902-1916 for St Anne's, Underwood Road, accessed at St Anne's R.C. Church, London. July 20th 1906.
For an image of the handwritten note see Appendix C, p. 219.

56 Beck, G.A. (Ed.), *The English Catholics, 1850-1950: Essays to commemorate the centenary of the restoration of the Hierarchy of England and Wales* (London: Burnes Oates, 1950), p. 27.

A group of Marist Brothers pictured at Grove Ferry, thought to be early in the 1900s. Brother Walfrid, the oldest in the group is given due prominence in the seating arrangement immediately to the right of the only priest in the photo.

CHAPTER 9

Grove Ferry 1906 – Dumfries 1912

Brother Walfrid's final teaching assignment would be at Grove Ferry – close to Canterbury – in the south of England county of Kent. Brother John Parker, in his biographical history titled 'Remembering the Marist Brothers', states that Brother Walfrid was moved to Grove Ferry in 1906 after reaching the school teaching retirement age of sixty-five during his headmastership of St. Anne's in London. Parker finds, while Walfrid was based at Grove Ferry in Kent, he 'taught for six years before retiring to Dumfries in 1912'.[1] Handley further explains 'after reaching compulsory retirement in 1906 he spent his remaining days first at Grove Ferry, which he had been instrumental in securing for the exiled French Brothers, and afterwards at Mount St. Michael' where he was eventually laid at rest in Dumfries.[2]

The establishment of a boarding school and community of Marist Brothers at Grove Ferry in Kent arose from secularisation legislation – known as the Combes Law – coming into effect in France in 1903.[3] Political developments in France towards the close of the nineteenth and beginning of the twentieth centuries were to have a direct influence on the life of Brother Walfrid. Lanfrey characterises the period as one of difficulty and upheaval for the Marist Brothers in their nation of origin, who found themselves 'confronting a hostile State and a society which was gradually shaking off the influence of the Church'.[4]

Where before Catholic institutions enjoyed varying degrees of legal protection and financial support from the French government, the watershed 'Dreyfus Affair', occurring over the course of the 1890s and early 1900s, heightened anti-religious sentiment and a Radical reform government was formed in 1899.[5] Beginning with the 1901 Law of Associations signalling withdrawal of state support for Catholic teaching congregations like the Marist Brothers, the Radical government embarked on a programme of formally separating the church and state in France. Between 1902 and 1905, under Prime Minister Emile Combes, legislation was passed ratifying the process of secularisation, effectively exiling the Marist Brothers and similar religious orders from France.[6] In response, the senior administration of the Brothers hastily made plans ahead of the Combes Law coming into effect, arranging a General Chapter at the Mother House in Lyon under the direction of Superior General Brother Théophane (Adrien Durand, b. 1824).

One commentator writes that the 'upheaval of 1903 could easily have turned into a disaster; however, it would eventually prove to provide new opportunities' in the longer term.[7] The Marist Brothers were forced to suddenly increase expansion internationally from their native France and Brother Walfrid was to play an important role in this process. The London-based *Standard* newspaper reports on September 15th 1903:

> The Marist Brothers, one of the religious Orders who have had to quit France under the Associations Law, have purchased a mansion at Grove Ferry, midway between Canterbury and Ramsgate, together with four adjoining houses, where a number of students have already arrived and commenced their studies. These will be followed at the end of the month by fifty or sixty more, in addition to the teaching staff, which will consist of about twenty members of the Order.[8]

Lanfrey finds that the dispersal of Marist Brothers based in France began on a considerable scale in 1901, immediately following the anti-religious Law of Association which signalled the beginning of aggressive secularisation on behalf of the French state. Numbers of Brothers leaving France peaked in 1903 with over five hundred members of the Institute reassigned to new continents. Thirty-one new Marist foundations were instituted, most notably in China, North America and Brazil. A further cohort of over five hundred French Brothers were relocated within Europe and Grove Ferry in rural Kent, England was decided upon as one such location equipped to rehouse both Brothers and Marist boarding school pupils.[9] This would involve the relocation of historic provincial houses from France to neighbouring European countries including Italy, Belgium and Spain in particular.[10] Grove Ferry was to serve as one temporary extension of the Beaucamps province, where Brother Walfrid had his formation as a Marist and taught as a teacher of English to French pupils, over thirty years prior.[11]

Some temporary foundations such as at Battle on the English south coast were utilised to prepare the mostly French national Brothers for missionary work by facilitating study of the English language. Handley states that Brother Walfrid, in his final assignment as an active Marist Brother, 'had been instrumental in securing' the more permanent Grove Ferry residence 'for the exiled French Brothers'.[12] Handley notably does not elaborate on Walfrid's specific role in the procurement in his history of the province, but given the site's proximity to London it is likely Walfrid visited to assess the suitability of the buildings on behalf of the Marist Brothers in France. Prendergast, historian of the Irish Marist Brothers, writes:

> . . . enforced closures included the Novitiate House at Beaucamps where Walfrid and so many other Brothers had studied. At that time it was home to over 150 boarding pupils and 30 Brothers who needed to be moved lock, stock and barrel to a different country. While some transferred to Belgium and others left for Brazil, a move across the Channel was the French superiors' preferred destination for the novitiate school. And so it was that they appealed to Dumfries that the organisational genius of Walfrid be released to them for the move. . . The scout in him soon set his eyes on Grove Ferry, a venerable mansion in an idyllic setting on the Great Stour River, six miles from Canterbury and 70 miles from London.[13]

As headteacher and director of St. Anne's in the East End of London, Brother Walfrid was by then one of the most experienced and senior Marist Brothers in the south of England. His reputation for 'organisational genius' is notable within the historiography of the Marist Brothers – largely gained through his charitable work, particularly in Glasgow with his fundraising achievements with Celtic FC. Walfrid's personal experience of spiritual formation at Beaucamps and command of the French language would also further distinguish him as an ideal candidate to help facilitate the relocations enforced upon the Brothers in France, as noted by his superiors in Dumfries charged with assigning the work of Brothers based in the United Kingdom and Ireland.

By October of 1903, the boarding school ran by the Marist Brothers in Paris was also forced to close, with an additional one hundred and ten pupils and thirty-six teaching Brothers decamping to the newly purchased establishment in Kent at Grove Ferry. Though based in England, Grove Ferry remained the property of the Beaucamps province - governed in exile from Grugliasco in Italy – until 1929 when the boarding school was purchased by the province of Great Britain and Ireland.[14] Rob Williams, a former pupil of the college, produced the only dedicated history of Grove Ferry held by the archives of the Marist Brothers, offering singular insight into the community Brother Walfrid was transferred to in May 1906 three years after it was established.[15]

Williams describes how the religious teaching Institute:

> . . . formed the Marist Brothers' College, Grove Ferry – a daughter house of the College at Beauchamps [sic] – to continue their task of providing 'a thoroughly Catholic education to enable pupils to pursue honourably and successfully the profession they may adopt'.[16]

The collection of buildings dates back to the eighteenth century and belonged to the Denne family who owned extensive land in the Chislet parish in Kent. Brother Benedict (James Blake, b. 1864), Brother

Godwin (Richard Mooney, b. 1860), along with Brother Walfrid's former colleagues in Glasgow, Brother Dorotheus and Brother Ezechiel, completed the purchase on the recommendation of Walfrid.[17] All five Marist Brothers, including Walfrid, had served as headmasters and directors of communities in either Britain or Ireland, so Brother Walfrid's experience within the Institute was drawn on and trusted by the French Brothers to facilitate their relocation.

Williams describes that the area totalling of around seven acres 'comprised the mansion, stabling, outbuildings, park and pasture land, a double cottage with garden and orchard (Greengorgon on the banks of the River Stour), four semi-detached villa residences (fronting the Thanet road), and lakes known as The Fishponds'.[18] Handley confirms that the mansion known as 'The White House' served as the hub of the Brothers' religious community and describes how 'some sixty trucks of books, furniture and fittings from an opulent boarding school in the Rue Pernety' arrived there from Paris.[19] For Brother Walfrid and his London confreres who began travelling to Grove Ferry for the annual summer retreat in 1904, the new establishment surely represented a stark contrast to the urban want witnessed in the East End of London.[20]

The original director of the community of Marist Brothers and headmaster of the school was a Frenchman, Brother Chumald, assisted by his compatriot from Beaucamps, Brother Andre. Williams describes a 'predominantly French College with French language, customs, food and games; and they became known locally as The Frenchmen'.[21] Indeed, at the blessing of the newly constructed chapel in March 1904, the *Faversham Times* reports the 'College has 105 pupils, all, with the exception of five, being Parisians' who followed their teachers from France.[22] Although 95% of the pupils at the outset were French nationals, Williams describes an international teaching staff. Brother Walfrid would join Spanish, German and British Marist Brothers who had decamped from France when he was moved to Kent in 1906.[23]

The 1906 list of placements recorded annually by the Marist

Brothers reads 'Walfrid teaching English' at Grove Ferry to the French students.[24] As the school progressed Williams finds increasing numbers of English boarders attending: by the time Walfrid retired to Dumfries in 1912 English had become the official language of the establishment, while 'games such as cricket and soccer were introduced'.[25] Local newspaper reports highlight the 'Marist Brothers' Upstreet College' taking part in the 'Faversham and District League'.[26] It is fitting that a connection with football followed Brother Walfrid to each of his placements during his active years as a Marist Brother.

Walfrid's time at Grove Ferry, Kent ended in July of 1912 with the sudden onset of ill health. On 27th July 1912, the Catholic newspaper of London *The Monitor and New Era* carried the following report:

> Rev. Brother Walfrid, at present residing in the Marist College, Grove Ferry, Kent, is slowly recovering from the recent attack of paralysis. He is about to celebrate his 73rd birthday. Brother Walfrid founded the famous Celtic FC.[27]

The short report also carries a photograph of Brother Walfrid in advanced years, most likely captured in Grove Ferry at one of the annual retreats held by the Marist Brothers. The image is one of only four previously known photographs of Walfrid, in a sequence beginning with the most well-known image of him posed as a young man in Glasgow to mark the opening of the Sacred Heart school in 1874. Handley (Brother Clare, b. 1900) recalls the typical scene at Grove Ferry at annual retreats for the Marist Brothers based in London, held each summer from 1904:

> Before the visitor in summertime unrolled the rich green of the marches sweeping down to the sparkling white of the chalk cliff and the deep blue of the sea, the shimmering bronze of wheat and the scarlet flare of the poppies, between the pale gold of barley, the white ribbons of roads that looped the undulating fields, the silted loam and sombre green of the hop gardens, clusters of red apples and black cherries peeping over orchards where comical sheep, smothered from nose to trotters in wool, wandered in full-

bellied ease, the mellow rust of ancient farm walls, the deep copses, and over all, a flood of yellow sunlight… It was the one patch of paradisal earth that we owned in all the Province.[28]

A photograph taken at Grove Ferry during one such retreat was located during archival research in Lyon, France showing Brother Walfrid, for the first time, amongst his fellow Marist Brothers. Held by the Archives of the Marist Brothers of France in St. Genis Laval, the undated photo was taken between 1904 when the first summer retreat was held at Grove Ferry and Walfrid's eventual departure in 1912. Rather than posed individually, Walfrid is captured at ease and smiling in a large group of fellow Brothers in Kent. His seniority earned within the order of Catholic teachers is illustrated by his position seated directly to the right of the priest directing the retreat on behalf of the Marist Brothers. Walfrid is pictured seated third from the left in the middle row [see photo on facing page at the start of this chapter].

The census of England and Wales records that Brother Walfrid remained engaged as a 'Professor in College' at Grove Ferry as of 2nd April 1911 making him, in his seventy-first year, the oldest member of the Marist community teaching there.[29] Walfrid evidently remained steadfast in his devotion to his religious vocation and was fit enough to travel to London weeks later where Tom Maley – a member of the original Celtic side – recorded some final thoughts on the football club he remains most closely associated with:

> Four years before he died Walfrid was the guest of honour at a celebration dinner in London where the Celtic team, one of the most successful in the Club's history, was passing through after a successful European tour. That night the Marist told Tom Maley, then a journalist, "Well, well, time has brought changes; outside ourselves there are few left of the old brigade. I know none of the present lot, but they are under the old colours and quartered in the dear old quarters, and that suffices".[30]

Brother Walfrid, in travelling to meet with members of the Club in London, displays an awareness and close interest in the progress of Celtic FC, an affection maintained in his final retirement years in Dumfries. Writing in his weekly *Glasgow Observer* column 'Maley's Football Notes', Tom Maley includes a section titled 'An Old Friend', dedicated to his meeting with Walfrid and the Celtic party at Charing Cross Station. Maley describes how:

> The good Brother retains his youthfulness almost, and seems as vigorous and fit as in the days when he was architect-in-chief of the Celtic. Situated in a place nigh Folkestone, the good Brother couldn't resist the temptation of meeting the party and doing the journey to London with them.[31]

One member of the Celtic coaching staff, Pat Hearne, claimed the distinction of having been a former pupil of Walfrid's. Having travelled from Folkestone to London in the company of the Celtic players and management, Brother Walfrid pronounced 'truly a meeting of the original conspirators' to Maley on arrival.[32] The elderly Marist Brother, signed off stating, 'It's good to see you all so well, and I feel younger with the meeting. Goodbye. God bless you'.[33]

Maley subsequently describes how 'the old man hurried into the bustle and life of the station and the big city it links up'. He writes:

> The onlookers who watched curiously the Celtic party little dreamt that the cleric who so lightly stepped out and who seemed so unconventional in his style, etc, was the central figure in the foundation of the greatest and best of athletic and football institutions, and that in the spare figure there was harboured the determination and the perseverance which gave Glasgow an additional leaf to the laurel it claims. The works of charity that the good Brother performed through the channels that the Celtic Club sent out have been many. The countless little ones who were fed and clothed, the many whose lives were made brighter and healthier and happier, remember the dear old man with gratitude, and no doubt in prayer, and we who were privileged to be at his disposal, nay, I would say in his service, rejoice and are exceedingly glad the opportunity

was ours. Long may the Club flourish, and may the good Brother live the fulness of years and witness its success afield and the frequency of its charitable functions.[34]

Brother Walfrid, therefore, was remembered with fondness as the 'central figure' and 'architect-in-chief' of Celtic FC in Glasgow, his most famed and enduring achievement. Evidently the feeling of fondness was reciprocated on the part of the Marist Brother who enjoyed meeting with old friends from his more youthful years in Glasgow.

The 'recent attack of paralysis', reported one year later at Grove Ferry in the summer of 1912, marked the first of several strokes suffered by Walfrid in his final years, bringing to a close fifty-one years of active service in the community as a teaching Marist Brother.[35] The same month, July 1912, Brother Walfrid was retired to the Marist Brothers' provincial house at Dumfries to live out the last years of his life in 'repos': rest.[36]

Notes

1 Microfiche of Brother Walfrid, No. 2998 held at the General Archive for The Institute of Marist Brothers, Rome.

2 Parker, Br. J., *Remembering the Marist Brothers* (2009), p. 112.

3 Handley, J.E., *A History of the Marist Brothers Province of the British Isles* (1968), p. 158.

4 Chalmers, Br. C, 'Administrative History of Marist Brothers of Great Britain', information received from the General Archives of the Marist Brothers in Rome, 2018.

5 Lanfrey, Br. A., *History of the Institute of the Marist Brothers: From the village of Marlhes to expansion worldwide (1789-1907)* Volume 1 (Rome: Institute of the Marist Brothers, 2015), p. 289.

6 Merriman, J., *A History of Modern Europe: From the Renaissance to the Present* (London: W.W. Norton & Company, 2004 Second Edition), p. 812.

7 Lanfrey, *History of the Institute of the Marist Brothers: From the village of Marlhes to expansion worldwide (1789-1907)* Vol. 1, pp. 336-339.
For more on the political context in France see Guerlac, O., 'The Separation of Church and State in France', *Political Science Quarterly*, Vol. 27, No. 2 (June, 1908), pp. 259–296.

8 Delorme, Br. A., *Marvellous Companions of Marcellin Champagnat* (Rome: Institute of the Marist Brothers, 2011), p. 250.

9 *The Standard*, September 15th 1903, p. 6.

10 Lanfrey, *History of the Institute of the Marist Brothers: From the village of Marlhes to expansion worldwide (1789-1907)* Vol. 1, pp. 339-340.

11 Delorme, *Marvellous Companions of Marcellin Champagnat*, pp. 255-256.

12 Chalmers, Br. C, 'Administrative History of Marist Brothers of Great Britain', information received from the General Archives of the Marist Brothers in Rome, 2018.

13 Handley, J.E., *A History of the Marist Brothers Province of the British Isles* (1968), p. 158.

14 Prendergast, N., *Before You We Stand: The Story of the Marist Brothers in Ireland* (Ireland: Naas Printing, 2021), p. 113.

15 Chalmers, Br. C, 'Administrative History of Marist Brothers of Great Britain', information received from the General Archives of the Marist Brothers in Rome, 2018.
The Grove Ferry school closed in 1941 and the property was sold by the Marist Brothers in 1946.

16 Williams, R., 'The Marist Brothers of Grove Ferry' (c. 1980s - 1990s), photocopies and handwritten notes held at the Scottish Catholic Archives, Edinburgh, SCA/MB/11/4.
Microfiche of Brother Walfrid, No. 2998 held at the General Archive for The Institute of Marist Brothers, Rome.

17 *Ibid.*

18 *Canterbury Journal, Kentish Times and Farmers' Gazette*, 19th September 1903, p. 8.

19 Williams, 'The Marist Brothers of Grove Ferry', p. 137.

20 Handley, *A History of the Marist Brothers Province of the British Isles*, p. 148.

21 *Ibid.*
The Monitor and New Era, July 15th 1904, p. 4.

22 Williams, 'The Marist Brothers of Grove Ferry', p. 138.

23 *Faversham Times and Mercury and North-East Kent Journal*, 26th March 1904, p. 7.

24 Williams, 'The Marist Brothers of Grove Ferry', p. 139.

25 'Liste de Placements', (1906) held at the Scottish Catholic Archives, Edinburgh, SCA/MB/1/6/3.

26 Williams, 'The Marist Brothers of Grove Ferry', p. 138.

27 *Herne Bay Press*, November 29th 1913, p. 3.

28 *The Monitor and New Era*, July 27th 1912, p. 12.

29 'Retraitants Anglais' (English Retreatants) Photograph held by Archives of the Marist Brothers of France in St Genis Laval.

30 1911 England, Wales and Scotland Census, accessed online at findmypast.co.uk.

31 'In Memory'of the Founding Fathers of Celtic Football Club' – pamphlet produced by the Celtic Graves Society (2013), p. 9.

32 *Glasgow Observer*, June 10th 1911.

33 *Ibid.*

34 *Ibid.*

35 *Ibid.*

36 *The Monitor and New Era*, July 27th 1912, p. 12.

St. Joseph's College, Dumfries. The statue is of the founder of the Marist Brothers, Saint Marcellin Champagnat.

CHAPTER 10

Dumfries 1912 – 1915

The community of Marist Brothers based in St. Joseph's, Dumfries came to be the centre of the Institute's presence in Britain and Ireland by the summer of 1912. The Marist teaching community in Dumfries can be traced to the 'transference of Father McDonald from Dundee to Dumfries' in 1869. In 1909, the transformation of the province of Britain and Ireland from missionary territory attached to France to a distinct province in its own right, was confirmed when Brother James was appointed in charge of The Province of Great Britain and Ireland, with its centre in Dumfries.[1]

Having retired there on account of his poor health and advanced years, the final three years of Brother Walfrid's life were thus spent at the heart of the mission of the Marist Brothers in Britain, to which Walfrid had devoted his adult life in living out his religious vocation in service over the course of half a century.

Further property had been acquired along with an additional 12.5 acres in 1877 as the St. Joseph's school and novitiate expanded and the provincial centre of the Marist Brothers in Dumfries had been given the title of Mount Saint Michael, after the patron saint of the town located in south-west Scotland.[2] The surroundings of Mount Saint Michael were not new to Brother Walfrid on his arrival in late July, 1912. Walfrid had been guest in Dumfries on at least three occasions, with visits documented in 1888, 1890 and 1891 during his time as Brother Superior of the Marist community in Glasgow. The 1890 college annual reports that Brother Walfrid was invited to take part in the feast day celebrations at St. Joseph's on 19th March during which 'the Chaplain, the Rev. Dr Crowther, sang the Solemn Mass' and 'the College Choir, assisted by an efficient orchestra' provided musical accompaniment. The article then states:

> In the evening, Brother Walfrid, Glasgow, exhibited a series of views of the most celebrated and picturesque Abbeys of Scotland, by means of a very powerful oxyhydrogen projection. These were followed by a large number of beautifully coloured scenes illustrating Henry Glassford Bell's well-known poem on Mary, Queen of Scots. Needless to say that all enjoyed heartily this entertainment, which brought to close a happy and memorable day.[3]

Walfrid, at that stage approaching his fiftieth year, evidently held a keen interest and knowledge of the religious history of his adopted country of Scotland. In utilising 'oxyhydrogen projection' – more commonly known as a 'magic lantern' – Walfrid also exhibits an ability to engage with the most modern teaching methods available at the time. The 'Mary, Queen o' Scots' poem, for example, authored by Glassford Bell and published in 1831 recounts the tragic fate of Catholic heiress Mary Stuart, executed for laying claim to the English throne at the height of the Reformation.[4] Interestingly, as well as sharing the same Catholic faith, Mary Stuart – like Walfrid – received education in France in her younger years. The Third Marquess of Bute, John Stuart-Crichton, descended directly from the Stuart dynastic line regularly attended such occasions in Dumfries as the prime benefactor of St. Joseph's College. The Marquess of Bute led the list of subscriptions collected for the establishment of the novitiate in Dumfries during the 1870s – which also included Archbishop Eyre of Glasgow and Father Noonan of Walfrid's own Sacred Heart parish – in donating £105 and his patronage continued until his death in 1900.[5]

In his history of St. Joseph's College, Taylor refers to Brother Walfrid's presence at two more visits to Dumfries – in 1888 and 1891 – which both represented sporting occasions. Held in the grounds of Mount St. Michael, the annual sports programme held by St. Joseph's College reflected a proud sporting tradition encouraged by the Marist Brothers in Dumfries, as well as close connections with Walfrid's Celtic

FC. Taylor records that in 1888, the inaugural report of the sporting events describes how proceedings were opened by the College Band:

> ... playing perhaps with greater gusto than usual, since they were invited to perform at the International Exhibition in Glasgow that year, which was a great honour for the boys, Herr Ludwig, their conductor, and Brother Mary Ambrose, who also instructed them. It is interesting to note that they were accompanied to the event by the Headmaster, Brother James, the College Chaplain, the Reverend Doctor Crowther, and Brother Walfrid, who founded Celtic Football Club that same year.[6]

Indeed, the Glasgow International Exhibition of 1888 showcasing the industrial wealth of the city opened at Kelvingrove on the same day Celtic FC played its first fixture at Celtic Park in the East End, in contrast, for the expressed purpose of ameliorating poverty there.[7] By 1891, Celtic FC had quickly established itself as one of the biggest crowd-pullers in British football, and were invited to play an Easter tour exhibition matches against English opposition, including Bolton Wanderers and FA Cup holders Blackburn Rovers. Sweeney finds that upon returning to Scotland:

> The Celts fulfilled a promise to Brother Walfrid to visit Saint Joseph's College in Dumfries, ran by the Marist Brothers. The annual College Sports Day finished on the Wednesday and who better than Celtic to close the meeting with a light hearted match against the College team.[8]

With Celtic players turning out for the St. Joseph's team comprised of past and present pupils, the match ended in a 3-3 draw.

> The college band led both teams on and off the field and an after match dinner was arranged in the College Refectory with speakers from both Celtic and St Joseph's giving thanks.[9]

Brother Walfrid, therefore, was instrumental in establishing a close connection between the Club he was foremost in establishing in 1887 and the flagship provincial school of the Marist Brothers in Dumfries.

The close connection with St. Joseph's endured – principally through former pupil Sir Robert Kelly who later became chairman of Celtic FC – long after Walfrid's short stay there in retirement.[10]

On 9th May 1910, Tom Maley delivered a lecture on the history of Celtic FC to the Marist Brothers and students of St. Joseph's College, just over two years before Brother Walfrid arrived there in ill health. Maley, brother of the Celtic manager Willie Maley, was introduced by William Kivlichan a former pupil at Dumfries and then player for the Glasgow side having left Rangers FC in 1907. Kivlichan held the rare distinction of having been a practising Catholic who played for Rangers in that era. The school annual describes how:

> Mr Maley lost no time in launching forth into his subject, and from start to finish there was not a dull moment. He showed how the Celtic Club, instituted in the beginning as a charity organisation by Brother Walfrid and a few friends, had grown by leaps and bounds to be the premier football team of Scotland, but at the same time they had never lost sight of the primary object for which they had been founded.[11]

Celtic had recently won an unprecedented sixth consecutive league championship and Maley's recounting of the Club's origins brought 'great bursts of applause from the pupils' over the course of a lecture which 'captivated the attention of one and all', including the senior Marist Brothers in attendance.[12] In this context, the transfer of an ailing Brother Walfrid – famed for his early connection to Celtic FC – to Dumfries in July, 1912 would have been experienced as a notable event for both the Brothers and, especially, the pupils based at St. Joseph's.

One such pupil attending St. Joseph's novitiate during Brother Walfrid's short period there was Joseph Patrick Robb, born on 1st March 1897. Thanks to the Robb family a private recording of a conversation taped in 1982 between Joseph Patrick Robb, his son Louis and grandson Andrew was made available for the research project on which this book is based. Joseph Patrick Robb, then aged 85, recalled his memories from his teenage years as a novice of the Marist Brothers spent in Dumfries, coinciding with Brother Walfrid's retirement there between 1912 and his passing in 1915. The recording offers a remarkable personal insight into Brother Walfrid's final years and is reproduced as an epilogue following this chapter.

As is vividly conveyed in Robb's 1982 recollection of his memories of Brother Walfrid in retirement, the Marist Brother's final three years in Dumfries were beset by health problems. To this end, Brother Gaetanus (Emile Van Ryckeghem, b. 1852) is listed in 'care of Bro Angelo + Walfrid' in the list of placements submitted to the General House in August of 1913.

In fulfilment of his vow of poverty, Brother Walfrid is recorded contributing substantially to an appeal made on behalf of the provincial council of the Marist Brothers in Britain and Ireland for a new novitiate fund designed to relieve the strain on Dumfries. The appeal was initiated by Brother James (Thomas McCann, b. 1844) in 1910, during his period in charge of the province, and aimed to raise £1,500 towards the purchase of the new property. The goal was achieved by December 1915, just months after Walfrid's death, when a new novitiate opened in Ballieborough in County Cavan, Ireland.[13] That Brother Walfrid, whilst effectively retired in his last years, gathered over £100 [several donations are listed on behalf of 'A Friend'] towards the total raised 'for the grand cause of Catholic Education' is testament to his historic association with charitable giving and reputation as a humanitarian.[14] The hastened establishment of Ballieborough – the first Marist Brothers novitiate of its kind in Ireland – is deemed a 'prudent measure' by Handley, owing to increasingly trying wartime conditions in Britain during the First World War.[15]

Against the backdrop of unprecedented casualties from the front, Brother Walfrid died at a quarter past six in the morning of 17th April, 1915 of a final cerebral haemorrhage.[16] Two prior episodes of stroke are also recorded by the doctor attending, one three years prior which forced his retirement to Dumfries as well as one occurring ten days before his death, as remembered by Joseph Patrick Robb.[17] Also present was Auguste Barton (Brother Killian), listed as an 'Intimate friend'. Born in the northern French commune of Wormhoudt in 1858, Brother Killian spent the bulk of his working life teaching French and carpentry at St. Joseph's, but also spent time under the directorship of Walfrid whilst engaged in the London schools of the Marist Brothers.[18] Having committed his earthly life in service to the Marist Brothers in 1886, it is right and proper that a fellow Brother accompanied Walfrid in his passing aged seventy-four.[19]

As was then customary for Marist Brothers who died at Dumfries, a humble funeral service took place in the college chapel on Monday 19th April, 1915.[20] Brother Conrad recalled 'that he was buried with a Celtic football jersey thrown on top of his coffin', in a distinguishing departure, for Brother Walfrid, from the normally simple funerals conducted for the Marist Brothers of the day.[21] A service for the repose of his soul was said at Sacred Heart, Glasgow in addition to requiem mass at St. Anne's, London.[22]

As fate would have it, Celtic FC – the Club so closely associated with the memory and legacy of Brother Walfrid – won the Scottish league championship on the same day that its Marist founder passed away.[23]

An obituary, titled 'Founder of Celtic F.C – Death of Rev. Brother Walfrid', carried by the *Glasgow Observer*, references those defining contributions and legacies of Walfrid's life in religion: in terms of education, community and football. It reads:

> Brother Walfrid has died. Glasgow Catholics, and particularly those of Bridgeton and Calton, will learn with profound regret of the death of their old and well-beloved friend, whose name was, and is, a household word in the East End, where for many years he did splendid work as a Marist. Some twenty-seven years ago he founded the Celtic Football Club, and to the end of his days he never lost interest in the doing of the Celts. Brother Walfrid, after being transferred from Glasgow, did excellent educational work in the South of England. In London his health broke down, and he came to the Marist house at Dumfries, where, after a prolonged illness, he passed away.[24]

Buried alongside fellow Marist Brothers in the cemetery attached to St. Joseph's in Dumfries, Walfrid's grave is marked in the same uniform and simple style as his confreres, save for the presence of an occasional green and white Celtic scarf recalling his connection to the football Club which distinguished him in life and in death. Celtic, of course, is the legacy with which Brother Walfrid remains indelibly associated, but his endeavours and achievements elsewhere in terms of service to religious education and charity further substantiate a far-reaching, impactful and symbolic life.

Notes

1 Taylor, M.G., *The Blue and Gold: St Joseph's College, Dumfries 1875 - 2000* (Glasgow: John S Burns 2000), p. 3.

2 *Bulletin of the Institute*, Vol. I, No. 6 (November, 1909), pp. 299-305. Chalmers, Br. C, 'Administrative History of Marist Brothers of Great Britain', information received from the General Archives of the Marist Brothers in Rome, 2018.

3 *Ibid.*

4 St Joseph's Commercial College annual (Dumfries: Currie & Co., 1890), p. 31.

5 *The Universe*, July 2nd 1887.

6 'Contributions to Marists' Novitiate, Dumfries [late 19th century]', GD517/2 held in the local archives of the Ewart Library, Dumfries.

7 Taylor, *The Blue and Gold: St Joseph's College, Dumfries 1875 - 2000*, p. 98.

8 *Glasgow Herald*, 29th May 1888, p. 11.

9 Sweeney, B., *Celtic, The Early Years: 1887-1892* (Scotland: CQN Books, 2015), p. 321.

10 *Ibid.*

11 Taylor, *The Blue and Gold: St Joseph's College, Dumfries 1875 - 2000*, p. 93.

12 St Joseph's Commercial College annual (Dumfries: Currie & Co., 1910), p. 63.

13 Chalmers, Br. C, 'Administrative History of Marist Brothers of Great Britain', information received from the General Archives of the Marist Brothers in Rome, 2018.

14 'Papers relating to novitiate fund at 'Mount St Michael's' (c. 1910-1916), held at the Scottish Catholic Archives, SCA/MB/8/5/9/2.

15 Handley, *A History of the Marist Brothers Province of the British Isles*, p. 148.

16 Microfiche of Brother Walfrid, No. 2998 held at the General Archive for The Institute of Marist Brothers, Rome.

17 'Statutory registers Deaths 821/ 206 (1915) Deaths in the District Dumfriesshire in the County of Dumfries', p. 69.

18 *Ibid.*

19 Parker, *Remembering the Marist Brothers*, p. 317.

20 Microfiche of Brother Walfrid, No. 2998 held at the General Archive for The Institute of Marist Brothers, Rome.

21 Taylor, *The Blue and Gold: St Joseph's College, Dumfries 1875 - 2000*, pp. 20, 48. *Glasgow Observer*, April 24th 1915.

22 Parker, *Remembering the Marist Brothers*, p. 113.

23 *Glasgow Star*, April 30th 1915.
1915 month's mind records (unarchived) held at the Roman Catholic Church of St Anne, Underwood Road, London.

24 *Glasgow Herald*, April 19th 1915. Celtic secured the league championship with a 3-1 victory over Third Lanark at Cathkin Park, Glasgow on Saturday the 17th of April 1915.

The 1982 recording of a conversation between Joseph Patrick Robb and his son Louis and grandson Andrew includes an interview granted to the author on a Zoom call under pandemic lockdown conditions in 2020. It begins with Joseph Patrick Robb, then aged 82, explaining his memories of Walfrid during his time as a teenaged pupil of the Marist Brothers at St. Joseph's College in Dumfries:

> Oh yes I knew Brother Walfrid
> and since, eh. . . his dying day
> I know now that he died,
> he must've died in 1916.

> Yes. Did you know that?

> About 1916 because I was still in Dumfries
> at the time myself.

> Where he was, and eh I was no longer in Dumfries.

> I went up to Glasgow in 1917.

> **But it was before that?**

> So he died before that so that's what
> makes me say 1916.

> **Yes**

> Now at the time I was 19 years of age
> and eh. . . Brother Walfrid had retired long before that.

> He had had a stroke, he was very badly paralysed.

> **Yes**

In fact I think he'd had two strokes by that time
and he was very badly paralysed all down one side.

And the picture I have of him is one arm in a sling
from around his neck just to hold that up.

And it was his right arm, no it was his left arm
paralysed down the left side.

But I also recall that he had a tremendous sense of
humour.

Under all these difficulties, because he wouldn't
use a stick, he wouldn't use anything!

Wherever he wanted to go he'd go there, struggle there
and if you happened to go over there or even just
to pass him by you would get one mighty thump
in the back or somewhere from the one arm
that was still his, but we had to dodge him.

[Laughter]

Had to dodge it, because it wasn't a tap!

You got, it was one good old thump.

And then he was so badly paralysed, you see,
the side of his face was also paralysed.

The appearance of his face, it was absolutely hideous,
it was all twisted to one side, you know.

But he was a tremendous character as I say,
full of beans, full of fun in spite of being so badly
handicapped.

The picture of Brother Walfrid which emerges from Joseph Patrick Robb's oral testimony is one of a strong-willed, resilient and physically imposing man who maintained his strength and complexity of character, along with a sense of humour, despite his advancing years and challenges relating to ill health. The original conversation also throws up notions surrounding Celtic's charitable origins as flowing from Brother Walfrid's guiding influences: faith, community and football.

Epilogue

Yes but he founded Celtic, that was 1887 wasn't it?

Yes well he must've been in Glasgow at that time

So that was before he went down to London?

Yes. . . and eh. . . what else can I say?

Was he still interested in the Celtic?

Yes, oh yes. He'd already know,
he got his telegram every Saturday.

Oh I remember you telling me that, that's right yes.

He got the telegram of the Saturday results.

They were telegrammed to him?

Whether it was a win, a draw or a lose,
he got his telegram at Dumfries, to the hotel.

To tell him the result?

And it was kept until the old man died.

That's tremendous.

But eh. . . that's about the limit of my knowledge of him. . .

**So how long were you at Dumfries, while he was there?
How long was this association?**

I would say about. . .

You went. . .

I would say. . . 3 years.

About 3 years yes?

I was transferred up to the Mount in Dumfries in 1913, August
and I was there until 1916, end of 1916.

So you were there when he died?

Oh yes, oh yes.

Walfrid

And was that quite a big event?

His death [Laughter] his death was one huge joke [Laughter]

Really?

Because what happened to him, eh. . . was
he got a third stroke which knocked him out.

He was completely unconscious.

There was no means of getting communication with him.

But he had a heart the size of a bell.

His heart kept going.

Yes?

You couldn't feed him.

Oh Lord, and he lay.

He had a wee room of his own, bed and a chair I suppose.

But I can see a picture in my own mind of his little room
and he lay, more or less, just on top, top of the bed,
with a sheet over him, and he snored and snored and snored.

Twenty-four hours a day, it was a steady [Imitates Snoring]

[Laughter]

Just like that, and that went on for the best part of eight days,
day and night. Poor. . .

Dear God!

Now the Brother Superiors at that time
and the Doctor concerned. . .
'oh yeah he won't last much longer'
'. . . give him another day, another day or two.'

And in the day or two extra that were being added on,
the undertakers were up at least three times
to take his measurements.

Epilogue

And he was still snoring them out.

[**Laughter**]

He was still snoring away.

And we were all young. At that time I told you I was about. . .

About 19?

About 19 and there were others the same age
and a bit younger perhaps.

He got no. . . nothing!

When he established himself there snoring,
people stopped going to see him.

There was nobody sitting at his bedside.

No?

To see. . . well I suppose there was at the beginning. . .

Yeah, yeah.

'Cos even the undertaker didn't know what was happening.

And in the end he just had that room to himself
and, God knows, we used to go in to try and waken him.

We didn't, you know, try to waken him by shaking him
but there was a coal fire and a coal scuttle.

Yes?

And we used to take the poker out, bang away at the scuttle
and that was to see if he was showing any signs of. . .

But no it was [Imitates Snoring]

And it went on and on
until at the end I think it was about the end of a week,
it was certainly a week at least,
he stopped. He stopped snoring.

              Yes.

And was his funeral quite a big event? I mean were there people. . . ?

I don't. . .

             Celtic?

From the Club?

No, I don't recall there was any special ceremony.

You would have it in mind, I suppose. . .

  I'm just wondering if representatives from the Club came down?

I don't recall any, eh. . . special service
as performed by the Celtic Club.

              No.
      It was during the war of course?

Yes, 1916, so it would be I suppose.

But he was a huge weight.

He was a tall man to start with
then all the extra weight he put on
because his appetite was alright.

             Yeah.

He was a very heavy man in the end.

          Well there you are!
    Andrew [grandson] couldn't believe it when I told him. . .

Oh no, he was the founder of the Celtic Football Club.

He founded the Club for the benefit of the poor of Parkhead.

      That's right yeah, around the Gallowgate district.

And, eh. . . the Celtic Football Club ever since
its foundation has been.

Epilogue

The Club is run as
a good first-class Club should be run
with a good ground and facilities and fans. . .

The conversation between members of the Robb family demonstrates an awareness of the charitable, religious origins of Celtic FC, especially as regards the role of Brother Walfrid at its outset. The fact that J.P. Robb recalls Walfrid receiving telegrammed results from the Club in Glasgow offers a fascinating testament to the then-retired and elderly Marist Brother's continued interest in, and keen fondness for, the Club, as well as an awareness of his own role in its historical development. Following email contact and gathering of the requisite ethical permissions, a follow-up interview was recorded as part of this research project on 31st August 2020 with Louis and Andrew Robb, son and grandson of Joseph Patrick respectively, who both feature in the original 1982 tape recording.

Further biographical details emerged which shed light on some details recollected by their relative, lending further credence to the validity and originality of the transcribed source material. The recent conversation conveys aspects of Brother Walfrid's legacy through the prism of generational support for Celtic FC and its cultural significance to the Irish Catholic diaspora in Scotland.

Do you know if your father was aware of, or would he have been aware of who Brother Walfrid was prior to his arrival in Dumfries?

Louis – Oh yes, oh definitely. Yes I would think Brother Walfrid was discussed frequently you know, at Dumfries. When did you say he came back there, up from London?

MC – It would have been late 1912.

Louis – Yeah, oh my father would have been definitely, my father he was very, very conscious of the Celtic connection all of his life. I'm sure he would then. . .

MC – As a young boy growing up?

Louis – By then, I mean, Celtic was becoming quite a notable
feature on the Scottish football scene. So Brother Walfrid's
Celtic connection would have been a prime topic of
conversation.

Andrew – I'm fairly sure, Michael. You'll know as well, were the
Celtic team not taken down to London on a charity tour and
met Walfrid in London and you know, he was recognised very
much for his, at a very early stage, for his part in founding the
Club? So I think you're bound to be right, Dad, your father
would certainly have no doubt known how significant this
man was.

Louis – Oh no question about that.

Andrew – and as you say growing up as a Catholic family in
Dundee in difficult circumstances then Celtic would have
been your football team, kind of default option. Correct me if
I'm wrong.

**When did you Louis and yourself Andrew, when did you first
become aware prior to recording the conversation with
your Dad, of Joseph's association with Brother Walfrid in his
younger years?**

Louis – It's impossible for me to say what age I was when I first
became aware of that. I mean I first saw Celtic in 1946
straight after the war, Celtic was a team. . . I was certainly
aware of it before that. When precisely I became aware of it
I'm really not quite sure. Football was always a great topic of
conversation in the house.

MC – So it was something your Dad would certainly have
mentioned before?

Louis – Oh I'm sure, I'm sure yes. Including his life with the
Marists and so on, yes we were all very aware, very aware of
that. But I can't really put, say what age I was I first became
aware.

Andrew – Yeah for me it was early 1970s when I started to become
interested in Celtic and I would have been told before then

but it was a fairly constant piece of family history there was a connection going back. I've got a boy of my own who likes football and he was told when he was very young so it's clearly the line is going on, so it's when you're old enough to stand and try and kick a ball that's when you were told. I think I knew around the age of 8 when I went to my first game that this was something more than just an outing.

The follow-up interview with Louis and Andrew Robb built on understanding the circumstances surrounding the original 1982 taped conversation. In terms of setting, with the original, informal conversation recorded in familiar surroundings by close relatives for private use, what emerges is an authentic recollection of memories relayed in a candid fashion. By revisiting and engaging with the conversation decades later, Louis and Andrew Robb echo and expand upon key themes which emerged such as the immigrant origins of the Irish Catholic community in Dundee, sense of familial duty and the significance of education as a route out of poverty.

1) So my next question was kind of linked to that idea of growing up and football, your formative years. So why do you think Joseph Robb decided to pursue an education with the Marists at St. Joseph's at Dumfries?

Louis – Well I wouldn't think he chose at all. He would've been told you know, that was what was gonna happen. He was subject to rules there and they probably singled him out as somebody who you know had the necessary intellectual, brain qualities to be worth putting through as a teacher. But I don't think it would have been something that he debated with them; he would have been told what was going to happen.

MC – So this capacity or potential to go on and be able to complete an education at Dumfries, this would have been noted in his education in Dundee?

Louis – Oh yes I'm sure, yeah. Of course, yeah.

Andrew – He was one of quite a large family wasn't he, Dad? If you remind me how many brothers and sisters he had. . . I daresay if there was opportunities to have education they would have been if not limited, then valued highly.

Louis – My father was the only one, he came from a large working class Catholic family in Dundee – two brothers Tom and Gus who lived quite long lives, Aunt Liz who was my favourite aunt and there were two aunts who became nuns with the Little Sisters of the Poor and there were at least another two children who died in infancy. So it was a big, a big family. I have no doubt they were a clever family too although my father was the only one who benefited from a real education.

2) From your own memory what other key recollections or memories would your Grandad talk about in terms of anything linked to those years in Dumfries or his memories of Brother Walfrid himself?

Andrew – He was pretty reticent about talking about Celtic or football by the time I knew him. He had more kind of day to day concerns in terms of what was on the television or the newspapers. In some way I remember going to his flat in Dundee and thinking. 'Is he definitely going to talk about this?' and, you know, without him feeling a bit too on the spot. He was quite an elderly gent by this stage and he was completely switched on. In case we all needed to ask he knew exactly what was going on, but he was setting the agenda as to what he talked about. I think we got as a full a story of Walfrid as we heard on any other occasion.

Andrew – did your father ever talk about the Order's view of Brother Walfrid?

Louis – I don't recall any such discussions but I can't imagine they did not, you know even at that time Celtic were very much a notable professional football team by that time. I'm quite sure that would have been a regular topic of discussion – you know the fact that Brother Walfrid was the guy who kicked the whole thing off.

Andrew – did your Dad talk about Brother Walfrid, I was just saying to Michael before I recall this being the first time I remember your father talking about Brother Walfrid, and really he must have done before?

Louis – it would have been talked about from time to time but, you know, he had other concerns. It was certainly a topic of conversation from time to time and it was something we were all very, very aware of.

For both interviewees, the memories of Walfrid and Celtic FC evoked by the recorded conversation with their relative produced a conscious connection with those themes of faith, immigration, education and football which endure as emblematic features of the life of Brother Walfrid. On the personhood and interests of Walfrid as an individual, the informal interview threw up some elucidating new perspectives on a lesser-known period of his life.

MC – one of the really interesting parts of the conversation I found was your father remembers Brother Walfrid receiving the telegram with the Celtic results on a Saturday and his voice really comes alive there in that he really vividly remembers that happening. That's something I found really fascinating anyway. . .

Louis – That was a lovely little nugget that, really. And bearing in mind how difficult communication was at that time. Virtually no telephone, most people just. . . the normal communication would have been by post, you know, sending a letter. Telegram, you know, were probably quite expensive I would think.

MC – Your Dad explains that the telegrams were sent to the hotel in Dumfries, so I'm thinking that someone would have been sent to, you know, fetch the results?

Louis – Well, that's right, yes of course. I'd forgotten that detail, it wouldn't even have been delivered to the college.

MC – He also goes on to speak in quite, you know, real detail about the final days, the final week of Brother Walfrid's life.

How he basically had a third and final stroke which, in his words, knocked him unconscious so he was more or less, he was on his deathbed for a week in a room on his own. But interestingly your father recalls that the younger Brothers in particular of whom he would have been one, took the time to go and visit Brother Walfrid. What do you think that says about their view of Brother Walfrid?

Louis – Well I think it says more about the life of total boredom in Dumfries at that time, you know that any kind of diversion was welcome.

Andrew – I think if you're a young man or boy coming to the Order it sounds as if that was someone you wanted to say you had seen or to have seen. It must have been a tie with the Club for that, for what he had done with the Club before. But not just in football terms creating a Club, but for those purposes to have started a football club.

MC – And your Dad talks about this – something that Celtic's charitable status, perhaps not quite so strong these days, but at the time that was a remarkable feature of it and he had raised a lot of money for charities.

Louis – That's right, well that was the whole purpose of the Club's formation.

Andrew – He'd have been famous for this as well.

MC – You certainly get the sense or the idea that for the younger novices Brother Walfrid was some kind of celebrity. . .

Louis – Oh yeah, oh I'm sure. I can't imagine. . . and he was obviously quite a formidable personality in his own right. You know 'a big man'. With quite a very substantial presence.

MC – So just overall, in terms of. . . what sense did you get from your father that his experience in Dumfries with the Marist Brothers and Brother Walfrid especially, how impactful did you get the sense that those years were for your father Joseph?

Louis – Oh they were absolutely critical, critical years for him and he never ever forgot how much he owed to the Marists for in a sense giving him an education he never would have had otherwise. Had it not been for that, as a young boy in Dundee he'd have gone into the jute mills at age 14, as his two brothers did and that would have been the life for him. He was given a wonderful education at Glasgow University and, you know, went on to enter the professions. . . so he owed everything to them. And he never ever forgot that debt.

MC – And Andrew, so I suppose my question to you would be from your memories of your Grandad, you've gone on to become a solicitor, did you get the sense that education was something really important to your Grandad and the family in general growing up?

Andrew – Yeah Michael, no doubt about it. It's this interlinking of different branches of life that struck me, or strikes me looking back – that it's not just about Celtic Football Club, or Dundee, but the coming together of his religious faith with football, his fairly austere upbringing in a tough environment in Dundee and where he came from, all of these strands came together and certainly, Dad, I know you and your brothers were always encouraged in education and you never got the feeling that you were going to be getting a great deal in life all that easily, I would imagine. I don't mean that in any kind of unpleasant way, but you know it's these various strands coming together that I think were significant for him because with Celtic and Brother Walfrid it was certainly to do with the idea that Celtic was putting back into the community and had been raised for specific purposes, and linking that also to the very hard upbringing that he and his forebears had had in Dundee and coming over from Ireland. So it was all of these strands coming together, I can look back and pick up on now being a little bit more older, more able to understand.

The simple gravestone at St. Joseph's College is often
adorned with green and white Celtic scarves.

Legacy

Andrew Kerins [Brother Walfrid] was one of the most significant Irish immigrants to Scotland, an outstanding individual in relation to Catholic education and charity in Glasgow and a major contributor to the emergence of organised sport in Scotland in the late nineteenth century. Andrew Kerins was but one individual, amongst countless thousands of victims, who survived the catastrophe of *An Gorta Mor* in Ireland, only to be forced to leave behind family, community and homeland in the hope of finding a better life overseas. Over one million others perished owing to the prevalence of starvation and disease during Ireland's darkest period of its history. Kerins left for Glasgow as a fifteen-year-old boy and the spectre of hunger, accompanied by a concern for the spiritual and physical well-being of others, are motifs which endured throughout his long and impactful life.

Walfrid's achievements in life reflect his origins in famished Ireland, as well as the three major themes which motivated his most memorable actions in life thereafter with the Marist Brothers, namely, his Catholic faith, community-based charitable action alongside a close and enduring association with football, and Celtic Football Club in particular. He played a leading role in originally founding Celtic in order to support the impoverished Irish Catholic diaspora in Glasgow.

The meaningfulness of the Club with regard to its historic supporting community has been analysed by others in a modern context.[1] A fuller consideration of the exact role and function Brother Walfrid performed in the embryonic stage of Celtic's existence, however, has not been achieved until now. The period between the founding of Celtic FC in 1887 and Walfrid's departure for London, in accordance with the requirements of the Marist Brothers at the time, has been reappraised and sheds new light on the understanding of the totemic role he played.[2]

Newspaper reports, new primary source evidence and reminiscences of contemporaries found through the research for this book demonstrate that Walfrid was integral to the instillation of the distinctive charitable, Irish and Catholic identities of Celtic at birth, and for which it remains known to the present day. His departure was keenly felt by the community he served in Glasgow, a fact reflected in the letters published in the newspapers of the day focusing on the original charitable function that Walfrid envisaged for the Club.

For many, the memory of Brother Walfrid continues to embody the ideal of charity, and a responsibility on the part of the Club to maintain that original vision, up to the present day. In addition, Walfrid retained an enduring association and affection for Celtic until his dying day. In journeying to London in 1911 to meet with Club officials in his eighth decade, he displays an awareness of his place in its history and a continued concern for its progress. Similarly, in arranging for weekly telegrams to Dumfries to inform of the Celtic match results, it has been evidenced that contact was maintained between Club and spiritual founder, demonstrating how that awareness and concern was reciprocated. The enduring legacy of Walfrid – in terms of sporting charity – reflects his motivations and achievements in life.

Brother Walfrid's unwavering religious faith is one enduring theme and the outstanding characteristic of his life. The notion of a 'Devotional Revolution' occurring in Ireland in the immediate aftermath of *An Gorta Mor* is utilised to understand and exemplify the subsequent achievements of Walfrid.[3] In the individual life of Brother Walfrid, commitment to Catholic education with the Marist Brothers, pride in his Irishness and a concern for the welfare of the poor and hungry, especially children, are evidenced in each chapter of this critical biography. These motivating factors typified his own response to the trauma of *An Gorta Mor* experienced in his formative years.

New information uncovered demonstrates the centrality of his childhood to the formation of his character, sense of social justice and the choices he made later in life. As a refugee of the Great Hunger and immigrant to Britain, the life of Brother Walfrid is both reflective and illustrative of the reinvigoration of the Catholic faith witnessed in Ireland in the years which followed.[4] His strength of faith, in terms of devoting his life to Catholic educational service as a Marist Brother, living out his religious vow of poverty through charitable works, can be traced back to his upbringing in County Sligo.

By researching and analysing the genealogy of the Kerins family – who agreed to participate in the research project – new light is shone on the familial origins of Brother Walfrid. For the young Andrew Kerins, privations engendered by the humanitarian disaster in Ireland caused his hasty exile from Ireland, away from his immediate family and wider community. As a bilingual speaker of both Irish and English, education evidently offered a path forward in life for Kerins and, together with his Catholic faith, contributed to his decision as a young man to first engage in evening classes with the Marist Brothers in Glasgow.

Aspinwall evoked the idea of 'Portable Utopia' in terms of how ideals such as voluntarism, self-help, social responsibility and charity carry a universal potential.[5] For Walfrid, these values characterise his subsequent itinerant career as a Catholic teaching Brother. His faith and passion for education, forged amidst the most challenging of circumstances in Ireland, proved truly 'portable', demonstrated by his achievements working in diverse religious communities in Scotland, France and England.

The historic Irish tradition of primogeniture dictated that, as second-born son in the Kerins family, he, like many young Irish male contemporaries from a rural upbringing, was forced overseas and away from the land which could no longer sustain him. Records of the Beaucamps register in France show that a majority of his contemporaries who joined the Marist Brothers shared similar origins in Ireland.

Mastery of the French language, evidenced in his later career teaching English to French postulants at Grove Ferry, along with his native Irish and English, illustrates the picture of a worldly individual far-removed from his humble roots. Those Irish roots, however, served as the source and foundation for the faith which came to inspire the humanitarian work which defines him.

The lived experience of individual male religious, including Marist Brothers like Walfrid, has thus far been under-researched in the historiography of Catholic education in Britain. In light of the centenary anniversary of the Education (Scotland) Act of 1918, this research contributes to reconsideration of the roles played by religious orders in a general sense, in an age when state funding was minimal.[6]

The willingness of Marist Brothers, such as Walfrid, to live out their vows of poverty – labouring under difficult and poorly-compensated conditions – has been discussed in a general sense in the biography. A more focussed consideration, however, of the individual lives of male religious has been called for, as a means of understanding more closely the ways in which the sometimes difficult experience of life in communities was negotiated.[7] In this sense, this critical biography of Brother Walfrid's life – including struggles as well as achievements – offers a fresh perspective on the impact and legacy of the Marist Brothers in terms of their role in the education of the multi-generational Irish Catholic diaspora. Walfrid's negotiation of religious life in diverse Marist communities in England in later life, as a senior Brother, provides supplementary evidence of his ability to adapt and respond to the requirements of different contexts.

Within the historiography, this Irish Catholic diaspora community is often described as ghettoised or insular in outlook. Walfrid's faith, indeed, is rooted in his Irishness but through his formation as a Marist Brother in Beaucamps and charitable actions as a member of the Saint Vincent de Paul Society, a somewhat overlooked French influence on the re-emergence of Catholicism in post-Reformation Britain during the nineteenth century is exemplified.

Similarly, it has been shown that the Irish Catholic communities Brother Walfrid operated in, whether in Glasgow or later in London, were found to be outward-looking both in terms of their awareness of causes distinct from their own faith or ethnic origin, as well as their motivation to raise funds in aid of such issues. Brother Walfrid's involvement in raising monies for people suffering amid a series of famines in colonised India, whilst based in London in early 1897, is one significant example of this.

Owing to his religious attire of black cassock and white habit, Brother Walfrid has often been misunderstood and popularly misrepresented as a Catholic priest, cleric or preacher. In reality he was none of these. Travelling to France as a religious postulant, Walfrid took vows of chastity, obedience and poverty, in much the same way as Catholic priests do. In taking the habit of the Marist Brother, Kerins chose, however, to devote his adult life to the teaching profession as a Catholic educator engaged in the teaching of young boys, often from deprived backgrounds. A far-travelled career followed, taking Walfrid from teaching posts in Glasgow to France, England and to his final resting place in Dumfries, Scotland. His dedication and aptitude as a Marist Brother are evidenced by his elevation to positions of seniority over the course of over half a century served in community with his fellow confreres.

In terms of Brother Walfrid's interior life, the few surviving handwritten sources offer an insight into what factors motivated the Marist Brother. By analysing examples uncovered and collected though archival research, closer insight into his personal character is offered and a more complex and nuanced picture of Brother Walfrid is produced.

Concern for the spiritual and physical welfare of children is one consistent feature of the surviving letters written by Walfrid. Whether appealing for the assistance of those in the upper echelons of society, such as the Marquess of Bute, or in simple notes to his Marist colleagues, the welfare of the 'poor children' remains at the forefront of Brother Walfrid's mind. This contrasts with reminiscences of some former pupils and contemporaries who recall a sometime-brusque, quick-tempered and resolute individual who prized discipline in the classroom.

Chiefly, however, Walfrid is recalled fondly by those who knew him personally, and the picture which emerges is one of a warm, kind and idiosyncratic character who maintained an active sense of humour until the end. His humanity is conveyed in his own writing, as well as secondary accounts and oral testimony. Thus, what is certain and evidenced by his letters of appeal and continuing engagement in works of charity, is that Walfrid, above all, was a man of practicality and action.

The most recognisable and enduring of these works came, of course, in 1887 as he played a leading role in organising the foundation of Celtic FC in Glasgow. Those contemporaries who worked alongside him to establish Celtic FC hold him as the main stimulator and organising force behind its creation in 1887. Thus, he is celebrated by the Club as its 'Founding Father' to the present day.

Celtic carries the distinction of having been originally formed with the expressed aim of raising monies for the maintenance of the school feeding programme Walfrid set up with the assistance of Brother Dorotheus – The Poor Children's Dinner Table. In this sense the origin of Celtic reflects the Marist charism of charity. As a senior and leading member of the original group of Irish Catholics engaged in the beginnings of the Club, Brother Walfrid has come to be recognised as the founder who did most to imbue Celtic with a distinct Irish, Catholic and charitable identity with which it remains associated for many to this day.

The statues which memorialise him, in both his birthplace of Ballymote and outside the stadium at Celtic Park, make explicit reference to his role in the charitable foundation of Celtic FC. To this end, the work of the Celtic FC Foundation, in recent years, has sought to continue Walfrid's legacy of 'Football for Good' in an official recognition of his role. A focus on charity has endured in varying forms and degrees since its inception. The Celtic FC Foundation – the charitable arm of the Club – rightly remembers Brother Walfrid as the originator of the Club's charitable function.[8]

Charity 'Sleep Out' events were held by the Foundation in November and December 2021 at Celtic Park in Glasgow, in the grounds of Walfrid's former parish school in London and, for the first time, in his birthplace of Ballymote in County Sligo, where a statue featuring his likeness and the crest of Celtic FC was unveiled in 2004.[9] The choice of sites key to Walfrid's lived experience is significant in evoking his far-reaching and ongoing charitable legacy. Since 1996, the charitable function of Celtic FC has raised in excess of seven million pounds: fitting tribute to the original purpose Brother Walfrid envisaged for the Club.[10]

Canon Tom White, parish priest of St. Mary's Catholic church in Glasgow where Brother Walfrid convened the meeting to found Celtic FC in 1887, has raised the case for Walfrid to be considered for sainthood. As an 'apostle for the poor' who endeavoured to alleviate poverty alongside his duties as a Catholic educationalist, the late Archbishop Tartaglia also lent support for beginning to reappraise Brother Walfrid's achievements in this vein.[11]

Brother Walfrid's life is of historical significance primarily because of the way his memory – a product of his achievements in life – continues to evoke the concept of charity and inspire similar endeavours to the present day. His life's work was remembered in 2019, fittingly at his final resting place – the cemetery of the Marist Brothers in Dumfries. At the installation and blessing of commemorative stones in June 2019, the following prayer was recited:

> We gather here today, During the week of the celebration of the life of St. Marcellin Champagnat, Founder of the Marist Brothers,
>
> To install and bless these stones which commemorate the lives of the Brothers of the Province of Britain and Ireland, many of whom are buried in this cemetery.
>
> In particular we commemorate the life of Brother Walfrid, Founder of Celtic Football Club,
>
> Whose life and ministry exemplify the dedication and values of the followers of St. Marcellin.[12]

Notes

1 *Glasgow Observer*, April 24th 1915.

2 Bradley, J.M, *Celtic Minded: Essays on Religion, Politics, Society, Identity and Football* (Argyll: Argyll Publishing, 2004).

3 Finn, G.,"Racism, Religion and Social Prejudice: Irish Catholic Clubs, Soccer and Scottish Society - II Social Identities and Conspiracy Theories', *The International Journal of the History of Sport*, Vol. 8, No. 3 (1991), p. 388.

4 Allen, N., 'Kerins, Andrew (Brother Walfrid)' available online at https://www.dib.ie/biography/kerins-andrew-brother-walfrid-a4519 accessed December 2021.

5 *Ibid.*

6 Aspinwall, B., *Portable Utopia: Glasgow and the United States 1820-1920*, pp. 185-186.

7 McKinney, S.J. and McCluskey, R., *A History of Catholic Education and Schooling in Scotland: New Perspectives* (London: Palgrave Macmillan, 2019).

8 O'Donoghue, T., 'The Role of Male Religious Orders in Education in Scotland in the Decades Leading up to the Education (Scotland) Act, 1918', in McKinney, S.J. and McCluskey, R., *A History of Catholic Education and Schooling in Scotland: New Perspectives* (London: Palgrave Macmillan, 2019), p. 98.

9 Available online at https://charity.celticfc.com/brother-walfrid/ accessed November 2021.
Active fund-raising appeals - such as 'Walfrid's Wish' and the 'Founding Fathers' Fast' - feature his name and image.

10 Available online at https://charity.celticfc.com/news/ accessed December 2021.

11 Available online at https://www.celticfc.com/celtic-fc-foundation accessed December 2021.

12 Available online at https://www.stir.ac.uk/news/2017/10/new-study-into-celtic-fc-founder-brother-walfrid accessed September 2021.

Walfrid

APPENDIX A: Celtic FC Circular (1888)

CELTIC FOOTBALL AND ATHLETIC CLUB
CELTIC PARK, PARKHEAD
(Corner of Dalmarnock and Janefield Streets)

Patrons
His Grace the Archbishop of Glasgow
and the Clergy of St. Mary's, Sacred Heart
and St. Michael's Missions, and the principle Catholic
laymen of the East End

The above club was formed in November 1887
by a number of the Catholics of the East End of the City.

The main objective of the club is to supply the East End
conferences of the St. Vincent De Paul Society with funds for
the maintenence of the 'Dinner Tables' of our needy children
in the Missions of St. Mary's, Sacred Heart, and St. Michael's.
Many cases of sheer poverty are left unaided through lack of
means. It is therefore with this principle object that we have
set afloat the 'Celtic', and we invite you as one of our ever-
ready friends to assist in putting our new Park in proper
working order for the coming football season.

We have already several of the leading Catholic football
players of the West of Scotland on our membership list. They
have most thoughtfully offered to assist in the good work.

We are fully aware that the 'elite' of football players belong to
this City and suburbs, and we know that from there we can
select a team which will be able to do credit to the Catholics of
the West of Scotland as the Hibernians have been doing in the
East.

Again, there is also the desire to have a large recreation
ground where our Catholic young men will be able to enjoy
the various sports which will build them up physically, and we
feel sure we will have many supporters with us in this
laudable object.

APPENDIX B: BROTHER WALFRID LETTER OF APPEAL (1885)

Sacred Heart Boys' School
42 Old Dalmarnock Rd.,
Glasgow

26 Oct. 1885

My Lord Marquis,

I trust your Lordship will pardon my troubling you once more.

I presume you are aware of the depressed state of Trade in and around the City just now. Nearly a year ago, with the kind assistance of the Brotherhood of St. Vin. de Paul, we were enabled to put into shape the 'Penny Dinner' system, in a Room adjoining the School. Since then, we have been giving a good bowl of Soup and a slice of Bread for a penny, and when the parents send bread with the children they can have the soup for a halfpenny.

This did well enough as long as they could patronize it and till our funds went down. There are also about 150 adults, who have, I may safely say, almost nothing to subsist on, and who receive daily, what the Society of St. Vin. de Paul can afford to give them.

I know the Society have very little money on hand, and I am therefore not inclined to ask their ever ready assistance, for our poor children just now. Hence I am compelled to apply, to those who are always willing to assist the Poor and the Orphan, for some help.

Therefore my reasons for encroaching on your Lordship's generosity.

I may state that since the 'Dinners' were started, last January, our school attendance has gone up considerably.

By accident, I came across some poor children last week who had not tasted a morsel for days, except what they received from us gratis, during school hours.

We are about to try and give the needy children, such as those mentioned last, a breakfast of Porridge and Milk daily till Trade becomes brisker and the severity of the Winter has passed by.

Trusting Your Lordship will take a favourable view of the matter.

I am, My Lord Marquis,
Yours most respectfully, Br. Walfrid

Sacred Heart Boys' School,
42 Old Dalmarnock Rd.,
Glasgow.
26th Oct. 1885.

My Lord Marquis,
I trust your
Lordship will pardon my
troubling you once more.
I presume you are aware of
the depressed state of Trade
in and around the City just now.
Nearly a year ago, with the
kind assistance of the Brotherhood
of St. Vin. de Paul, we were
enabled to put into shape the
'Penny Dinner' system, in a

Room adjoining the School.
Since then, we have been giving
a good bowl of Soup and a
slice of Bread for a penny,
and when the parents send
bread with the children they
can have the soup for a halfpenny.
This did well enough as long
as they could patronize it and
till our funds went down.
There are also about 150 adults,
who have, I may safely say,
almost nothing to subsist on,
and who receive daily, what the
Society of St. Vin. de Paul can
afford to give them.
I know the Society have very
little money on hand, and
I am therefore not inclined to

ask their, ever ready assistance,
for our poor children just now.
Hence I am compelled to apply,
to those who are always willing
to assist the Poor and the Orphan,
for some help.

Herefore my reasons for
encroaching on your Lordship's
generosity.

I may state that that since the
'Dinners' were started, last January,
our school attendance has gone
up considerably.

By accident, I came across some
poor children last week who had
not tasted a morsel for days,
except what they received from
us gratis, during school hours.

We are about to try and

give the needy children, such as those mentioned last, a breakfast of Porridge and Milk daily till Trade becomes brisker and the severity of the Winter has passed by.

Trusting Your Lordship will take a favourable view of the matter,

I am,

My Lord Marquis,

Yours most respectfully,

Br. Walfrid.

APPENDIX C: Summary of Research Dissemination

Publications

'Searching for Brother Walfrid: Faith, Community and Football', published online by the Irish Diaspora History Network in August 2018.

'Searching for Brother Walfrid: Faith, Community and Football', published online by Catholic Heritage in November 2019.

Conference papers

'Searching for Brother Walfrid: Faith, Community and Football', a presentation given at the 'Sporting Heritage' conference held at Hampden Park, Glasgow in February 2018.

'Searching for Brother Walfrid', a presentation given online for the 8th Annual Education Studies PGR Conference hosted by Warwick University in April 2021.

Public Engagement

'Brother Walfrid – The Bhoy from Sligo', a talk given online on behalf of the Irish Diaspora in Scotland Association as part of the St. Patrick's Day festival in March 2020.

APPENDIX D: BIBLIOGRAPHY

Secondary Sources

Anderson, B., *Imagined Communities: Reflections on the Origin and Spread of Nationalism* (London: Verso, 1983)

Aspinwall, B., 'A Glasgow Pastoral Plan, 1855-1860: Social and Spiritual Renewal', *The Innes Review*, Vol. 35, No. 1 (Spring, 1984), pp. 33-36.

Aspinwall, B., 'Catholic Teachers for Scotland: the Liverpool Connection', *The Innes Review*, Vol. 45, No. 1 (1994), pp. 47-70.

Aspinwall, B., 'Children of the Dead End: the Formation of the Modern Archdiocese of Glasgow, 1815-1914', *The Innes Review*, Vol. 43, No. 2 (Autumn, 1992) pp. 119- 144.

Aspinwall, B., 'Popery in Scotland: Image and Reality, 1820-1920', *Scottish Church History Society* (1986), pp. 235-257.

Aspinwall, B., *Portable Utopia: Glasgow and the United States 1820-1920* (Aberdeen: Aberdeen University Press, 1984)

Aspinwall, B., 'Some Aspects of Scotland and the Catholic Revival in the Early Nineteenth Century', *The Innes Review*, Vol. 26, No. 1 (Spring, 1975), pp. 3-19.

Aspinwall, B., 'The Child as Maker of the Ultramone', *Studies in Church History*, Vol. 31 (1994), pp. 427-445.

Aspinwall, B., 'The Scottish Dimension: Robert Monteith and the Origins of Modern British Catholic Social Thought', *The Downside Review*, Vol. 97, No. 326 (Jan., 1979), pp. 46-68.

Aspinwall, B., 'The Welfare State within the Welfare State: The Saint Vincent de Paul Society in Glasgow, 1848-1920', *Studies in Church History*, Vol. 23, (1986), pp. 445-459.

Barr, C., *Ireland's Empire: The Roman Catholic Church in the English-Speaking World, 1829-1914* (Cambridge: Cambridge University Press, 2019)

Beck, G.A. (Ed.), *The English Catholics, 1850-1950: Essays to commemorate the centenary of the restoration of the Hierarchy of England and Wales* (London: Burnes Oates, 1950)

Benton, M., 'The Aesthetics of Biography – And What It Teaches', *The Journal of Aesthetic Education*, Vol. 49, No. 1 (Spring, 2015), pp. 1-19.

Blum, M., Colvin, C. and McLaughlin, E., 'Scarring and Selection in the Great Irish Famine' (May, 2018), Available at http://www.quceh.org.uk/uploads/1/0/5/5/10558478/wp17-08.pdf, pp. 27-28.

Appendices

Boyce, G.D. and O'Day, A., *The Making of Modern Irish History: Revisionism and The Revisionist Controversy* (London: Routledge, 1996)

Boylan, D.M., 'Centenary of the St. Vincent de Paul Society', *An Irish Quarterly Review*, Vol. 22, No. 86 (June, 1933), pp. 313-320.

Boyle, M., *Metropolitan Anxieties: On the Meaning of the Irish Catholic Adventure in Scotland* (Surrey: Ashgate, 2011)

Bradley, J.M, *Celtic Minded: Essays on Religion, Politics, Society, Identity... and Football* (Argyll: Argyll Publishing, 2004)

Bradley, J.M., *Ethnic and Religious Identity in Modern Scotland: Culture, politics and football* (Aldershot: Avebury, 1995)

Bradley, J.M., 'Football in Scotland: a history of political and ethnic identity', *The International Journal of the History of Sport*, Vol. 12, No. 1 (1995), pp. 81-98.

Bradley, J.M., 'Sport and the contestation of cultural and ethnic identities in Scottish society', *Immigrants & Minorities*, Vol. 17, No. 1 (1998), pp. 127-150.

Brown, S.J., ''Outside the Covenant': The Scottish Presbyterian Churches and Irish Immigration, 1922-1938', *The Innes Review*, Vol. 42, No. 1 (Spring, 1991), pp. 19- 45.

Cahill, A.E., 'Moran, Patrick Francis (1830-1911)', *Australian Dictionary of Biography*, Vol. 10 (1986) accessed online on 1st February 2018.

Canning, Rev. B.J., *Irish-Born Secular Priests in Scotland 1829-1979* (Inverness: Bookmag, 1979).

Carey, H.M., 'Book Review: Rome in Australia. The Papacy and Conflict in the Australian Catholic Missions, 1834-1884 by Christopher Dowd', *Church History and Religious Culture*, Vol. 91, No. 1-2, (2011), pp. 281-309.

Celtic Graves Society, 'In Memory of the Founding Fathers of Celtic Football Club' (2013).

Chalmers, Br. C, 'Administrative History of Marist Brothers of Great Britain', information received from the General Archives of the Marist Brothers in Rome, 2018.

Checkland, O., *Philanthropy in Victorian Scotland: Social Welfare and the Voluntary Principle* (Edinburgh: John Donald Publishers, 1980).

Checkland, S.G., *The Upas Tree: Glasgow 1875-1975. . . and after 1975-1980* (Glasgow: University Press, 1981).

Cohen, G., 'Missing, biased and unrepresentativeness: the qualitative analysis of multisource biographical data', *Historical Methods*, Vol. 34, No. 4 (2002), pp. 166-176.

Collins, B., 'Early evidence of Irish immigration to Scotland: a note on a Catholic parish register', *Local Population Studies*, Vol. 32 (1984), pp. 28-33.

Collins, B., 'The Origins of Irish Immigration to Scotland in the Nineteenth and Twentieth Centuries', in Devine, T.M. (et al), *Irish Immigrants and Scottish Society in the Nineteenth and Twentieth Centuries* (Edinburgh: John Donald Publishers, 1991)

Cooper, S.E., 'Irish migrant identities and community life in Melbourne and Chicago, 1840-1890' (Edinburgh University thesis submitted November 2017, as yet unpublished)

County Sligo INTO Millennium Committee, *The National Schools of County Sligo* (Sligo: Carrick Print, 2000)

Cousens, S.H., 'The Regional Pattern of Emigration during the Great Irish Famine, 1846- 51', *Transactions and Papers (Institute of British Geographers)*, No. 28 (1960), pp. 119-134.

Crowley, J., Smyth, W. J. and Murphy, M., (eds), *Atlas of the Great Irish Famine* (Cork: University Press, 2012).

Cummins, N., and O'Grada, C., 'On the Structure of Wealth-Holding in Pre-Famine Ireland', *Irish Economic and Social History* (Feb, 2021), pp. 1-27.

Daly, M., 'Revisionism and Irish History: The Great Famine', in Boyce, G.D. and O'Day, A., *The Making of Modern Irish History: Revisionism and The Revisionist Controversy* (London: Routledge, 1996).

Danaher, N., 'Irish Studies: A Historical Survey across the Irish Diaspora', in O'Sullivan, P. (et al), *Volume Two: The Irish in The New Communities* (Leicester: Leicester University Press, 1992).

Darragh, J., 'James Edmund Handley, 1900-1971, *The Innes Review*, Vol. 22, No. 1 (1971), pp. 2-5.

Davis, G., *The Irish in Britain, 1815-1914* (Dublin: Gill and Macmillan, 1991).

Deignan, P., *Land and People in Nineteenth Century Sligo* (Sligo, 2015)

Deignan, P., *Land and People in Nineteenth Century Sligo: from Union to Local Government* (Sligo, 2010).

Delorme, Br. A., *Marvellous Companions of Marcellin Champagnat* (Rome: Institute of the Marist Brothers, 2011).

Devine, T.M. (et al), *Irish Immigrants and Scottish Society in the Nineteenth and Twentieth Centuries* (Edinburgh: John Donald Publishers, 1991).

Devine, T.M., and Findlay, R.J., *Scotland in the 20th Century* (Edinburgh: Edinburgh University Press, 1996).

Devine, T.M., The Scottish Nation 1700-2007 (UK: Penguin, 2006)

Dilworth, M., 'Religious Orders in Scotland, 1878-1978', *The Innes Review*, Vol. 29, No. 1 (Spring, 1978), pp. 92-109.

Dingle, A.E., and Harrison, B.H., 'Cardinal Manning as Temperance Reformer', *The Historical Journal*, Vol. 12, No. 3 (1969), pp. 485-510.

Appendices

Donaldson, I., 'Biographical Uncertainty', *Essays in Criticism*, Vol. 54, No. 4 (Oxford University Press, 2004), pp. 305-322.

Donaldson, M., 'The Voluntary Principle in the Colonial Situation: Theory and Practice', *Studies in Church History*, Vol. 23 (1986), pp. 381-390.

Dowd, C., *Rome in Australia: The Papacy and Conflict in the Australian Catholic Missions, 1834-1884* (The Netherlands: Brill, 2008).

Duffy, M., 'The Perils of Published Missionary Letters', *International Bulletin of Mission Research*, Vol. 1 (2018) pp. 1-11.

Edwards, O.E., 'The Catholic Press in Scotland since the Restoration of the Hierarchy', *The Innes Review*, Vol. 29, No. 2 (1978), pp. 156-182.

Erben, M., 'The purposes and processes of biographical method' in Scott, D. and Usher, R. (eds) *Understanding Educational Research* (London: Routledge, 1996).

Feheny, J.M., 'Delinquency among Irish Catholic Children in Victorian London', *Irish Historical Studies*, Vol. 23, No. 92 (Nov., 1983), pp. 319-329.

Feheny, J.M., 'The London Catholic Ragged School: An Experiment in Education for Irish Destitute Children', *Archivium Hibernicum*, Vol. 39 (1984), pp. 32-44.

Fernandez-Suarez, Y., 'An Essential Picture in a Sketch-Book of Ireland: The Last Hedge Schools', *Estudios Irlandeses*, No. 1 (2006), pp. 45-57.

Finn, G.P.T., 'Racism, Religion and Social Prejudice: Irish Catholic Clubs, Soccer and Scottish Society – I The Historical Roots of Prejudice', *The International Journal of the History of Sport*, Vol. 8, No. 1 (1991), pp. 72-95.

Finn, G.P.T., 'Racism, Religion and Social Prejudice: Irish Catholic Clubs, Soccer and Scottish Society – II Social Identities and Conspiracy Theories', *The International Journal of the History of Sport*, Vol. 8, No. 3 (1991), pp. 370-397.

Fitzpatrick, T.A., *No Mean Service: Scottish Catholic Teacher Education 1895-1995* (St Andrew's College Bearsden: John S Burns and Sons, 1995).

Fitzpatrick, T.A., 'The Marist Brothers in Scotland before 1918', *The Innes Review*, Vol. 49, No. 1 (1998), pp. 1-10.

Flores, R., book review article of Turner, A., Cox, L. and Bocking, B. (eds), *The Irish Buddhist: The Forgotten Monk who Faced Down the British Empire* (New York: Oxford University Press, 2020), published by the Irish Journal of Sociology (2021), pp. 1-3.

France, P. and St. Clair, W. (eds), *Mapping Lives: The Uses of Biography* (Oxford: University Press, 2004).

Gallagher, T., Glasgow: *The Uneasy Peace* (Manchester: Manchester University Press, 1987).

Gallagher, T., 'The Catholic Irish in Scotland: In Search of Identity', in Devine, T.M. (et al), *Irish Immigrants and Scottish Society in the Nineteenth and Twentieth Centuries* (Edinburgh: John Donald Publishers, 1991).

Gilley, S., 'English Catholic Attitudes to Irish Catholics', *Immigrants & Minorities*, Vol. 27, No. 2-3 (2009), pp. 226-247.

Gilley, S., 'The Roman Catholic Mission to the Irish in London, 1840-1860', *Recusant History*, Vol. 10, No. 3 (1969), pp. 123-145.

Glassie, H., 'The Irish Folklore Commission: International Scholarship, National Purpose, Local Virtue', *Béaloideas*, Vol. 78 (2010), pp. 1-18.

Green, A., 'Individual Remembering and "Collective Memory": Theoretical Presuppositions and Contemporary Debates', *Oral History*, Vol. 32, No. 2, (Autumn, 2004), pp. 35-44.

Guerlac, O., 'The Separation of Church and State in France', *Political Science Quarterly*, Vol. 27, No. 2 (June, 1908), pp. 259-296.

Gunning, P.I., 'Association Football in the Shamrock Shire's Hy Brasil: The 'Socker' Code in Connacht, 1879-1906', *Soccer & Society*, Vo. 18, No. 5-6 (2017), pp. 608-630.

Handley, J. E., *Brother Clare's History of The Province*, New Edition (Glasgow: Marist Brothers, Easter 2011).

Handley, J.E., *A History of St. Mary's Boys' School, Calton, Glasgow, 1863-1963* (Glasgow: J. Burns & Sons, 1963).

Handley, J.E., *A History of the Marist Brothers Province of the British Isles* (1968).

Handley, J.E., *The Celtic Story: A History of Celtic Football Club* (London: Stanley Paul, 1988).

Handley, J.E., *The History of St. Mungo's Academy* (Paisley, 1958).

Handley, J.E., *The Irish in Modern Scotland* (Cork: Cork University Press, 1938).

Hannan, M., 'The Children don't sing here anymore', *Corran Herald 1999/2000*, Vol. 32 (2000), p. 20.

Harland-Jacobs, Jessica L., 'Incorporating the King's New Subjects: Accommodation and Anti-Catholicism in the British Empire, 1763-1815', *Journal of Religious History*, Vol. 39, No. 2 (June, 2015), pp. 203-223.

Harthwick, S. C., 'The Clergy Relief Fund, 1831: Tithe Defaulters', *Irish Genealogy*, Vol. 8, No. 1 (1990), pp. 82-102.

Healy, A., *The Man Who Started Celtic* (as yet unpublished).

Hennesey, J.J. 'Immigrants Become the Church', in Hennesey, J.J., *American Catholics: A History of the Roman Catholic Community in the United States* (Oxford: Oxford, 1983).

Hickey, J., *Urban Catholics: Urban Catholicism in England and Wales from 1829 to the present day* (London: Geoffrey Chapman, 1967).

Holmes, A., 'Researcher Positionality – A Consideration of Its Influence and Place in Qualitative Research – A New Researcher Guide', *International Journal of Education*, Vol. 8, No. 4 (Sep., 2020), pp. 1-10.

Holmes, R., 'Introduction' in France, P. and St. Clair, W. (eds) *Mapping Lives: The Uses of Biography* (Oxford: University Press, 2004), pp 1-18.

Horton, P., 'Athleticism and the Elite Catholic Boys Schools of Colonial Australia', in Horton, P. (et al), *Manufacturing Masculinity. The Mangan Oeuvre: Global Reflections on J.A. Mangan's Studies of Masculinity, Imperialism and Militarism* (Berlin: Logos Verlag, 2017).

Horton, P., *Manufacturing Masculinity. The Mangan Oeuvre: Global Reflections on J.A. Mangan's Studies of Masculinity, Imperialism and Militarism* (Berlin: Logos Verlag, 2017).

Johnson, C., 'Development in the Roman Catholic Church in Scotland, 1789 – 1829' (University of Strathclyde: unpublished thesis, 1980).

Kay, J., and Vamplew, W., 'Beyond altruism: British football and charity, 1877-1914', *Soccer and Society*, Vol. 11, No. 3 (2010), p. 21.

Keenan, W.J.F., 'Death figures in religious life: Components of Marist death culture 1817-1997', *Mortality*, Vol. 3, No. 1 (1998), pp. 7-26.

Kehoe, S. K., 'Catholic Relief and the Political Awakening of Irish Catholics in Nova Scotia, 1780-1830', *The Journal of Imperial and Commonwealth History* (Oct. 2017) pp. 1-20.

Kehoe, S. K., *Creating a Scottish Church: Catholicism, Gender and Ethnicity in Nineteenth-Century Scotland* (Manchester: Manchester University Press, 2010)..

Kehoe, S. K., 'Women Religious and the Development of Scottish Education', in McKinney, S.J. and McCluskey, R., *A History of Catholic Education and Schooling in Scotland: New Perspectives* (London: Palgrave Macmillan, 2019) pp. 61-81.

Kelly, E., 'Challenging Sectarianism in Scotland: The Prism of Racism', *Scottish Affairs*, No. 42 (Winter, 2003), pp. 32-56.

Kelly, M., and Fotheringham, A.S, 'The online atlas of Irish population change 1841-2002: A newresource for analysing national trends and local variations in Irish population dynamics', *Irish Geography*, Vol. 44, No. 2-3 (2011), pp. 215-244.

Kidd, C., 'Race, Empire and the Limits of Nineteenth-Century Scottish Nationhood', *The Historical Journal*, Vol. 46, No. 4 (Dec., 2003), pp. 873-892.

Kinealy, C., *A Death-Dealing Famine: The Great Hunger in Ireland* (Chicago: Pluto Press, 1997).

Kinealy, C., King, J. and Moran, G., (eds), *Children and the Great Hunger in Ireland* (Quinnipiac, University Press, 2018).

Lanfrey, Br. A., *History of the Institute of the Marist Brothers: From the village of Marlhes to expansion worldwide* (1789-1907) Volume 1 (Rome: Institute of the Marist Brothers, 2015).

Langan, M.D., Reviewed Work(s): Migration in Irish History, 1606-2007 by Patrick Fitzgerald and Brian Lambkin, Studies: An *Irish Quarterly Review*: What Do We Do Next? Solving Ireland's Problems, (Autumn, 2009), Vol. 98, No. 391, pp. 347- 350.

Larkin, E., 'The Devotional Revolution in Ireland, 1850-75', *The American Historical Review*, Vol. 77, No. 3 (Oxford: Oxford University Press, Jun. 1972), pp. 625-652.

Le Chevallier, I., *Rendez-vous Leicester Square: The History of Notre Dame de France 1865-2015*, (Notre Dame de France: London, 2015).

Lugton, A., *The Making of Hibernian* (John Donald: Edinburgh, 1999).

McBrearty, R., 'Glasgow Before The Explosion: the role of migration and immigration in the development of football cultures in the city prior to 1873', article published online at https://scottishfootballorigins.org/2021/08/26/glasgow-before-the- explosion-the-role-of-migration-and-immigration-in-the-development-of- football-cultures-in-the-city-prior-to-1873/ accessed August 26th 2021.

McCaffrey, J.F., 'Politics and the Catholic Community since 1878', *The Innes Review*, Vol. 29, No. 2 (1978), pp. 140-155.

McCaffrey, J.F., 'The Irish Vote in Glasgow in the Later Nineteenth Century: A Preliminary Survey, *The Innes Review*, Vol. 21, No.1 (1970), pp. 30-36.

McClelland, V.A., 'A Hierarchy for Scotland, 1868-1878', *The Catholic Historical Review*, Vol. 56, No. 3 (October, 1970), pp. 474-500.

McClelland, V.A., 'The Irish Clergy and Archbishop Manning's Apostolic Visitation of the Western District of Scotland, 1867', *Historical Review*, Vol. 53, No. 2 (July, 1967), pp. 229-250.

McDermid, J., 'Catholic women teachers and Scottish education in the nineteenth and early twentieth centuries', *History of Education*, Vol. 38, No. 5 (2009), pp. 605- 620.

MacDonald, R., 'The Catholic Gaidhealtachd', *The Innes Review*, Vol. 29, No. 1 (1978), pp. 56-72.

McDowell, M., 'The origins, patronage and culture of association football in the west of Scotland, c. 1865-1902' (University of Glasgow: PhD Thesis, 2010).

Appendices

McDowell, M., 'Football, migration and industrial patronage in the west of Scotland, c. 1870-1900', *Sport in History*, Vol. 32., No. 3 (2012), pp. 405-425.

McFarland, E., 'A Reality and Yet Impalpable: The Fenian Panic in Mid-Victorian Scotland', *The Scottish Historical Review*, Vol. 77, No. 204 (Oct., 1998), pp. 199- 223.

McFarland, E., 'The Making of an Irishman: John Ferguson (1836-1906) and the Politics of Identity in Victorian Glasgow', *Immigrants & Minorities*, Vol. 27, No. 2-3 (2009), pp. 194-211.

McGettrick, B., 'From Portinch to Glasgow', *Corran Herald*, Vol. 29 (1996), p. 13.

McGettrick, T., 'Townlands & Place Names', *Corran Herald*, Vol. 22 (1992), p. 6.

McKee, Eliza, 'The origins and development of the Public Record Office of Northern Ireland, 1922-1948', *Archives and Records*, Vol. 40, No. 2 (2019), pp. 164-178.

McKinney, S.J. and McCluskey, R. (Eds.), *A History of Catholic Education and Schooling in Scotland: New Perspectives* (London: Palgrave Macmillan, 2019).

McKinney, S.J., '100 Years of the Education (Scotland) Act, 1918', *Pastoral Review*, Vol 14, No. 3 (2018), pp. 22-27.

McKinney, S.J., 'A Scottish Education Milestone', *Open House*, Vol. 275 (Glasgow: Glasgow University, 2018), pp.9-10.

McKinney, S.J., 'Catholic schools in Glasgow and caring for the needs of those who are poor' in Sean Whittle (ed.) *Vatican II and New Thinking about Catholic Education: The impact and legacy of Gravissimum Educationis* (London: Routledge, 2016), pp. 96-111.

McKinney, S.J., 'The Journey towards the Education (Scotland) Act of 1918', *Open House*, Vol. 274 (Glasgow: Glasgow University, 2018), pp. 7-8.

McLeod, H., 'Building the "Catholic Ghetto": Catholic Organisations 1870-1914', *Studies in Church History*, Vol. 23, (1986), pp. 411-444.

McManus, A., *The Irish Hedge School and its books, 1695-1831* (Dublin: Four Courts Press, 2004).

McMurrich, P., 'Book Review: Verguet's Sketchbook: A Marist Missionary Artist in 1840s Oceania by Mervyn Duffy and Alois Greiler', *Journal of the Australian Catholic Historical Society* Vol. 35 (Dec., 2015) pp. 122-115.

McQuade, P., 'Glengarry – Glasgow's Sacred Heart', (2016) accessed online at https://the-shamrock.net/2016/09/18/glengarry/ on 15th February 2018.

McQuade, P., 'The Brother Walfrid Story', (2015) accessed online at https://the- shamrock.net/2015/04/06/the-brother-walfrid-story/ on 22nd January 2018.

McRoberts, D., 'The Restoration of the Scottish Catholic Hierarchy in 1878', *The Innes Review*, Vol. 29, No. 1 (Spring, 1978), pp. 3-29.

McTernan, J. C., *Worthies of Sligo: Profiles of Eminent Sligonians of Other Days* (Sligo: Avena Publications, 1994)

McTernan, J., 'The Tighes of Tighe's Town', *Corran Herald* 1999/2000, Vol. 32 (2000), p. 4.

Maley, W., 'Celtic Memories' in *St. Peter's College Magazine*, Vol. 20, No. 76 (June, 1951), p. 16.

Mangan, J.A., 'Missing men: schoolmasters and the early years of Association Football', *Soccer & Society*, Vol. 9, No. 2 (2008), pp. 170-188.

Marmion, Rev. J.P., 'Newman and Education', *The Downside Review*, Vol. 97, Issue 326 (1979), pp. 10-29.

Mason, J., 'Mixing methods in a qualitatively driven way', *Qualitative Research*, Vol. 6, No. 1 (2006), pp. 9-25.

Maver, I, *Glasgow* (Edinburgh: Edinburgh University Press, 2000).

Maver, I., 'The Catholic Community' in Devine, T.M., and Findlay, R.J., *Scotland in the 20th Century* (Edinburgh: Edinburgh University Press, 1996).

Maynard, J. O., *History of the parish of St. Anne's Underwood Road Volumes I – IV*, accessed at Tower Hamlets Local History Library and Archives, LC13903/024.

Meister, D.R., 'The biographical turn and the case for historical biography', *History Compass* (2017), pp. 1-10.

Merriman, J., *A History of Modern Europe: From the Renaissance to the Present* (London: W.W. Norton & Company, 2004 Second Edition).

Mitchell, M. J. (et al), *New Perspectives on The Irish in Scotland* (Edinburgh: Birlinn, 2008).

Mitchell, M.J., 'Anti-Catholicism and the Scottish Middle Class 1800-1914' in C. Gheeraert-Graffeuille, G. Vaughan (eds.), *Anti-Catholicism in Britain and Ireland, 1600-2000, Practices, Representations and Ideas* (London: Pallgrave MacMillan, 2020), pp. 219-237.

Moore, M., 'Early association football in Ireland: Embryonic diffusion outside Ulster, 1877-1882', *Sport in History* (2021), pp. 1-25.

Morris, R.J., 'Voluntary Societies and British Urban Elites, 1780-1850: An Analysis', *The Historical Journal*, Vol. 26, No. 1 (March, 1983), pp. 95-118.

Nally, D., '"That Coming Storm": The Irish Poor Law, Colonial Biopolitics, and the Great Famine', *Annals of the Association of American Geographers*, Vol. 98, No. 3 (2008), pp. 714-741.

Nasaw, D., 'AHR Roundtable: Historians and Biography Introduction', *The American Historical Review*, Vol. 114, No. 3 (Jun., 2009), pp. 573-578.

O'Connell, A., 'The Irish Hedge Schools: Rejection, resistance and Creativity (1695- 1831)', *Revue Civilisations* (2011), pp.55-86.

O'Donoghue, T., *Catholic Teaching Brothers: Their Life in the English-Speaking World, 1891-1965* (New York: Pallgrave, 2012)

O'Donoghue, T., 'The Role of Male Religious Orders in Education in Scotland in the Decades Leading up to the Education (Scotland) Act, 1918', in McKinney, S.J. and McCluskey, R., *A History of Catholic Education and Schooling in Scotland: New Perspectives* (London: Palgrave Macmillan, 2019), pp. 81-103.

O'Farrell, P., *The Catholic Church and community: an Australian history* (Kensington New South Wales: N.S.W. University Press, 1985).

O'Gorman, J.J., 'Canada's Greatest Chaplain', *The Catholic Historical Review*, Vol. 8, No. 2 (July, 1922) pp. 217-228.

O'Grada, C., *Black '47 and Beyond: The Great Irish Famine* (Princeton: Princeton University Press, 2000).

O'Hagan, F.J., and Davis, R.A., 'Forging the compact of church and state in the development of Catholic education in late nineteenth-century Scotland', *The Innes Review*, Vol. 58, No. 1 (Spring, 2007), pp. 72-94.

O'Hagan, F.J., *The Contribution of the Religious Orders to Education in Glasgow during the period 1847-1918* (Wales: Edwin Mellen, 2006).

O'Laughlin, M. C., *The Book of Irish Families: Great and Small; 1* (Irish Genealogical Foundation, 2002).

O'Sullivan, P. (et al), *Volume Two: The Irish in The New Communities* (Leicester: Leicester University Press, 1992).

O'Tuathaigh, M.A.G., 'The Irish in Nineteenth-Century Britain: Problems of Integration', *Transactions of the Royal Historical Society*, Vol. 31 (1981), pp. 149-173.

Parker Kinch, D.A., 'Seeking a "Steadfast Aim": A Cultural Historical Biography of Bessie Rayner Parkes Belloc (1829-1925)' (University of Portsmouth thesis submitted June 2021).

Parker, Br. J., *Remembering the Marist Brothers* (2009).

Pittock, M., *Celtic Identity and the British Image* (Manchester: University Press, 1999).

Pooley, C., 'Newspaper Reporting of Migrants in England 1851-1911: Spatial and Temporal Perspectives', *Journal of Migration History*, Vol. 5 (2019), pp. 31-52.

Pooley, C., 'Segregation or integration? The residential experience of the Irish in mid- Victorian Britain', in Swift, R. (ed), *The Irish in Britain 1815-1939* (1989), pp. 60- 84.

Possing, B., 'Biography: Historical' in Wright, J. D. (ed.), *International Encyclopedia of the Social & Behavioral Sciences* (Amsterdam: Elsevier, 2015).

Power, M., 'Reviewed Work(s): The Untold Story: The Irish in Canada by Robert O'Driscoll and Lorna Reynolds', *The Canadian Journal of Irish Studies*, Vol. 15, No. 2 (Dec., 1989) pp. 115-118.

Prendergast, N., 'A Brother called Walfrid' (The Marist Brothers in Ireland, 2021).

Prendergast, N., *Before You We Stand: The Story of the Marist Brothers in Ireland* (Ireland: Naas Printing, 2021).

Prendergast, N., 'Irish Marist Brothers in Oceania', *Champagnat: An International Marist Journal of Charism in Education*, Vol. 21, No. 1, (May, 2019) pp. 6-19.

Prentis, M.D., 'Scottish Roman Catholics in Nineteenth-Century Australia', *The Innes Review*, Vol. 33, No. 33 (Aug., 2010) pp. 58-70.

Quinn, J., 'Reviewed Work(s): The Last Conquest of Ireland (Perhaps) by John Mitchel and Patrick Maume', *Irish Historical Studies*, Vol. 35, No. 138 (Nov., 2006), pp. 255-257.

Rawlyk, G., 'Religion in Canada: A Historical Overview', *Annals, The American Academy of Political and Social Science*, Vol. 538 (Mar., 1995) pp. 131-142.

Reid, J., 'Irish Famine refugees and the emergence of Glasgow Celtic Football Club', in Smyth, W.J., 'The province of Connacht and the Great Famine' in Crowley, J., Smyth, W. J. and Murphy, M., (eds), *Atlas of the Great Irish Famine* (Cork: University Press, 2012), pp. 513-520.

Rodchenko, J.P., 'An Irish-American Journalist and Catholicism: Patrick Ford of the Irish World', *American Society of Church History*, Vol. 39, No. 4 (Dec., 1970), pp. 524- 540.

Rogers, N., *Ballymote Aspects Through Time*, second edition (Sligo: Orbicon Print, 2010).

Ross, A., 'The Development of the Scottish Catholic Community, 1878-1978', *The Innes Review*, Vol.29, No. 1 (Spring, 1978), pp. 30-55.

Ross, D. M., 'Penny Banks in Glasgow, 1850-1914', *Financial History Review*, Vol. 9, No. 1 (2002), pp. 21-39.

Saarinen, I.M., 'Making Roman Catholic priests in the nineteenth century: a prosopographical study of Scottish Mission's France-trained students and seminarian social identities, 1818-1878' (Edinburgh University thesis submitted July 2017, as yet unpublished).

Salmon, Rev. D, *A Short History of the Parish of St. Anne's*, Underwood Road (London: Salesian Press, 1950).

Scott, M.W., 'Book Review: Verguet's Sketchbook: A Marist Missionary Artist in 1840s Oceania by Mervyn Duffy and Alois Greiler', *The Outrigger*, Vol. 58, No. 10 (Spring, 2015)

Sharp, J., 'Juvenile Holiness: Catholic Revivalism among Children in Victorian Britain', *Journal of Ecclesiastical History*, Vol. 35, No. 2 (April, 1984), pp. 220-238.

Sheppard, F.H.W. (Ed.), 'Mile End New Town', in *Survey of London: Volume 27, Spitalfields and Mile End New Town* (London, 1957), pp. 265-288.

Skinnider, M., 'Catholic Elementary Education in Glasgow, 1818-1918' in Bone, T.R. (ed), *Studies in the History of Scottish Education 1872-1939* (London: University of London Press, 1967), pp. 13-71.

Smyth, J.J., 'The Power of Pathos: James Burn Russell's Life in One Room and the Creation of Council Housing', *The Scottish Historical Review*, Vol. 98, No. 1 (2019), pp. 103-127.

Smyth, J.J., 'Thomas Chalmers, the 'Godly Commonwealth', and Contemporary Welfare Reform in Britain and the USA', *The Historical Journal*, Vol. 57, No. 3 (2014), pp. 845-868.

Smyth, W.J., 'Exodus from Ireland – patterns of emigration', in Crowley, J., Smyth, W. J. and Murphy, M., (eds), *Atlas of the Great Irish Famine* (Cork: University Press, 2012) pp. 494-503.

Smyth, W.J., 'The province of Connacht and the Great Famine' in Crowley, J., Smyth, W. J. and Murphy, M., (eds), *Atlas of the Great Irish Famine* (Cork: University Press, 2012) pp. 281-290.

Strachey, L., *Eminent Victorians* (London, 1918).

Strachey, L., *Eminent Victorians* (Oxford: University Press, 2003).

Sutton, D. A., 'The public-private interface of domiciliary medical care for the poor in Scotland, c. 1875-1911' (University of Glasgow: unpublished PhD thesis, 2009).

Sweeney, B., *Celtic, The Early Years: 1887-1892* (Scotland: CQN Books, 2015).

Sweeney, B., *Celtic: The Battle for the Club's Soul 1892-1897*, Vol. 1 and 2 (Scotland: CQN Books, 2020).

Sweeney, J.P., 'The Church in the United States', *The Furrow*, Vol. 2, No. 7 (Jul., 1951) pp. 445-457.

Swift, R., *Irish Migrants in Britain, 1815-1914* (Cork: Cork University Press, 2002).

Swift, R., 'The Outcast Irish in the British Victorian City: Problems and Perspectives', *Irish Historical Studies*, Vol. 25, No. 99 (May, 1987), pp. 264-276.

Taylor, J., *Jean-Claude Colin: Reluctant Founder* (Adelaide: ATF Press Publishing, 2008).

Taylor, M.G., *The Blue and Gold: St. Joseph's College, Dumfries 1875 – 2000* (Glasgow: John S Burns 2000).

Tenbus, E.G., '"We Fight for the Cause of God": English Catholics, the Education of the Poor, and the Transformation of Catholic Identity in Victorian Britain', *Journal of British Studies*, Vol. 46, No. 4 (October, 2007), pp. 861-883.

Thomas, E., 'From Sligo to Wales – the flight of Sir Charles Phibbs', *History Ireland*, Vol. 12, No. 1(Spring, 2004).

Tierney, D., 'Financing the Faith: Scottish Catholicism 1772-c.1890' (Aberdeen University thesis submitted May 2014).

Tranter, N., *Sport, Economy and Society in Britain, 1750-1914* (Cambridge: University Press, 1998)

Treble, J.H., 'The Development of Roman Catholic Education in Scotland, 1878-1978', *The Innes Review*, Vol. 29, No. 2 (Autumn, 1978), pp. 111-139.

Valley, P., *Philanthropy: from Aristotle to Zuckerberg* (London: Bloomsbury, 2020).

Vaughan, G. 'The Distinctiveness of Catholic Schooling in the West of Scotland Before the Education (Sco) Act, 1918', in McKinney, S.J. and McCluskey, R., *A History of Catholic Education and Schooling in Scotland: New Perspectives* (London: Palgrave MacMillan, 2019).

Walker, W.M., 'Irish Immigrants in Scotland: Their Priests, Politics and Parochial Life', *The Historical Journal*, Vol. 15, No. 4 (December, 1972), pp. 649-667.

Walsh, Rev. J., 'Archbishop Manning's Visitation of the Western District of Scotland in 1867', *The Innes Review*, Vol. 18, No. 1 (Spring, 1967), pp. 3-18.

Watters, D.M., '"Our Catholic school": themes and patterns in early Catholic school buildings and architecture before 1872', *The Innes Review*, Vol. 71, No. 1 (2020), pp. 1-66.

Primary Sources

Champagnat, M., Spiritual Testament, May 18th 1840. Accessed online at: https://champagnat.org/es/marcelino-champ/testamento-espiritual-de- marcelino-champagnat/

'In Memory of the Founding Fathers of Celtic Football Club' – pamphlet produced by the Celtic Graves Society.

'Names of Subscribers' – accessed online at www.thecelticwiki.com

'The Marist Brothers of the Schools: Their Life and Work' (1955) held at Dumfries and Galloway Council Archives, GD517/10.

Accs-10691 – Collection of letters and papers of PD Thomson concerning the history of Hibernian FC, held at the National Library of Scotland, Edinburghhttp://census.nationalarchives.ie/reels/vob/IRE_CENSUS_1821- 51_007250687_00971.pdf.

Appendices

Annals of (St. Andrews) St. Josephs Monastery, 71 Charlotte St. Glasgow – 'Copies of Letters 1860-1916 – B. Walfrid, B. Procope A.G, B. Nestor S.G. A.B. Glasgow'.

Beaucamps Admissions Register, SGL/01-0702/02: Freres Renseignements – 1854-1877.

Beaucamps Freres-Communautes, SGL/01-07-03: Registres des Vêtures 1844-1886.

Beaucamps Vie de la Province, SGL/02-02-09: Annales Maison de Beaucamps et Province.

Brother Colins Chalmers, 'Administrative History of Marist Brothers of Great Britain', information received from the General Archives of the Marist Brothers in Rome, 2018.

Brother John Parker, 'Names and Particulars transcribed from the Register of Admission to the Novitiate of Beaucamps', received April 2020.

BU/21/214/101 – Brother Walfrid letter to the Lord Marquess of Bute, 26 October 1885.

Bulletin De L'Institut, publication of the Marist Brothers (1909-1984) held at Archives of Bulletin of the Institute, historic issues accessed online at www.champagnat.org .PS/ IZ/ NP/ S/ 23/ 1-7.champagnat

Carleton, W., Illustrated Stories and Tales of the Irish, Vol. 3 (Project Gutenberg Edition, 1843).

Census of Ireland (1901) and (1911), accessed online at http://www.census.nationalarchives.ie/

Census Records for Scotland – the Mitchell Library, Glasgow.

Charles Booth Survey B221; B223; B224; B3181; B387.notes held at the Scottish Catholic Archives, Edinburgh, SCA/MB/11/4.The Salesian Press, 1950) – the Marist House Archive, Glasgow.

Clyde Bill of Entry and Shipping List 1855, Glasgow City Archives, FCN 26.9.

De Beaumont, G., Ireland: Social, Political, and Religious. Vol. 1 (1839)

Expenses Book 1896-1901 for St. Anne's, Underwood Road, accessed at St. Anne's R.C. Church, London.

Gaume, J., Catechism of Perseverance: An Historical, Doctrinal, Moral and Liturgical Exposition of The Catholic Religion. Translated from the French of Abbe Gaume by Rev. F.B. Jamison (Dublin: John Duffy, 1866).

Glasgow Archdiocese Archives:
GC17/68/1 – Letter from Brother Walfrid to John Long, August 2 1885.
GC18/16/1 – Letter from Brother Walfrid to Archbishop's secretary Father Maguire, March 10 1886.
GC18/16/2'– Letter from Brother Walfrid to Archbishop's secretary Father Maguire, June 1 1886.

Glasgow City Council Registrars information at the Genealogy Centre of the Mitchell Library.

Glasgow nineteenth century overlay maps – accessed online at https://maps.nls.uk/townplans/overlays.html

Glassford Bell, H., 'Mary, Queen o' Scots' (1831) accessed online at https://digital.nls.uk/broadsides/view/?id=16318.2005

Griffiths Valuation (1858). Accessed online.

Irish Folklore Project – The Schools' Collection 1937-38, Vol. 0170, p. 0128. Accessed online at https://www.duchas.ie/en/cbes/4701702/4694113

'Installation and Blessing of Commemorative Stones, Cemetery of the Marist Brothers Dumfries', June 7th 2019 (commemorative booklet).

Lewis, S., *County Sligo in 1837: A Topographical Dictionary* (The County Sligo Heritage and Genealogical Society: Sligo, 2003).

Maley, W., *The Story of the Celtic, 1888-1938* (Essex: Desert Island Books, 1939).

Marriages, Apr. 1837 to June 1837, Emlefad and Kilmorgan; County of Sligo; Diocese of Achonry.

Microfiche of Brother Walfrid, No. 2998 held at the General Archive for The Institute of Marist Brothers, Rome.

Minutes of the Christian Young Men's Society – Scottish Catholic Archives, Edinburgh.

Muir, J.H., *Glasgow in 1901* (Glasgow: William Hodge & Company, 1901).

O'Rourke, Canon J., *The Great Irish Famine* (Dublin: Veritas, 1989).

Pat Woods' private collection held at the Mitchell Library – newspaper cuttings and materials pertinent to the history of Celtic FC.

Personal papers and writings of Brother Clare (James E. Handley).

Post Office Glasgow Directories – the Mitchell Library, National Library of Scotland website.

Salmon, Rev. D, *A Short History of the Parish of St. Anne's, Underwood Road* (London: Salesian Press, 1950).

Sisters of Charity Glasgow Children's Refuge Annual Reports, 1889-1930 (Glasgow: P. Donegan & Company)

Sligo Prison General Register 1843-1878, Book No. 1/34/3.

Society of St. Vincent de Paul, Manual of the Society of St. Vincent de Paul (20th Edition).

Society of St. Vincent de Paul, Society of St. Vincent de Paul: 150 Years in Glasgow (Glasgow: Network Ltd, 1998).

St. Anne's Boys School Registers 1886-1905, accessed at Tower Hamlets Local History Library and Archives.

St. Anne's log books of the Saint Vincent de Paul Society, accessed at St. Anne's R.C. Church, London.

St. Anne's School Inspector Reports 1904 – 1908, accessed at London Metropolitan Archives, LCC/EO/ PS/ IZ/ NP/ S/ 23/ 1-7.

St. Joseph's Commercial College annual (Dumfries: Currie & Co.).

Strang, J., 'Statistics of Glasgow 1841-62', DTC 7.5.3A held at Glasgow City Archives, the Mitchell Library.

SVDP – Romero House archives, London.

The Brother Walfrid Memorial booklet published by the Brother Walfrid Commemoration Committee to mark the unveiling of a statue to Walfrid at Celtic Park on the 5th of November 2005.

The Catholic Directory, Ecclesiastical Register, and Almanac (London, Burns and Lambert).

Tithe Applotment Books 1833, Parish of Emlafad. Accessed online at https://www.nationalarchives.ie/article/tithe-applotment-records

Williams, R., 'The Marist Brothers of Grove Ferry' (c. 1980s – 1990s), photocopies and handwritten notes held at the Scottish Catholic Archives, Edinburgh.

Records accessed via Glasgow City Archives at the Mitchell Library, Glasgow:
D-ED7/190/1 – Log Book of St. Alphonsus' R.C. Boy's School, 1874-1899
D-ED7/192/1.1 – Log Book of St. Andrew's R.C. Boy's School, 1865-1881
SR-10/3/894/1.1 and SR10/3/894/1.2 – Log Books of St. Mary's R.C. Boy's School, 1864- 1894
D-ED7/247/1.1 – Log Book of St. Mungo's R.C. School, 1864-1899
GB-0243/D-TC6/319/7'– St. Mary's Catholic Burial Ground, Register of Lairholders 1870
DTC-6/317 – 'Records of Petitions by Sanitary Department for the Closure of Certain Burying Grounds, 1870-76'
D-HE/1/5/3 —'Report on Certain Recent Outbreaks of Enteric Fever in Glasgow', October 11 1875

Newspaper Publications
Canterbury Journal, Kentish Times and Farmers' Gazette
Catholic Herald
Dundee Courier
Faversham Times and Mercury and North-East Kent Journal
Glasgow Evening News
Glasgow Examiner

Glasgow Herald
Glasgow Observer
Glasgow Star
Herne Bay Press
Irish Free Press
London Monitor
North British Daily Mail
Roscommon and Leitrim Gazette
Scottish Referee
Scottish Sport
Scottish Umpire
The Catholic Times
The Daily Record
The Dublin Evening Post
The Dundee, Perth, and Cupar Advertiser
The East London Advertiser
The Freeman's Journal
The Glasgow Free Press
The Monitor and New Era
The Sligo Champion
The Standard
The Tablet
The Universe
The Weekly News

Acknowledgments

I first wish to thank Emma O'Neil of the Nine Muses arts company in Glasgow who funded my research project which has enabled this book. Without her passion, commitment and constant support the PhD thesis on the life of Brother Walfrid and hence this book simply could not have come to fruition. I would also like to express a special note of thanks to Dr Joe Bradley for sharing his expertise, experience and encouragement throughout the project, from start to finish. Without this guidance I would not have been able to get the job done, thanks Joe!

I am indebted to my PhD supervisors, Stephen Morrow and Dr April Henning at the University of Stirling, for always making the time to provide insightful feedback, supportive advice and positive words of encouragement. I also thank all of the staff and fellow students in the Faculty of Health Science and Sport, past and present, I have met along the way. It has been a pleasure to work and learn alongside you.

To the University of Stirling community of staff and students as a whole, my thanks for the various forms of support and inspiration I have experienced during the last four years.

My sincere thanks to the Archdiocese of Glasgow, particularly the late Archbishop Tartaglia and Canon Tom White, for their kind support for the research on Brother Walfrid from the outset. Similarly, my thanks to everyone at Celtic Football Club for their backing of the project throughout, especially then chief executive Peter Lawwell, the staff of the Celtic FC Foundation and Frank Rafters, along with his team of expert tour guides. A huge thank you to Brendan Sweeney and Paul McQuade from the Celtic Graves Society for their insights, enthusiasm and readiness to help at every stage of the project.

I owe a huge deal of gratitude to the Marist Brothers of Glasgow for allowing me access to their archives, their generous hospitality and for offering me exemplary insight into the charism of their religious tradition. Thanks to Brother Colin Chalmers, previously head of the general archives of the Brothers in Rome, for providing expert insight and supplementary information. I would also like to extend special thanks to Brother Brendan Geary who was a constant source of support and answered all of my queries with kindness and customary patience. In addition, thank you for helping to facilitate a research trip to France which was such a valuable experience and so important to the project overall. *Merci beaucoup* to Brother Adrien, Carles Domenech and the Marist Brothers of Lyon for making me feel so welcome and part of their community during my stay there. In particular, thank you to Brother Lanfrey for arranging a trip to view and experience the sites of historic significance to the origins of their Institute. To Brother Alois, who travelled from Germany to work alongside me, thank you so much for your patience and assistance in translation.

In Ireland, my thanks go to the extended Kerins family for their engagement, contributions and support for the research project. To those family members elsewhere who helped contribute to the project via email, my sincerest thanks also. Thank you to Professor Bart McGettrick for his insights ahead of my research trip to County Sligo, where – amongst others – Neale Farry of the Ballymote Heritage Group, Carmel Wims, Michael Mooney and John McGettrick were so accommodating and generous with their time.

Thanks to Dr Irene O'Brien and her staff at the Mitchell Library in Glasgow for their patience, kind words and help along the way. Likewise, thank you to the staff at the Ewart Library in Dumfries and the Tower Hamlets Local History Library and Archives. I am very grateful to the past and present priests and staff of St. Anne's Roman Catholic Church and school in Whitechapel, London. Thanks also to

Bernadette Jones, headteacher of St. Joseph's College in Dumfries. My gratitude to Donna Maguire at the Scottish Catholic Archives for offering such comprehensive access to their collections and for facilitating the completion of archival research in both Glasgow and Edinburgh. Thank you also to the Saint Vincent de Paul Society in Glasgow, Richard McBrearty and the staff of the Scottish Football Museum at Hampden Park for allowing me access to their collections and likewise Lindsay Nairn and the staff at the Bute Collection at Mount Stuart.

Lastly, my thanks to the Robb family, Pat Woods, Tom Campbell, Peter MacKinnon, Michael Annis and Michael Small for some particularly kind and much-appreciated contributions to the research. So many contributed in some way to this project on Brother Walfrid – too many to mention – but know that I will always be grateful for even the simplest words of encouragement received. And last but not least, my thanks to Derek Rodger of Argyll Publishing who took on as editor the job of helping me to convert a thesis into what I hope is an engaging biography and of bringing the production to a satisfactory and timely completion.

Above all else, I would like to thank my Mum, Marie Connolly, for instilling in me a passion for reading from my earliest years and my Dad, Phil Connolly, for imparting a love for football – especially Celtic Football Club. Without these two influences, along with their support and patience while I was completing the thesis, this research project would have been impossible. This book is dedicated to you both, with all my love.

The most well-known image of Brother Walfrid
posed as a young man in Glasgow

Index

Index

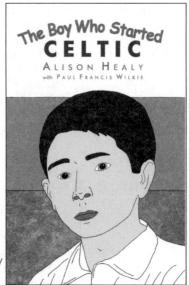

£9.99 HARDBACK
www.thirstybooks.com/
bookshop

The first children's book on the life of the founder of Celtic Football Club. Illustrated in colour throughout, this book is the story of a boy, a calf and one of the biggest football clubs in the world. It is also a story of how one person can change many people's lives.

All great journeys begin with a single step. As a boy, Brother Walfrid did not know he was starting a great journey when he sold a calf at County Sligo's Ballymote Fair and took the boat to Scotland.

Every day, people are starting great journeys and they don't even know it. They are just trying, like Walfrid, to make people's lives better by helping others who are not as fortunate as them. Walfrid helped people and started one of the world's most well-known football clubs. Perhaps readers of Brother Walfrid's story may start a great journey of their own one day?

Alison Healy is an Irish writer from Ballymote, Co Sligo. She remembers being very excited when she first heard she was related to Brother Walfrid. He was her mother's grand uncle. She also writes for *The Irish Times*.

'Andrew Kerins was a refugee from Ireland who fled economic, social and religious subjugation to begin a new life in Glasgow, amongst many other Irish immigrants and their offspring in Scotland's west-central belt. In later becoming a Marist Brother and missionary, he dedicated his life to the meanings and virtues of the Gospels, as an educator, community activist, organiser, leader, and a spiritual example for everyone touched by the fruits of his labour. A significant aspect of his work led to the foundation and formation of Celtic Football Club. In this biography, Dr Michael Connolly explores Walfrid in the context of late Victorian Scottish life and in the process explains the reasons why Celtic, a football institution in Scotland as well as a socio-cultural Irish diasporic symbol, means so much to so many. This book adds to knowledge and understanding of charity, education, Catholicism, Irishness and football in modern Scotland and further afield.'

Dr Joseph M Bradley
University of Edinburgh

'St. Mary of the Assumption Church in Glasgow with its memorial to *An Gorta Mòr*; Celtic Park with its memorial to Brother Walfrid; and the humble brother from County Sligo himself – all are inextricably linked. And each in turn have a strong connection to the multi-generational Irish community in Glasgow today as they had during the terrible years of poverty and hunger which befell our people in the late nineteenth century. The writing of this book arose as much from this shared love and gratitude for Brother Walfrid as from any academic endeavour and places author Michael Connolly in the footsteps of all who came before him who have made sure that the story of Andrew Kerins is never forgotten. The book's focus on Kerins' early life, and the events which made him the man he was, is invaluable in understanding those terrible times and the actions of those, like Walfrid, who tried to make life better for the Irish in Glasgow. This is a story which requires telling and re-telling down the generations and Michael Connolly has made an outstanding contribution to that endeavour.'

Professor Jeanette Findlay,
Chair, *Coiste Cuimhneachain An Gorta Mòr*
(Famine Memorial Committee)

'Examining Walfrid's life from an impressive range of sources, this book locates his contribution in broader contexts of history and geography. The book traces Andrew Kerins' path from a small farm in County Sligo at the time of the Great Hunger to a young emigrant's desperate move to Glasgow where he eventually became a teacher. His deep concern to alleviate poverty, especially amongst children, led him to establish Celtic Football Club to raise money and provide recreation for many people on the margins of life in Victorian Scotland. By joining the Marist religious community Walfrid was part of a much larger European religious culture which involved training in northern France and later working in the East End of London. The book engages deeply with the masculine worlds of Catholic religious Brothers and football players but it also explores struggles to support Irish multigenerational immigrant communities with education and basic living needs.'

Bronwen Walter
Emeritas Professor of Irish Diaspora Studies,
Anglia Ruskin University, Cambridge